# Why Engagement Matters

Heather O'Brien • Paul Cairns
Editors

# Why Engagement Matters

Cross-Disciplinary Perspectives of
User Engagement in Digital Media

 Springer

*Editors*
Heather O'Brien
University of British Columbia
Vancouver, BC, Canada

Paul Cairns
University of York
York, United Kingdom

ISBN 978-3-319-80142-1          ISBN 978-3-319-27446-1     (eBook)
DOI 10.1007/978-3-319-27446-1

Springer Cham Heidelberg New York Dordrecht London

Printed on acid-free paper

Springer International Publishing AG Switzerland is part of Springer Science+Business Media
(www.springer.com)

*For Silas, Eleanor, and Patrick:*
*Constantly engaging ...*

# Foreword

When Wittgenstein first heard the expression "it takes all sorts to make a world", it struck him as profound. For most native English speakers, this idiom would be conversational wallpaper too commonplace to be noticed: "you pays your money and you takes your choice", "one man's meat is another man's poison", "there's nowt so queer as folk." But for the Austrian philosopher "it takes all sorts to make a world" seemed to him a "beautiful and kindly saying" [3]. And the saying is, or should be, important to anyone interested in user engagement. As O'Brien and Cairns point out in their introduction to this volume—engagement is a complex phenomena because users bring to it their "personal histories, knowledge, skills and emotion". For this reason, the exact same phrase can be for one person a bland cliché while for another it is sublime poetry.

Slavoj Zizek argues that the fundamental contribution of psychoanalysis is to distinguish between simple pleasures and enjoyment which is often "disturbed pleasure" or indeed pain [4]. Even in a context like games, pain (or at least frustration) is an important aspect of engagement. The Wittgenstein story is almost too good to be true for a philosopher more interested in family resemblances between phenomena than essentialist definitions. But stories don't have to be true to be useful. It is perhaps for this reason that Design Fiction is being taken up by researchers in human–computer interaction (HCI) (e.g. [1, 2, 5]). Computing technology is now being applied to every area of our lives: personal, social, political, sexual and spiritual. In each of these areas, designers aim to create engaging interactions, but how to do this for different sorts of people? The obvious answer is personalisation, but the equally obvious question is—what if your user doesn't like personalisation? Design Fiction allows us to consider character and context in ways that conventional scenarios do not. The extract below is an extract from a Design Fiction novel that explores what the care industry of the near future might look like. As O'Brien and Cairns point out, engagement is a diverse topic that requires multiple approaches. It could be argued that fiction has no place in science, even social science, but it takes all sorts to make a book.

**Fig. 1** Our heroes, Boris and Annabel Bide (Copyright Mark Blythe)

## The Centenarians

Boris and Annabel Bide are centenarian spies called out of retirement to track down
their old enemy @tak. Their search takes them through the care sectors of the
twenty-first century from the Careslums of Walmart Mansions to the Experiential
worlds of Albion and Horny Pines. Here they are having dinner at an AppleCare
facility.

## Digitally Tinted Glasses

Light shimmered through a waterfall that spanned the length of the restaurant. The
Bides sat at their table watching the torrent twist and lash against the glass in streaks
of white foam. Their menus showed only one choice each with a message saying that

the dish had been specially selected to meet their exact physiological requirements and also to be exactly what they happened to fancy.

"Tuna and asparagus salad," she looked over the card at Boris, "That's not what I had in mind at all".

"Well Eggs Benedict is exactly what I wanted," said Boris, "and I didn't even know it!"

"The power of suggestion."

"The power of totally awesome technology!"

Service bots placed large glasses of chilled white ecoholic wine on the table.

"Look at this" Boris marvelled "it's uncanny. How did they know I wanted white wine?"

"Yes, that's an incredible mystery isn't it?"

"Alright that was a safe bet, but how did they know I wanted it served by R2D2 out of Star Wars?"

When the food arrived Annabel poked at it suspiciously, "I'd rather have had beans on toast," she looked down on the busy street scene on the table, "I suppose it might be quite nice to see what's going on back home sometimes but while you're having lunch it's distracting isn't it?" She gestured to the cataract outside the window, "I mean there's an actual waterfall just there."

"Still," Boris was staring at the table, "it's pretty impressive, I mean how does it even know this is our home town?"

"The same way it knows about our dietary requirements." The image below the plates began to fade away.

"Look, it knows we're talking about it," Boris pointed, "it's going to try something else."

A patchwork of green and yellow now filled the table.

"It's a landscape," Boris enthused. "It's as if we're in a hot air balloon. Admit it, that's fantastic," the floor around the table began to show the same display.

"Oh for goodness' sake," Annabel tutted, "now I'm getting vertigo," the aerial scene crept back onto the confines of the table.

Boris said he could change the table display if she wanted and before Annabel could answer he started flicking through the default settings: a tropical reef teaming with fish, an ice hole opening onto deep, mysterious water, a lake of fire and lava inside a volcano. Annabel told him to stop fiddling and he left it drifting through space.

There was a lull in the conversation and the planet their table was drifting by faded to white.

"What's it doing now?" Annabel frowned.

Golden letters shimmered up out of the white background, "*blessed is the man,*" the words appeared in the table one at a time "*who having nothing to say, abstains from giving us wordy evidence of this fact* ... **George Eliot**"

"Christ! It's doing quotations now," Annabel stared.

"*A facility for quotation,*" more golden words emerged from the table, "*covers the absence of original thought* ... **Dorothy L. Sayers**."

"Bloody impertinence!" Annabel rolled up her sleeve.

*"My thoughts be bloody, or be nothing worth …* **Hamlet**"

"For goodness' sake!" She flicked at the table until it returned to drifting over the landscape, "everything in this place is a gadget! The tables, the chairs, the floors, the plates! Why can't they leave anything alone? Cups more or less the same for five thousand years but not good enough now. Now they've also got to provide horoscopes or psychotherapy."

"Speaking of gadgets!" Boris took a pair of spectacles from his jacket pocket and put them on the table with a roguish look, "have you tried these yet? They're amazing!"

"No they're not amazing," Annabel eyed them balefully.

"They're rose tinted glasses: you get them in your welcome pack," Boris put them on and grinned, "they're incredible. They take decades off you."

"What do you mean?"

"They process the image they're pointed at and enhance it. So right now they've smoothed out all of your wrinkles, given back your hair and turned it brown again. I won't say too much about what its done to your bosom but suffice it to say you look like you could nurse the thirstiest of infants."

"What?" Annabel leaned over and snatched them from his face. She put them on warily and stared for a moment at Boris with her mouth open before doubling over with laughter, "they're beer goggles! Ha! Let's both wear them tonight and see what happens!"

"Look at that guy," Boris nodded over at a man sitting at the table next to them.

"He looks like a teenager!"

"You can make the default setting any image you like. Look over there," Boris pointed across the room and Annabel saw an owl in a blouse sitting next to a man with a cat's head coming out of his neck.

When they finished their meal and started the long process of getting to their feet Boris gawped at a beautiful woman stepping lightly towards them.

"Hallo there!" her smile seemed full of love though they had never seen her before, "you must be Annabel and Boris, I've been looking forward to meeting you so much. I'm here to give you the tour of the rest of our facilities," she linked arms with them, "I'll be your Angel for the afternoon."

"Our Angel?" Boris raised his eyebrows in a roguish way that Annabel clearly disapproved of, "my dear, are you going to take us to heaven?"

"We do have a heaven if you want to go," she led them across the glimmering floor, "but it's not easy to get into."

"I should think not," it was clear that the spring in Boris' step was not solely the result of the supportive catsuit he wore beneath his clothes, "you don't want just anyone getting into heaven eh? What's the dress code? Blameless life, good deeds?"

"Of course not," the Angel laughed, "just an upgrade. It's an artificial heaven you see. We thought—if there is no afterlife then we had better make one. We create an avatar with your memories, thought patterns, opinions, personality traits and let it loose in a digital paradise."

"And the avatars enjoy that do they?" Annabel raised a wispy eyebrow.

"Of course, they're programmed to be happy."

"What on earth is the point of that?"

"Well it's not for everyone," the Angel conceded, "but we sometimes find that bereaved relatives find it comforting. The avatars are capable of conversation and say the sorts of things that their loved ones would have said."

"What like—where are my socks?" Annabel asked, "or how does this work? Or—it's a bloody disgrace."

The Angel laughed

Annabel handed the digitally tinted glasses back to Boris. "You know old walnut I think I prefer looking at you just the way you are."

"Well," Boris ran a bony hand over his few remaining hairs, "sometimes there's no alternative to the real thing."

As they left the restaurant the waterfall became a flow of molten lava and the room was bathed in a hellish red light.

York, UK                                                                                     Mark Blythe
September 2015

# References

1. Bleecker, J.: Design Fiction: A Short Essay on Design, Science, Fact and Fiction. From blog. nearfuturelaboratory.com (2009). Accessed October 2015
2. Blythe, M.: Research through design fiction: narrative in real and imaginary abstracts. In Proc of (CHI '14), pp. 703–712. ACM, New York, NY (2014)
3. Eagleton, T.: Reason, Faith, and Revolution: Reflections on the God Debate. Yale University Press, New Haven, CT (2010)
4. Fiennes, S., Zizek, S.: The Perverts Guide to Ideology. Zeitgeist Films, New York, NY (2014)
5. Sterling, B.: Shaping Things. MIT Press, Cambridge, MA (2005)

# Preface

Interest in user engagement (UE) has grown over the past several years. Influenced by the user experience movement in human-computer interaction [1, 2] and marketing and economics [3], UE has become a primary focus of researchers, developers, marketers, and technology users themselves. Across a variety of digital domains, including health, learning, marketing and commerce, information searching, social media, news, and entertainment, there is an impetus to construct, evaluate, and design engaging user experiences. Engagement is about creating satisfied consumers, learners, and searchers, but this is only part of the story. Engagement may be used as evidence that a business is meeting (or failing to meet) its performance outcomes and therefore has economic implications. Engagement may also mediate positive individual and social outcomes, such as learning and personal growth, collaboration and connectivity, civic participation, knowledge transfer, or health behaviour change. Thus, it is critical to understand user engagement in an era where so many experiences and transactions are digitally mediated and hinge upon the ability to motivate, captivate, and compel.

As the chapters in this book demonstrate, user engagement has been investigated by researchers in a variety of disciplines, each with their own unique lens. As UE scholars and professionals, we approach our work with particular ideologies and perspectives that have been shaped and honed through years of education and professional experience. Our theoretical stance informs how we propose to define, model, and measure UE. For example, let us imagine that we are interested in UE in eLearning.

1. One researcher may underscore how social variables, such as students' peer network in the learning environment, interact with media features and affordances (e.g. discussion forums, peer feedback on assignments) to foster engagement.
2. Another researcher may be more interested in the role of individual differences, such as learning style or self-efficacy, in engendering perceived engagement with course modules.

In these examples, the researchers' theoretical stance informs the variables and outcomes of interest and dictates how the study of UE is approached: the first researcher may draw upon social network analysis or communications theory, while the second researcher may adopt a cognitive or constructivist orientation. Both researchers seek to understand how factors within the eLearning environment—media, mode of instruction, content, and other students—facilitate engagement and, by extension, learning outcomes. Thus, each has similar goals in that they wish to understand UE and how it affects student learning, but each will likely take very different paths despite operating within the same domain.

User engagement, as with other aspects of subjective user experience, is a complex phenomenon. Users bring personal histories, knowledge, skills, and emotions to their interactions with technologies, while systems vary in terms of how they present and organize system features and content. When user and system meet, there is typically some kind of goal (i.e. what users hope to achieve) and one or more tasks (i.e. how users go about achieving their goal) instigating the interaction. Goals may be leisure or work oriented and therefore fuelled by different motivations; tasks may be clearly articulated or fuzzy in terms of how they will be performed and their anticipated outcome. Furthermore, all user-system interactions are situated in broader individual, organizational, and social contexts that both facilitate and constrain engagement. In short, UE is a complex concept to investigate.

Varied disciplinary perspectives allow us to work on individual pieces of this complex puzzle at different levels of granularity. Some of us try to understand user engagement at the level of the individual, whereas others look at UE across millions of searchers or hundreds of employees in an organization. At some point, however, we need to connect these pieces into a cohesive picture. When we see how researchers in other fields and domains are framing, exploring, measuring, and designing for user engagement, we gain a level of awareness that benefits our own work as well as collective efforts. We analyse and compare approaches and findings to lend insight into our own research questions and dilemmas while simultaneously working to identify research priorities, gaps, and opportunities for collaboration.

The purpose of this book is not to constrain UE to one perspective but to offer a well-rounded appreciation for UE across different domains and disciplines. We begin this text with foundational chapters that describe theoretical and methodological approaches to user engagement; the remaining contributions examine UE from different disciplinary perspectives and across a variety of computer-mediated environments, including social and communications media, online search, eLearning, games, and eHealth.

The chapters on "Theoretical Perspectives on User Engagement" and "Translating Theory into Methodological Practice" constitute the introduction to the book and can be read as distinct or continuing chapters. In the chapter "Theoretical Perspectives on User Engagement", user engagement as a concept is explored and exploded. By focusing on three key principles for evaluating concepts, clarity, scope, and meaning, and evaluating the literature to date that defines, dissects, and discusses UE, O'Brien raises several questions about what we mean by UE, what kinds of boundaries we can place on and around it, and what are its antecedents and outcomes. This chapter then addresses two theoretical frameworks from positive psychology (Flow Theory) and education (Dewey's Philosophy of Experience) that have informed much work on UE; two case studies featuring recent dissertation work demonstrate the integration of multiple theoretical perspectives and inform methodology and design. Lastly, a number of conceptual and measurement models are articulated and compared. The chapter concludes by drawing together evidence and ideas from the aforementioned sections to present a series of unifying propositions and open questions to inform future UE research.

Measurement of UE is the focus of the chapter "Translating Theory into Methodological Practice". Rather than review all of the various ways in which UE is being measured—which are diverse, exciting, context-dependent, and mirror current trends and practices in human-computer interaction—O'Brien looks at the robustness of the user engagement scale (UES) across various domains. Through a review of the literature that has adopted and adapted the UES, the author looks specifically at its reliability, validity, and generalizability within and across contexts as a measurement tool. The purpose of the chapter is to examine the strengths, weaknesses, and unknowns of the UES, but also the reciprocal relationship between theory and the development and application of measurement instruments using the UES as the example.

In the chapter "eLearning", Wiebe and Sharek begin by asking a pivotal question, "Why do we care about engagement in eLearning?" In learning environments, engagement is not an end in and of itself. Rather, it mediates learners' short- and long-term goals and the formal and self-evaluative outcomes that indicate progress toward those goals. The authors use an example of an engineering student to illustrate goal formation, schema development, and behavioural change, while also linking these ideas to the design of eLearning environments. The emphasis of this chapter is that engagement with instructional content is "a necessary precondition to learning" and this position is anchored in theory and application; case studies derived from an experiment and a massive open online course (MOOC) are used to reinforce the theoretically derived characteristics of engaging eLearning environments within these unique settings that vary in scale.

Digital games are the focus of the chapter "Engagement in Digital Games". Cairns draws upon O'Brien's Process Model of User Engagement (see chapter "Theoretical Perspectives on User Engagement") to situate the game experience (GX) literature on digital games. He fleshes out the temporal aspects of game play from the point of engagement, through sustained engagement, disengagement, and re-engagement and the attributes that characterize these stages. However, he points out that the Process Model fails to capture two essential aspects of digital game engagement: (1) individual differences, or why specific people play specific games; and (2) the way in which players engage *outside of the game*, for example, thinking about the game when they are not playing it, which may result in looking for information that will support and progress game play at a future point. A case could be made that these missing aspects are not exclusive to digital games. Cairns calls the latter point a "blurring" of the disengagement phase and questions how we should look at engagement: within a single gaming session or across a series of sessions.

Sutcliffe, in his chapter on designing for user experience and engagement, places clear limits on the temporal aspects of engagement, dealing with engagement at the single session level (chapter "Designing for User Experience and Engagement"). He presents a model that encompasses the *context* (e.g. who the users are and the domain in which they are interacting) and leads to the selection of *criteria* (e.g. interactivity, content, aesthetics) that influence decision attributes that inform the *evaluation of experience*. The chapter is rich in examples of "engaging" design, and the author emphasizes, in particular, the affective components of users—both their personal dispositions and the emotions engendered through interaction. However, Sutcliffe states that the goal of the chapter is not prescriptive and that design is something that continuously evolves; thus this chapter serves to provide design knowledge and inspiration rather than being a "how to" approach to engaging design.

In the chapter "User Engagement with Digital Health Technologies", Kostkova crafts her chapter on eHealth around four main areas of interest: knowledge or attitude change, impact at the point of care, integrative digital storytelling, and professional communities of practice (CoP). Each of these ideas is explored and illustrated with concrete examples of eHealth technologies designed and adapted to meet the needs of a specific group of health consumers or practitioners. The author underscores the need to articulate the *purpose* of an eHealth technology *before* determining what mode of delivery and design is most appropriate for engaging the user. She also raises the conundrum that while it is fine to design "engaging" eHealth portals and environments, engagement cannot occur without, first, the awareness that they exist and, second, the ability to access them physically and intellectually.

From eHealth we move to information searching in the chapter "Engagement in Information Search". Edwards and Kelly explore search engagement through small-scale and large-scale search studies, illuminating factors of systems, users (e.g. individual differences), and tasks (e.g. degree of complexity) that impact engaging outcomes. Their review includes a range of self-report, behavioural, and physiological measures of engagement and related concepts, such as interest, that speak to the range and growing sophistication of the measurement of search engagement. Yet, they also describe the limitations of measures—particularly when they are used in isolation. For example, behavioural signals are reliable when they are linked to cognitive and affective signals, yet on their own may be highly interpretive. Relatedly, measures that are not subjected to rigorous evaluation affect the quality of the conclusions that we can draw from the research.

Oh and Sundar approach user engagement from a communications perspective in their chapter "User Engagement with Interactive Media: A Communication Perspective", with interactivity at the heart of their model. Physical interactions with media facilitate cognitive and emotional involvement, which leads to content absorption, culminating in behavioural outcomes which the authors term "outreach". As such, they emphasize that user engagement has cognitive, affective, and behavioural components and that media—its content and interactive affordances—can affect people's experiences. However, the challenge for designers is translating conceptual findings into application. What is more, Oh and Sundar acknowledge the complexity of media engagement "that involves several precursors and moderators", speculating that individuals may be one such precursor. Thus a strength of this chapter—in addition to their model—is (similar to Cairns) their consideration of factors *outside* of the interactive media experience.

An additional model of user engagement is presented in the chapter "A Model of Social Media Engagement: User Profiles, Gratifications, and Experiences" by McCay-Peet and Quan-Haase to explain social media engagement. Their model includes several components: presentation of self, action and participation, uses and gratifications, positive experiences, usage and activity counts, and social context, which are discussed in depth with relevant evidence and examples. The model supports the main thrust of the chapter: "By examining both tangible indicators of engagement, such as usage and activity counts, as well as more abstract indicators relating to positive user experiences, we can begin to understand why people engage at the level they do, with what kinds of social media platforms, and to what effect". This chapter concludes with illustrative case studies, but also some thought-provoking questions to guide our inquiry in this area and which move us beyond individual outcomes of user engagement to ethical and social implications of social media engagement.

The book concludes by bridging the cross-disciplinary perspectives presented in each chapter and proposing an agenda for future research in this area. This agenda focuses specifically on building robust theoretical and measurement models of UE, ensuring that research informs design and that application informs research, and raising awareness of the larger ethical and societal issues within which our work is situated. It is our sincere hope that this book will appeal to established and emerging academic and industry researchers who will take up and pursue these various research challenges.

## Acknowledgements

We would like to thank everyone involved in helping us to bring this book into being, not least our contributing authors who spent considerable time and effort to produce insightful chapters that share their experiences of studying engagement. We would also like to thank the staff at Springer, especially Ralf Gerstner, who have patiently guided the production of the book. Paul Cairns would like to personally thank Heather O'Brien for pulling him onto this project late in the day. It has been a lot of fun! He would also like to thank Heather O'Brien for putting up with his late-evening LaTeX fettling. Heather O'Brien would like to thank and acknowledge the support of her colleagues at the iSchool, UBC, and beyond, including Elaine Toms with whom this engagement journey began. And to Paul Cairns for coming aboard, being the book's "Latex hero", and never being in short supply of humour and encouragement.

In the end, this book is for you, the reader. We hope you find here insight and inspiration that will lead you to produce exciting research and applications on UE in whatever field you belong to.

Vancouver, British Columbia, Canada                                              Heather O'Brien
York, UK                                                                                      Paul Cairns
September 2015

# References

1. Blythe, M.A., Overbeeke, K., Monk, A.F., Wright, P.C. (eds.): Funology: From Usability to Enjoyment. Springer, Netherlands, Dordrecht (2003)
2. Hassenzahl, M., Tractinsky, N.: User experience—a research agenda. Behav. Inf. Technol. **25**(2), 91–97 (2006)
3. Pine II, B.J., Gilmore, J.H.: The Experience Economy. Harvard Business School Press, Boston (1999)

# Contents

# Contributors

**Paul Cairns** University of York, York, UK

**Ashlee Edwards** University of North Carolina, Chapel Hill, NC, USA

**Diane Kelly** University of North Carolina, Chapel Hill, NC, USA

**Patty Kostkova** Department of Computer Science, University College London, London, UK

**Lori McCay-Peet** University of Western Ontario, London, ON, Canada

**Heather O'Brien** University of British Columbia, Vancouver, BC, Canada

**Jeeyun Oh** Robert Morris University, Moon, PA, USA

**Anabel Quan-Haase** University of Western Ontario, London, ON, Canada

**David Sharek** Playgraph LLC, Cary, NC, USA

**S. Shyam Sundar** Pennsylvania State University, State College, PA, USA

**Alistair Sutcliffe** Manchester Business School, University of Manchester, Manchester, UK

**Eric Wiebe** North Carolina State University, Raleigh, NC, USA

# Theoretical Perspectives on User Engagement

**Heather O'Brien**

## 1  Introduction

Over the past 30 years, and particularly the past decade, user engagement (UE) has become a buzzword in a variety of domain and application areas, including search engines, online gaming platforms, museum portals, and mobile health apps. It is clear, given the attention the concept is receiving within academia and industry, that UE is a vital part of users' interactions with technology. What is not clear, however, is what is meant by the term: What do we mean when we say that our goal is to engage users with technology, and what are the benefits of doing so? How we define UE conceptually is indicative of the larger set of values, contexts, and disciplinary perspectives that inform human relationships with technology and how we operationalize, measure, and design for human-computer experiences.

The purpose of this chapter is to explore user engagement using a theoretical lens. This review is not exhaustive, but aims to provide an introduction for engaging with subsequent chapters. Explicitly, this chapter synthesizes existing definitions and exposes their overlap and inconsistencies; it examines two theoretical approaches, Mihaly Csikszentmihalyi's Flow Theory and John Dewey's Philosophy of Experience, that have informed much work in the area of UE and describes published behavioural and measurement models that depict the engagement process, its influences, and its antecedents. Two case studies are used to illustrate the interconnectedness of theory and application.

This chapter is about showcasing current theoretical perspectives on UE and their origins. Yet it is also about highlighting resonance and dissonance within the UE literature for the purposes of advancing UE research and application. I conclude this chapter with a set of unifying propositions that highlight areas of consensus and

H. O'Brien (✉)
iSchool, The University of British Columbia, Vancouver, BC, Canada
e-mail: h.obrien@ubc.ca

© Springer International Publishing Switzerland 2016
H. O'Brien, P. Cairns (eds.), *Why Engagement Matters*,
DOI 10.1007/978-3-319-27446-1_1

1

may form the basis for a theory of user engagement. In addition, I address "open questions" in the study of UE that articulate future research directions. The intention is that these propositions and open questions will stay with the reader in subsequent chapters as we explore UE with different computer-mediated environments and multidisciplinary contributors, as well as to inspire emerging research to explicate theory and its role in application.

## 2   The Concept of User Engagement (UE)

The word engagement is part of our everyday vernacular; engagement can and often does mean a range of things, but the general premise is that to engage or be engaged is in some way beneficial. As we shift our focus to what engagement means in the realm of human-computer interaction (HCI), these general definitions become inadequate and nondescript: What do we *mean* when we say our goal is to engage people with and through technology? Defining UE may seem an unnecessary task to some; many researchers investigate UE in the absence of any articulated definition. In my view, however, it is the cornerstone of measurement, theory building, and system design. At the same time, many of us who grapple with the question of how to define UE see that it is not straightforward. Definitions of UE proposed over the past three decades show both consensus and variation. The purpose of this section is not to champion one definition over others. Rather, it is to describe various definitions and their overlap/divergence in order to shed light on some emerging questions that can inform readers' interactions with later chapters.

### 2.1   Defining User Engagement

In some of the earliest discussions of user engagement with technology, Brenda Laurel called UE "[t]he state of mind that we must maintain in order to enjoy a representation of an action" [31, pp. 112–113], and Quesenbery suggested that it is a component of usability (along with effectiveness, efficiency, ease of learning, and error tolerance) that "draws people in" and "encourages interactions"[49, p. 86]. Another strategy has been to define UE according to the characteristics it engenders in users (e.g. a sense of control [6]) or evokes through their interactions with systems (e.g. a "state of playfulness" [66, p. 64]). Jacques, for instance, focused specifically on the dynamic nature of users' attention and interest during interactions with educational multimedia systems when he defined UE as "a user's response to an interaction that gains, maintains, and encourages their attention, particularly when they are intrinsically motivated" [27, p. 103].

I built upon Jacques' work [27], proposing and testing additional attributes of engaging experiences in a series of qualitative and quantitative studies. Through an extensive literature review and interview study, I conjectured that UE was "a category of user experience characterized by attributes of challenge, positive affect, endurability, aesthetic and sensory appeal, attention, feedback, variety/novelty, interactivity, and perceived user control"[42, p. 941]. Later, through the construction and empirical validation of an experiential rating scale to measure user engagement, I honed this definition further. UE was recast slightly as "a quality of user experience with technology" characterized by the perceived usability and aesthetic appeal of the system, focused attention, novelty, felt involvement, and endurability [38, p. 131] and [44, p. 64]. Others have also viewed UE within the context of an overall interactive user experience [62] with an emphasis on what compels people to become engaged and sustain their use of a technology [29]. Dobrian et al. [18] added user involvement to this interactive view.

However, there are some ambiguities when we look critically at definitions of UE. For example, Brandtzaeg et al. [8] suggested the major component of engagement is control, whereas Webster and Ahuja [65] labelled engagement "Flow *without* user control" [emphasis added]. To better appreciate the differences, definitions can be compared according to principles for evaluating concepts, such as clarity, scope, and meaning [64].

Clarity: What is the object of emphasis in UE, that is, interface, system features, content, and other participants in the environment?
Scope: Does UE comprise affective, behavioural, and/or cognitive elements? What are the temporal, contextual, and conceptual boundaries of UE?
Meaning: What are the defining and accompanying features of UE?

The following sections examine these principles in more detail as they relate to UE; this analysis leads to a series of emerging questions for further consideration (Table 1).

## 2.2 Clarity

Peters et al. [48] addressed the question of what is being engaged with at the micro level of the interaction, that is, the object of focus, and the shifting of attention from person to object or from person to other actors in the environment. In addition to the micro level is the macro level of the interaction. The macro level may be thought of in terms of what people bring to the interaction, that is, individual differences, how the system facilitates or impedes engagement, and the setting in which the interaction occurs. The microview reveals the complexity of evaluating and designing interactions with technologies such as interactive displays, museum technologies, mobile applications, or virtual agents and robots where we must capture both individual and social activities and their contributions to overall UE. The macro-level perspective involves looking beyond the interaction itself to users' thoughts, feelings and behaviours prior to, during, and as a consequence of the interaction, as well as the content that is being delivered and system functionality.

This brings us to the important question of whether UE manifests within the user or is precipitated by the system. While many researchers emphasize users' perceptions of the interaction [38, 42], responses to the interaction [27], state of mind [31, 65], or feelings [8], others take a more design-orientated focus, tying UE to system qualities and emphasizing the designer's role in creating engagement [3, 49, 62]. Colbert and Boodoo [14], for example, tested two versions of a bicycle repair website, one that was compliant with guidelines for online content and one that was non-compliant. They found that, while there were no differences in bounce rates or number of pages visited for each of the sites, web users spent more time interacting with the compliant version and returned to it more frequently. Significantly, this study attributed differences in behavioural engagement to the presentation of web content, rather than to differences in individuals or the tasks they aimed to accomplish with the website, as these were unknown to the researchers. Based on these findings, we might speculate further on how users' evaluations of content (credibility, relevance, informativeness) contribute to UE; there is already rich scholarship in the disciplines of information science [53] and communications [60] that can contribute to this line of inquiry.

Other research demonstrates how changing the design of a system can change not only how users interact with it physically but also social interactions and the interpretation of the message. Aasbakken et al. [1] implemented a touch-screen and button-based installation of an interactive water conservation exhibit. Children were drawn to the familiar touch-screen installation, spending more time with it and physically interacting with it more frequently than the button-based version. Interestingly, the authors noted that the "artistic message" was interpreted differently depending on the installation and that the design could unintentionally alter the integrity of that message.

In addition to asking whether UE rests with the individual, the content, or the system, different types of UE have been identified. For example, I found that online news readers reported two distinct engagement paths: one group of participants emphasized the novelty and interestingness of news items, whereby interface features were sometimes seen as an unwanted distraction; another group described the interactive and participatory features as central to their engagement [40]. Patel et al. [47] found three types of engagement in their study of a photo sharing application. Small groups of friends participated in a city tour, followed by a picture sorting task of photos taken during sightseeing and, finally, a focus group. Data from the sorting activities and focus groups revealed that engagement occurred with the act of taking pictures, with other people in the group, and with the city environment. Thus, task, social, and contextual engagement were all part of the groups' overall engagement with the photo app. The role of the environment is especially pronounced in studies like [47] that investigate mobile technologies. For example, Cocciolo and Rabina [13] asked students to use an iPad to participate in the GeoStoryteller project, spending time in a physical neighbourhood as they learned about German immigration in New York. They found that being in the physical environment increased students' understanding of and interest in the topic, whereas augmented reality features of the interface did not, owing to usability issues and the challenges of "learn[ing] how to use a new technology on a conspicuous device in an uncontrolled environment" (p. 114). Thus engagement with place, rather than tool engagement, were defining aspects of engaging with immigration history in this study.

As a result, we must ask what the unit of analysis for UE is: user, system, content, or the broader social or physical context. This represents a complex problem for investigating UE and necessitates research that examines both micro- and macro-level interactions with one or more of these units.

## 2.3 Scope

As evidenced in this book, engagement is of interest to researchers from a variety of disciplines. Collectively, we investigate a range of computer-mediated experiences: for instance, how to motivate students in an online course, how to modify or track health behaviours, how to investigate search engagement, and why and to what extent people participate in online news and social media. The breadth of computer-mediated experiences across subject domains, applications, systems, and devices is such that identifying an all-inclusive definition is difficult if not impossible: overly specific definitions lead to disparate coverage for some contexts, while overly generalized definitions become meaningless and not applicable. But what boundaries can be drawn around user engagement?

One issue concerning scope is whether engagement is affective, behavioural, or cognitive in nature. Laurel [31] and Webster and Ho [66] described engagement as a cognitive state, while other definitions include behavioural components. For example, Jones [29] included "continued use" of the system and Quesenbery [49] and Sutcliffe [62] referred to being drawn into or participating in an interaction. Others have taken a more encompassing view: "Engagement describes their [users'] intrinsically motivated attraction [to a system] and is expressed in cognitive, behavioural and affective terms" [28, p. 57]. I have also taken this view, suggesting that UE consists of affective (e.g. motivation, positive and negative feelings), cognitive (e.g. challenge, interest), and behavioural (e.g. interactivity) components [38].

Existing definitions of UE are typically not limited to one type of technology (with the exception of [29]), but focus instead on the qualities of systems more broadly (e.g. aesthetic appeal) and how the system—and users' interactions with it—affects users' internal states (e.g. motivation, interest, attention). However, the temporal and contextual scope of UE is problematic, and we do not adequately distinguish it from other qualities of interactive experiences.

For instance, UE has been described as "a state of playfulness" [66]; UE and Play Theory share similar characteristics [38, 42], but play is a distinct concept from UE. Webster and Martocchio [67] define microcomputer playfulness as "a situation-specific characteristic [that] represents a type of intellectual or cognitive playfulness. It describes an individual's tendency to interact spontaneously, inventively, and imaginatively with microcomputers" (p. 202). Like play, UE may be specific to a particular situation. For example, I may find web searching tedious in some instances and highly engaging at other times, depending on what I am searching for, how interesting the search results are, or how much time I have to spend browsing the web. Webster and Martocchio [67] highlighted play as something that is cognitive in nature and that precipitates activity. This may also be the case for user engagement, but it could also be the case that physical interactions with technology facilitate cognitive involvement. Thus, UE does not assume directionality in terms of how cognitive and behavioural processes interact. In addition to cognition and behaviour, engagement involves an emotional or affective investment, which is not present in Webster and Martocchio's [67] definition of microcomputer playfulness. Lastly, though UE may lead people to interact "spontaneously, inventively, and imaginatively" with technology, engaged users may also interact routinely and predictably. An online news reader may habitually peruse local news and sports each morning and report their subjective engagement as high though there is nothing particularly novel about the interaction itself.

In addition to play, current definitions also do not distinguish UE from fun, cognitive absorption, or interest. In fact, some researchers have explicitly used engagement interchangeably with other terms including attention, interactivity [46, 61, 63], and cognitive load (i.e. the propensity to seek out and take on challenges) [57] because people need a means of operationalizing the concept. One way in which to distinguish some of these concepts would be to categorize some as personality driven, that is, cognitive absorption, and others as situational, that is, interest and fun [10], though we still need to consider the relationship amongst various kinds of subjective experiences in HCI.

With regard to the temporal boundaries of UE, Sutcliffe [62, pp. 3–4] distinguished UE as something that occurs "within a session" from user experience (UX) as the more long-term adoption and use of technology. However, other researchers have not delineated UE and UX as such, suggesting that "continued use" is part of engagement [29] and that engagement leads to short-term and long-term re-engagement [38]. In addition, intention to re-use has been called an indicator of engagement [66]. As a result, the temporal boundaries of user engagement are vague.

Related to this is the question of context and whether engagement is a process that occurs during the interaction, the product of the interaction, or both. The ways in which we are trying to measure user engagement would suggest that we believe it to be both: we are attempting to capture physiological or behavioural indicators over the course of an interaction while also gathering data on users' perceptions of and future behaviours with applications. UE is then both "in the moment" and a product of the users' reflections and evaluations of their interactions with technologies; this embeds engaging episodes within larger user experiences. However, this poses the challenge of trying to isolate and extract instances of UE within broader experiences and raises the conceptual dilemma of distinguishing UE and UX.

Law et al. [32] expressed that UX, as a field of research, is still maturing, with researchers continuing to struggle with questions of scope and measurement—

issues that are mirrored in UE research. Hassenzahl [25] defined UX as "momentary, primarily evaluative feeling (good-bad) while interacting with a product or service" whereby "UX becomes a temporal phenomenon, present-oriented and changing over time" (p. 12). Hassenzahl also stated that UX can be "made" by focusing on specific human needs and values in the design of technologies. UX researchers have described "meta-experiences," where cumulative experiences become part of personal histories and identities [4, 33]. I believe that UE is a catalyst within and component of these meta-experiences but that UE may or may not be part of the UX: users may describe a range of experiences in their interactions with technology, with engagement being only one type. Sutcliffe [62] has maintained that UE is a "quality of the interactive experience". This definition encompasses different types of interactive experiences (as opposed to passive activities, such as watching television), but does not specify the "quality" per se, and raises the question of whether UE occurs during passive interactions; media and communications scholars would likely say "yes".

In addition to UX, usability is another concept that is both distinct and inter-related. Quesenbery [49] categorized engagement as a component of usability, whereas I have argued that usability is a dimension of user engagement: usable systems do not necessarily evoke engaging experiences, but without a minimum level of usability, engagement with the system is not possible [38, 42]. Whether we look at usability as part of the engagement equation or UE as one aspect of usability determines the kinds of outcomes we expect from users' interactions with technology and our methodological and design approaches.

## 2.4 Meaning

In thinking about "meaning," it is useful to differentiate accompanying from defining features, where accompanying features as those that *predict* or *represent* *indicators or outcomes of* UE [64]. Accompanying features may be useful to include in models of user engagement or to develop hypothesis for theory building and testing in the context of research studies. Defining features, on the other hand, are present in the definition of engagement.

Many researchers have examined *attributes* as "defining features" of UE. Jacques [27] proposed the following attributes of engagement with educational multimedia systems: attention, motivation, perceived time, control, needs (experiential and utilitarian), and attitudes (feelings). I expanded this list to include ten different attributes of UE (aesthetic appeal, attention, challenge, endurability, feedback, interactivity, control, pleasure, sensory appeal, and variety/novelty) and looked at these in the narratives of gamers, searchers, online shoppers, and eLearners. I found that most—if not all—of these attributes manifested in users' engagement with these applications. In later work, I developed a self-report measure, the user engagement scale (UES), and reduced the number of attributes through factor analysis to perceived usability, aesthetic appeal, novelty, felt involvement, focused attention, and endurability [38, 42].

Jacques's work [27] heavily influenced my research, and there is much overlap in our approach to studying UE. For example, we both emphasized similar attributes, such as attention and motivation, though we looked at motivation from different perspectives. Jacques felt that intrinsic motivation was essential for UE within learning environments, whereas I explored utilitarian and hedonic motivations in my work with online shoppers [39]. This example of how motivation can be operationalized differently according to the domain of study suggests that attributes may be highly context dependent. To demonstrate this idea further, I found that novelty was a salient attribute of interacting with an online news environment [40] and an educational webcast system [43], but was not central to experiences with other types of technologies [44, 68]. McCay-Peet et al. [34] had similar findings in their Amazon Mechanical Turk study, where participants reported becoming "distracted" by news content that was not relevant to their information search task, but was nonetheless personally interesting and attention grabbing. In addition to context dependency, the manifestation and expression of attributes may be user dependent. In my interviews with video game players, I found that some players became "hooked" on particular games that had realistic graphics, whereas others escaped into non-aesthetic games with powerful storytelling elements [38].

Thus, the nature of UE's defining features—what they are and how they are manifested during engaging experiences—appears to be context and user dependent; this translates into the need for a fluid definition of UE. Constructing a flexible definition while maintaining some consistency is not an easy undertaking.

Less emphasis has been placed on accompanying features of UE, though there are some exceptions. Hyder devised and tested an elaborate model of engagement antecedents (e.g. aesthetics, product involvement, depth of navigation, etc.) and consequences (e.g. intention to purchase, perceived value, brand recall, etc.) in his study of e-commerce website engagement [26, p. 399]. He tested over 20 hypotheses, leading to the findings that aesthetics predicted website engagement, which consisted of positive affect, focused attention, challenge, curiosity, and involvement. Website engagement predicted consumers' perceptions of value, intention to purchase, the desire not to switch to competitors, as well as increased brand loyalty. Such studies can lead us to consider how to build more sophisticated models that take into consideration both antecedents and outcomes of UE so that we might evolve our understanding of UE's accompanying features.

## 2.5 Assessment of UE Definitions

The evaluation of existing definitions of user engagement reveals many issues pertaining to clarity, scope, and meaning. Based on this analysis, I summarize these issues as outstanding questions for defining UE (Table 1).

**Table 1** Emerging questions for defining user engagement

| Evaluation criteria | Questions relating to the evaluation of existing definitions |
| --- | --- |
| *Clarity* | What do we mean by user engagement?<br>How do we understand UE at both the micro and macro levels?<br>What is the emphasis of engagement? In other words, should we focus on users, systems, content, or some combination of these? Should we distinguish engagement with tasks, technologies, other people, and the experiential setting? |
| *Scope* | How do we (or can we) construct a definition of engagement that is appropriate for all computer-mediated contexts?<br>Is UE affective, cognitive, and/or behavioural?<br>What is the temporal nature of UE?<br>Is UE a product of interaction, a process, or both?<br>What is the relationship between UE and related concepts, such as UX, usability, fun, play, etc.? |
| *Defining and accompanying features* | What are the accompanying (i.e. predictors and outcomes) and defining (i.e. attributes) features of user engagement?<br>How stable are these across different contexts or user populations? |

These emerging questions suggest a number of research directions and should fuel theoretical discussions. How we define UE has implications for the theoretical perspectives we use to frame engagement, which I now explore in greater depth.

## 3 Theoretical Perspectives for Framing User Engagement

Theory helps us make sense of users' experiences: it informs how we design studies and interfaces; it allows us to derive and model user, system, and contextual factors that predict UE; and it places expected and unexpected outcomes of user studies and design experiments into a broader interpretive framework. Thus, theory is crucial for moving UE research and practice forward. However, the term theory is problematic.

> Like so many words that are bandied about, the word theory threatens to become mean-ingless. Because its referents are so diverse – including everything from minor working hypotheses, through comprehensive but vague and unordered speculations, to axiomatic systems of thought – use of the word often obscures rather than creates understanding [35, p. 39].

Indeed, the theory universe is vast, and there is a variety of associated terminology: paradigms, frameworks, metatheories, theories, and models that range from the general to the specific and from the abstract to the concrete. Each discipline has its own way of thinking about, defining and constructing theory, and as a multidisciplinary set of researchers, we bring these disciplinary lenses to bear on our work in UE. This chapter does not argue that one paradigm or theoretical perspective is superior for the purposes of framing UE, but presents some of the approaches that have been used in UE research, and shows the outcomes of these applications in terms of research findings, behavioural models, and new directions. I do not distinguish models, theories, metatheories, and paradigms here but rather take the more encompassing view that what follows are "theoretical perspectives".

In terms of what theoretical orientations have been used in UE research, Csikszentmihalyi's Theory of Optimal Experience or Flow Theory [15] is commonly cited. Other theoretical frameworks have included Aesthetic Theory [5], Interaction [56], Play Theory [59, 69], and Social Presence Theory [51]. In my own work [38, 42], I adopted McCarthy and Wright's Threads of Experience [33], which is rooted in John Dewey's pragmatist Philosophy of Experience [17]. In this section, I elaborate on two theoretical streams: Positive Psychology, specifically Flow Theory, and Dewey's Theory of Experience, with examples on how these theories have been applied in UE research.

## 3.1 Positive Psychology: Flow Theory

The Theory of Optimal Experiences, commonly referred to as Flow Theory, hails from positive psychology. Its founder, Mihaly Csikszentmihalyi, observed that activities such as rock climbing, reading, creating art, and meditating induced Flow in people. "Flow" is a state "in which people are so involved in an activity that nothing else seems to matter; the experience itself is so enjoyable that people will do it even at great cost, for the sheer sake of doing it" [15, p. 4]. According to Csikszentmihalyi Flow, Flow is characterized by enjoyment, challenge, intrinsic motivation, focused attention, positive reinforcement, clear goals, personal control, and temporal dissociation. Central to Flow Theory is the idea of meaning making: people are free to focus on their goals when their feelings, thoughts, and actions are aligned with their social motivations and biological needs [15, p. 27].

Positive psychology is finding new ground in HCI with the emergence of "positive computing" [11] and its emphasis on technology for human well-being. However, Flow Theory has been employed within HCI for some time. It has been used to explore users' reactions to and motivations to use various computer-mediated tools and interfaces [21, 30], to understand the role of situational and personality variables in users' interactions with computers [49], and to help designers build systems or measures to encourage or capture the Flow state [20].

Unfortunately, however, the adoption of Flow in HCI has resulted in "conceptual inconsistencies" where Flow is equated with engagement, immersion, presence, cognitive absorption, and other terms [55, p. 514]. Recognizing that "the ambiguity of the [Flow] concept has created a situation in which research in the area might be studying altogether different phenomena" [55, p. 515], Romero and Calvillo-Gámez proposed a phenomenological, embodied interaction framework for incorporating Flow Theory into HCI. Specifically they asked researchers to understand and distinguish effortful, effortless, and captive attention; recognize the centrality of the body in Flow activities and digital interactions; explore the sense of expansion users feel when in the Flow state; and differentiate between Flow experiences *with* versus *through* technologies.

Romero and Calvillo-Gámez's [55] embodied view of Flow is not only useful for HCI researchers interested in Flow experiences but is highly relevant for framing user engagement, particularly in terms of how it is related to and distinct from Flow. Engagement has been called a "subset of Flow" and "Flow without user control" [65], and it is felt that the focused attention of Flow is a central component of UE [48]. While UE may be part of the "Flow continuum" originally proposed by Csikszentmihalyi and taken up by Romero and Calvillo-Gáamez [55], saying that engagement is Flow without user control suggests that UE is suited for characterizing only passive interactions with technology or that engaged users are willing to forfeit control to the system, which I do not believe to be the case.

In earlier work [38, 42], I speculated that challenge, feedback, user control, attention, intrinsic motivation, meaningfulness, positive emotions, and goal directedness—all characteristics of Flow—might be part of UE. However, when I analysed my interviews with technology users, I observed some important differences between the characteristics of Flow and the experience of UE. First, challenge was not always necessary for UE—and in fact, it deterred engagement for some participants sharing experiences within particular domains; further, challenge manifested differently; for example, the physical challenge of manipulating and navigating a game space is different from the intellectual challenge of reading electronic news or books. In addition, users did not always have goals in mind when they became engaged. Web browsers, for instance, enjoyed surfing without any objective, and gamers played to pass the time. Furthermore, engaged users described both intrinsic and extrinsic motivations for initiating and sustaining their interactions with digital media, and this supports the idea that some technologically mediated activities are not self-selected. We use the systems our work and academic organizations purchase or license (or that we can obtain for free), and we perform tasks using those systems. If we are able to derive some level of UE within these mandatory use settings, it may enhance our productivity or at least make tasks feel less onerous.

While most of UE work has emphasized positive emotions, there needs to be more exploration and emphasis on the role of negative affect in UE and how this is a distinction between Flow and UE. In my work in the online news domain [40], I noted that some news readers were drawn into news items that were serious, controversial, sensational, and, frankly, grizzly; another work in online news [2] suggests a characteristic of engagement that is not an explicit part of Flow—interest. Arapakis et al. [2] performed a sentiment analysis of over 13,000 news articles and then created a corpus of 18 articles that varied in interestingness (high vs. low) and polarity (positive vs. negative). In a subsequent user study that employed eye tracking and self-report measures, the researchers found that interesting news content increased positive affect and led to more focused attention and longer fixations on new and popular news item comments. Results also indicated that affect, interest ratings, enjoyment, and curiosity heightened when news content increased in sentiment but became more negative. Thus both the cognitive (interestingness) and affective (polarity) elements of content informed users' perceptions of the news reading experience. Peters et al. [48] relay that interest is an affective state that is tightly coupled with attention: "attention is deemed to be required for varying degrees of affective processing while, conversely, emotional stimuli capture, maintain and may modulate attention" (Sect. 2.3, para 1). McCay-Peet et al. [34] demonstrated this in their study of visual saliency with online news content. They found that interest in content and wanting to find out more about news items based on headlines helped predict self-reported focused attention.

Thinking about the role of interest in particular and negative emotion more broadly, there is reason to pursue how negative affect predicts and sustains engagement—and this relates to the aforementioned point about mandatory system use. As researchers and designers, we may need people to engage with things that induce discomfortable or negative emotions. This line of thinking is linked with the emerging area of "uncomfortable HCI". For instance, Halbert and Nathan [22] explored the link between negative emotions and critical reflection for the purposes of facilitating transformative experiences around decolonizing pedagogies in the context of an online graduate course. Their work pushes back on the notion that UE should always be positive and provides a more nuanced view of UE: if UE is intended to result in learning, health behavioural change, political involvement, personal growth, etc., then we must anticipate that UE is more complicated emotionally, cognitively, and behaviourally.

In summary, Flow and UE share many of the same attributes, though the degree and manifestation of these attributes may be what sets these concepts apart. Cairns et al. [10] make a similar argument about the relationship between Flow and immersion in the context of gaming, where immersion is defined according to the level of involvement experienced by the player and "total immersion" is akin to the Flow state or being "in the game". In distinguishing UE and Flow, we see that Flow necessitates challenge or intrinsic motivation, whereas UE may not. There is a close coupling of attention, interest, and affect inherent in both UE and Flow, but the presence of negative and positive affect may be what sets these types of experiences apart; Flow is a pleasurable experience, whereas UE may involve a more complex range of emotions. We might also speculate that UE and Flow form part of the same continuum of subjective experience where UE is necessary for Flow, but Flow is not necessary for UE: the engaged user may or may not move into a Flow state before disengaging with a technology. Nonetheless, the impact of Flow, and positive psychology more broadly, on UE research is apparent and far reaching.

## 3.2   John Dewey's Philosophy of Experience

Dewey, a learning theorist, viewed experience as something that occurs within the individual and influences current and future attitudes and behaviours. Yet it is also something that is shaped by the past and acts in conjunction with the present or the "objective conditions under which experiences are had" [17, p. 39]. Dewey's Philosophy of Experience consists of two basic principles: continuity and interaction.

First, Dewey emphasized the quality of experience, which he proposed was both an immediate and long-term concern, where "[w]holly independent of desire or intent, every experience lives on in further experience" [17, p. 27]. This idea, called the principle of continuity, is linked to "habit":

> The basic characteristics of habit is that every experience enacted and undergone modifies the one who acts and undergoes, while this modification affects, whether we wish it or not, the quality of subsequent experiences. For it is a somewhat different person who enters into them. The principle of habit so understood obviously goes deeper than the ordinary conception of a habit as a more or less fixed way of doing things, although it includes the latter as one of its special cases. It covers the formation of attitudes; attitudes that are emotional and intellectual; it covers our basic sensitivities and ways of meeting and responding to all the conditions which we meet in living. From this point of view, the principle of continuity of experience means that every experience both takes up something from those which have gone before and modifies in some way the quality of those which come after [17, p. 35].

Continuity, which reflects the way in which previous experiences influence future ones, resonates with UE if we view its temporality as both in the moment and over time.

The second principle, interaction, states that experience is the interplay between "objective and internal conditions" (the world, the self) and that "taken together, or in their interaction, they form what we call a situation"[17, p. 42]. In Dewey's terms, objective conditions are those which "interact with personal needs, desires, purposes, and capacities to create the experience which is had" [17, p. 44]; these include not only material objects but also other people and the social setting where the experience plays out.

Early work in systems engineering viewed interaction as the inputs and outputs created between users and systems. Moran's [36] framework, for instance, consisted of the physical devices (e.g. screen, keyboard, etc.) that constituted the system, the syntactic actions to initiate tasks (e.g. a series of mouse clicks to save a document), the semantic representations of tasks in the form of icons and menu options, and operational tasks (e.g. text-editing tasks such as underline and italicize). Norman [37] considered the system but also sought to incorporate user and designer into the picture. Norman's Gulfs of Execution and Evaluation model envisioned the system as bridging the gap between users' and designers' conceptual models of how the system should appear and function by, on the one hand, enhancing the skills and experiences of users and, on the other hand, enforcing "proper design" [37, p. 45] through an understanding of users' psychological needs. In this way, Norman sought a richer understanding of the "situation" by appreciating the unique perspectives of user and designer and their intersection at the system interface.

As we investigate the manifestation of UE with different applications, we see the role that context plays in the manifestation of UE in terms of the dimensions that are most intensely experienced by users. We understand that it is not only qualities of the system being interacted with but the broader social and physical setting in which the interaction takes place. Dewey's interaction principle makes it challenging to, for example, measure and design for UE: humans, technology objects, and contexts are dynamic, diverse, and evolving. However, this principle stresses the holistic nature of experience and confirms that engagement operates along a continuum with many influences and outcomes, rather than being an all-or-nothing response to technology.

This view of interaction is evident in HCI. Both Shedroff [58] and Laurel [31] described interactive experiences with technology as a continuum. For [58], the continuum ranged from passive to active and consists of six elements: control, feedback, productivity, creativity, communication, and adaptation, all of which constituted dimensions of "The Experience Cube". Laurel [31] viewed the interactivity continuum as comprising three rather than six components: frequency and number of potential interactions; range of options available to the user; and the significance of these choices with respect to needs, tasks, and goals.

Dewey saw the two principles—continuity and interaction—as connected in an "active union" that underscored the significance of the experience [17, p. 44]. In addition to these two principles, Dewey also advocated for social control and social enterprise. By social control, he felt that adults could intervene in children's education by introducing rules and standards, yet do so "without the violation of freedom" [17, p. 53]; we see this idea later embodied in Play Theory, the physical activity that encourages learning and creativity, is psychologically and socially beneficial, and involves aspects of competition and collaboration [52]. Social enterprise recognizes that actors are not only part of but contribute to the shaped environment. We might operationalize social enterprise differently today than in Dewey's time, with the plethora and impact of social networking, crowdsourcing, and other online applications, but the premise remains valuable. Lastly, Dewey stated that experience is initiated by the "formation of purpose"[17, p. 68]. This purpose may develop and evolve over the course of interaction through observation and participation.

Dewey's Philosophy of Experience, originally intended for the field of education, is highly applicable to UX, as explored by McCarthy and Wright [33] with their "Threads of Experience" and more specifically to UE. In my own work, I derived a behavioural model of UE consisting of a point of engagement, sustained engagement, disengagement, and re-engagement and subsequently mapped it to McCarthy and Wright's spatio-temporal, compositional, emotional, and sensual threads [33]. For example, the point of engagement was characterized by sensual qualities including aesthetic or "attention getting" elements and the novel presentation of information; motivation and interest formed the emotional thread at this stage of the engagement process [42, p. 948]. Qualitatively constructing the Process Model of UE and placing it within the larger context of the Threads of Experience gave me a richer, more holistic picture of UE as well as its constituent parts.

Dewey put forward that the quality of experience depends on the moment of interaction, as well as how it shapes future interactions; this is echoed in models of UE that emphasize reengagement and the varying levels of engagement possible

[28, 38, 42, 66]. In addition to highlighting both short- and long-term interactions, Dewey emphasized the interaction between learners and their environments, the need for some form of imposed control in the setting that does not remove learners' agency, and the existence of social enterprise. As we consider today's users and the affordances of modern devices (e.g. touch screens) and applications (e.g. social media, online learning systems) that emphasize interactivity and participation, we recognize the perfection of Dewey's ideas when applied to UE. Designers attempt to create physical and virtual spaces for experiences to unfold, balancing system affordances with user agency and leveraging the power of social networks and crowds to motivate interactions.

While engagement research has already learned much from Dewey, though perhaps not articulated as such, there are two areas that have not been sufficiently explored. First, Dewey emphasizes "purpose," yet little is known about the influence of goals and tasks on user engagement. Second, Dewey stressed accumulated experience but also the role of the social enterprise; more efforts could be invested to specifically examine the role of social practices and context on user engagement.

## 3.3   Case Studies of Multi-Theoretical Approaches to the Study of User Engagement

Much of the work on UE has some connection to positive psychology and Dewey's Philosophy of Experience, though other frameworks in the areas of motivation theory and cognition are drawn upon. Research need not be limited to one theory. In this section, I feature recent research that utilizes multiple theoretical frameworks to make sense of UE.

### 3.3.1   Case 1: Flow, Cognitive Load, and Engagement in Adaptive Video Games

Sharek [57] used Flow Theory, cognitive load theory (CLT), and engagement to test static, user-controlled, and adaptive gameplay approaches in a series of three experiments. Sharek looked at the nature of each gameplay approach in terms of difficulty, complexity, and the nature of user control in the gameplay trajectory and then used this grounding to situate his multi-theoretical framework.

Sharek examined Flow attributes, namely, clear goals, the immediacy and quality of feedback, the balance between player skill and task challenges, control, focused concentration, loss of self-awareness and external awareness, and time distortion (p. 15). He used Csikszentmihalyi's Flow Model, which proposed that Flow increases linearly as skill and challenge increase; "boredom" is the result of high skill and low challenge, and "anxiety" equates with low skill and high challenge. This Flow Model was later adapted to a four-channel model that added apathy (low skill, low challenge) to Flow, boredom, and anxiety. Sharek modified the model, slightly using "effortlessness" for apathy and "frustration" instead of anxiety. Into this space, Sharek introduced CLT, which also looks at the balance of challenge and skill; load may be extraneous, intrinsic, or germane. He reasoned that high intrinsic load would result in frustration, low intrinsic load would lead to effortlessness, and germane load would "link to the intrinsic motivation and positive affect required for a person to enter the Flow, and thus become actively engaged" (p. 23). In other words, intrinsic or extrinsic motivation would lead to an engaged state where the desire to participate would induce Flow.

These theoretical frameworks—Flow and CLT—were used to develop and test hypotheses regarding the measurement of UE and performance outcomes with a linear, user-controlled (choice), and adaptive version of a game called Grid Blocker (see chapter "eLearning"). Flow Theory also informed the design of the Game-clock mechanism that was imbedded in the game. Game-clock was designed to look at users' level of temporal dissociation and awareness with the idea that "the more times they checked the Game-clock, the more aware they were of the passage of time and therefore the less they were engaged in the game". However, after initial testing, "Game-clock showed more promise as a measure (during intermissions) of affect and desire to play the game" (p. 32). In addition to Game-clock, Sharek used other measures of UE in his three studies including subjective self-reports, such as the game engagement questionnaire (GEQ) [9], UES [30], NASA-TLX (cognitive load) [24], and Intrinsic Motivation Inventory [16]; and performance measures, such as time spent playing the game, number of errors, and "over-moves". In studies two and three, a secondary monitoring task was added to the primary gameplay task to increase cognitive complexity.

Overall, Sharek found that the adaptive game was more successful than the linear or choice-based game design in motivating players to take on increasing levels of challenge while still maintaining engagement and appropriate levels of cognitive load. Returning to the linear Flow Model, he concluded that "a linear increase in difficulty can provide a scaffolding effect where people will be able to develop their skills in a gradual manner"; this was supported by the fact that participants in the three studies did not experience frustration due to the gradual increase in difficulty. While he speculated that "those in the Linear condition experienced a degree of Flow", they may not have truly been engaged, and this has implications for serious games:

> ...in a learning context, just being in the Flow may not be enough to push a person into situations where their full potential may be realized. This is where Flow Theory and engagement part ways. In the context of learning and serious games, being engaged requires a person to not only be in the Flow state but also to actively seek out more difficult challenges rather than simply balance their skill with the challenges of the task (p. 92).

For the purposes of this chapter, Sharek's work shows synergy between theory and design, where the attribute of challenge was derived from both Flow Theory and CLT and used to operationalize engagement. Further, the self-report and perfor- mance measures used in the three studies were selected on the basis of his theoretical approach and are used to iteratively test three different game designs. Thus, this example illustrates continuity and congruence between concept definition, theory, measurement, and design.

### 3.3.2 Case 2: Technology for Well-Being: Meditation in the Virtual World Sanctuarium (Contributed by Laura Downey)

New work by Downey [19] draws upon the emerging areas of positive technology and positive computing, specifically the framework outlined by Botella et al. [7] and Riva et al. [54]. Downey used a "Third Wave HCI" approach [6, 23] to design and evaluate UE and the experiential perspective of technology-supported meditation, a well-being activity. This was done via the creation and assessment of a meditative virtual world, Sanctuarium.

The theory of positive technology is grounded in well-being theory and provides a basis for the combination of positive psychology and technology to enhance the quality of people's lives both individually and collectively [7, 54]. Well-being theory comprises subjective or hedonic well-being and psychological or eudaimonic well-being [54]. Subjective well-being ("the enjoying self") refers to an individual's self-assessment of life satisfaction and positive and negative emotions [54]. Psychological well-being ("the growing self") associates happiness with a purposeful life. Social well-being ("the sharing self") extends psychological well-being to the group level and focuses on connections between individuals, groups, communities, and organizations [54]. The hedonic level of the positive technology framework involves using technology to induce positive pleasant experiences. The eudaimonic level uses technology to support engaging and self-actualizing experiences. Downey mapped technology-supported meditation to the eudaimonic level because meditation is an activity connected to personal growth and self-actualization. The social and interpersonal level of the positive technology framework includes using technology to support and improve social integration and connectedness.

With this theoretical foundation in place, Downey [19] explored engagement and experiential aspects of an engaging activity (meditation) supported by technology. The researcher examined how technology could be used to evoke and support positive, self-actualizing, and engaging experiences in Sanctuarium, a 3D island-scape for meditation. The virtual environment includes a seven-circuit labyrinth cut through a bamboo forest. Participants virtually walk the labyrinth visually following their avatar (walking meditation) and perform seated meditation in the center of the labyrinth in front of a soothing fountain surrounded by flickering candles. The meditation activity ends after the avatar walks out of the labyrinth and sits on the beach surrounded by the peaceful sounds of the ocean.

Sanctuarium was constructed and tested with 12 experienced meditators, whose experiences were explored qualitatively through pre- and post-interviews and quantitatively through the use of an adapted UES [44, 68] and the Effects of Meditation scale [50]. Phenomenological analysis provided a rich picture of the meditation experience with and without Sanctuarium. Integrated results indicated that meditation with Sanctuarium was not only engaging but that it facilitated meditation and guided meditation, making it suited for use even by those new to meditation. Downey concluded that the restorative environment was successful because of its pleasing visual and aural design elements and the facilitation aspects that "centered on the concepts of non-distraction, focus, and simplicity of design and instructions". As one meditator described it: "It's like being dipped into this peaceful world and your senses are stimulated ... it was visually very beautiful and I noticed myself being completely engaged in it". Another meditator offered this: "It kept me focused. It kept me noticing. It kept me with a still mind but an alert mind".

This work is an exciting case of theory informing design and measurement, with the outcome of a user study being used to validate design strategies and to inform theory development and evaluation. The design and evaluation of well-being technology is complex and challenging, and engagement was shown to be a critical aspect of meditation software. This emerging research contributes to enhancing well-being in the world through the creative and innovative use of technology and demonstrates that UE is a central aspect of positive technology experiences.

# 4  Models of User Engagement

Models of UE can be described as those that focus on engagement as an interaction process and those that examine relationships amongst variables with the goal of predicting or identifying outcomes of UE. Collectively these models are highly informative and rich. However, little work has been done to test and generalize many of the models, highlighting an important gap in the research.

The dissertation work of Richard Jacques in the mid-1990s made the first significant contribution to modeling UE. In a series of studies that ranged from card sorting to user-centered experiments, he proposed that engagement consisted of six attributes, each of which operated along a continuum. These components included the degree of attention (divided or focused), motivation to continue the task, perceived control (presence or absence), and needs satisfaction experienced by the user, as well as the user's perception of time ("dragging on" or "flying by") and attitude (negative or positive) [27, p. 67]. Jacques believed that the lowest and highest levels of engagement would be obtained when users rested completely on one or the other end of this spectrum for all attributes.

Jacques' work introduced two essential premises that I adopted and extended [38]. First, Jacques proposed that engagement is not an "all or nothing" interaction but that it ranges along a low to high continuum, and this relates back to Dewey's ideas of continuity discussed earlier. Second, he emphasized the importance of the attributes that constitute engagement (see Sect. 2.4). Thus, he introduced the notion that UE is multidimensional and that the attributes impact each other and the overall level of engagement that can be achieved:

> A high level of one attribute does not always mean a person is highly engaged, as low levels of the other attributes may outweigh it. For example, a person may feel motivated, but if the experience is not meeting their needs and they do not feel in control, then they will not feel very engaged [27, p. 67].

These premises were applied in my work over a decade later. The Process Model of UE (see also Sect. 3.2), based on critical incident interviews with users of different types of technologies, described a *point of engagement* that led to a *sustained period of engagement*; at some point, whether by choice or due to external factors (e.g. interruptions in the environment), participants *disengaged* from the interaction. This disengagement was sometimes followed by short-term or long-term *reengagement*. By segmenting engagement into concrete stages, I was able to identify attributes of UE that seemed most salient for that particular phase of the interaction. For example, the point of engagement was characterized by the aesthetic appeal and novelty of the interface, interest, motivation, or a specific or experiential goal to be achieved through the interaction [42].

The Process Model of UE depicted attributes as rising and falling over the course of an interaction as a way to convey how they operate at different levels of intensity during an engagement episode [38, 42]. While Jacques articulated that high levels of an attribute do not necessarily predict overall engagement, I proposed that ebbs and Flows are a natural part of the interaction trajectory and, depending on their intensity, contribute to users' overall evaluation of the experience. In addition, the attributes that initiate UE may be different than those required to sustain it. For example, an aesthetically appealing interface may draw a person into a game, but the right level of challenge, feedback, and control is essential for continuing to play. I have continued to look at the validity of the Process Model of User Engagement with different applications, such as online news browsing [40]. The Process Model of UE has shown good generalizability, but I have articulated the need to incorporate task and content variables into the model [40, 41].

In addition to building on Jacques' thinking around the attributes of engagement and their scalability, I confirmed Jacques proposition that engagement is multidimensional [38, 43] in my work to develop and evaluate a self-report measure of user engagement, the UES (see chapter "Translating Theory into Methodological Practice"). Through two large-scale surveys with online shoppers, I honed the attributes further using factor analysis techniques, perceived usability, aesthetic appeal, novelty, felt involvement, focused attention, and endurability, and examined the relationships between these factors. The resulting model (Fig. 1) showed interrelationships amongst the engagement factors: aesthetic appeal and novelty predicted

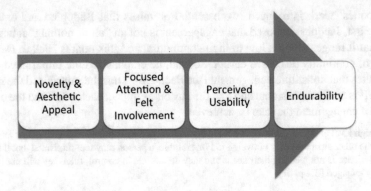

**Fig. 1** Model of relationship between engagement factors

users' focused attention and felt involvement, which predicted perceived usability. Endurability or users' overall evaluation of the experience was the outcome variable.

My attempts to model UE have been both conceptual and statistical. The Process Model of UE focused on the engagement episode and the attributes that contribute to each of its four stages; the measurement model tested hypothesized relationships about how the factors of UE, as measured by the UES, were related. The limitation of both models is that they relied solely on self-report data collected through interviews and surveys, methods which depend upon participants' ability to accurately recall a past event. The Process Model of UE has been tested in different domains using a qualitative approach, and I have tested the factor structure of the UES in subsequent work [45], but have not reexamined the path model. Both the behavioural and measurement models I proposed are narrow in focus and look specifically at the interaction between the user and the technology and the user's perspective of their engagement. However, other models incorporate non-perceptual variables, such as user behaviours or media conditions, and attempt to identify factors that influence engagement and the relationship between UE and other concepts, such as disorientation [12, 65].

Chapman [12], for example, used a self-report questionnaire to measure UE influences (control, challenge, feedback, bells and whistles, ease of use, aesthetics, and variety) on UE (intrinsic motivation, attention, curiosity, and engagement) in the context of an educational training system that was presented in one of three modes: video and text, audio and text, or text only; task performance was measured using behavioural data. Findings of the experimental study showed no relationship between mode and UE influences, but a significant relationship between mode and engagement. Further, it demonstrated that UE influences predicted UE and that higher engagement resulted in greater self-reported satisfaction and perceived usefulness of the system, as well as longer interactions. Thus, engagement was empirically linked to other self-report and behavioural measures, and it was confirmed that the way in which content was delivered (video, audio, text only) influenced users' perceptions of system engagement.

**Table 2** Summary of engagement models

| Researchers | Type | Variables in the model |
|---|---|---|
| Jacques [27] | Behavioural | Low ← Attention → High<br>Low ← Motivation → High<br>Low ← Perceived time → High<br>Low ← Attitude → High<br>Low ← Control → High<br>Low ← Needs → High |
| O'Brien [38]; O'Brien and Toms [42] | Behavioural | Point of engagement → Sustained engagement → Disengagement → Re-engagement |
| O'Brien [38]; O'Brien and Toms [44] | Measurement | Aesthetic appeal and novelty → Focused attention and felt involvement → Perceived usability → Endurability |
| Chapman [12] | Measurement | Engagement influences and mode of interaction → Engagement<br>Engagement → Satisfaction, perceived usefulness, interaction time |
| Webster and Ahuja [65] | Measurement | Navigation system → Perceived disorientation and user engagement → User performance → Future intention to use |

Webster and Ahuja [65] looked at UE in relation to the disorientation people can experience when navigating the Internet. They hypothesized and tested a measurement model whereby they confirmed that the navigation system used influenced perceived disorientation and user performance (as measured by number of correct answers to a task and time on task). In turn, perceived disorientation predicted UE and future intentions to use; UE and user performance also predicted future use intentions. The empirical results of this experiment illustrated how negative interactions with a web system influenced both user perceptions (engagement) and actions (performance) and the probability of reengaging with the system in the future.

Table 2 summarizes the various behavioural and measurement models of UE published to date. Within these models, we see evidence of both defining and accompanying features. Many try to hone in on the nature and characteristics of engaging experiences and the relationship between what people think, feel, and do during a UE episode. Thus far, the models focus on variables at the micro level of the interaction, and this opens up the potential for more macro-level modelling across episodes (e.g. patterns of engagement over the duration of an online course) or with the introduction of more sophisticated predictor (e.g. individual differences, task) and outcome (e.g. comprehension, long-term behavioural change) variables.

# 5   Conclusions

In this chapter, I have reviewed the varied definitions, theoretical orientations, and models that have been used to frame or emanated from UE research. This overview is not exhaustive, and in the upcoming chapters we will see different domain-specific approaches and research questions explored by the contributing authors of this book. While there is not a one-size-fits-all approach to UE, we are left, based upon the studies reviewed in this chapter, with a series of unifying propositions:

- User engagement is a process and product of people's interactions with computer-mediated environments. In other words, UE can be analysed *during* and *after* human-computer interactions and at the micro and macro levels. Variables of interest and methodological approaches and measures should be selected with this in mind.
- The main unit of analysis for UE varies according to the interactive setting: people interact with content, systems, and the environment to bring about UE. Research studies should clarify the unit of analysis being examined.
- User engagement has affective, behavioural, and cognitive aspects. Researchers should attempt to account for the multifaceted nature of UE or clarify the aspect of UE being examined or measured, e.g. "behavioural engagement".
- User engagement is a quality of UX that is characterized by the depth of the actor's investment in the interaction; this investment may be defined temporally, emotionally, and/or cognitively. The attributes of UE we focus on and measure in a given study should be aligned with the kind of investment we propose to investigate.
- User engagement operates along a continuum from shallow to deep; the continuum is influenced by the nature of the interaction but also situational constraints and users' conscious and unconscious goals and needs.
- Context is an important variable in user engagement. Context may be discerned at different levels, from the personal to the social to the task or situation that precipitates the interaction and to the overarching technology domain. We should make an effort to isolate and measure aspects of the context to better understand influences on UE.

In conclusion, this chapter ends with a call to action for researchers working in this space to adopt a theoretical orientation in their investigation of UE, its measurement and system design. The benefit of doing so is that we will build a more concrete foundation for UE as a concept for operationalizing it in our inquiry.

My own engagement with the literature has led me to a deeper appreciation of the extensive work that has been undertaken and yet also the "open questions" that need to be addressed. Specifically, I see the need to:

- Examine variables (individual, social, system, task) that predict engaging user experiences
- Critically evaluate the tangible and intangible outcomes of user engagement with technology on people, organizations, and society more broadly

- Investigate the attributes, articulated in definitions and models of UE, which are most salient for engaging computer-mediated interactions in specific domains and contexts

While we will surely not achieve perfect consensus on what engagement is, emphasizing theory and building a community of research and practice bring us ever closer to elevating UE from an overused and poorly understood concept to a solid field of inquiry for achieving a deeper appreciation of how technology impacts individuals, organizations, and society.

**Acknowledgements** I wish to express sincere thanks to Brett Lee for the thoughtful and sometimes rambling (though wonderfully so) discussions about user engagement and to Paul Cairns for helping me to see "the forest for the trees" in working through versions of this chapter. I would also like to acknowledge the generous support of the Social Science and Humanities Research Council of Canada (SSHRC) and the Network of Centres of Excellence in Graphics, Animation and New Media Project (GRAND NCE) for supporting my research over the past several years.

# References

1. Aasbakken, M., Jaccheri, L., Chorianopoulos, K.: Evaluation of user engagement and message comprehension in a pervasive software installation. In: Proceedings of the Second International Workshop on Games and Software Engineering: Realizing User Engagement with Game Engineering Techniques, pp. 27–30. IEEE, Piscataway (2012)
2. Arapakis, I., Lalmas, M., Cambazoglu, B., Marcos, M., Jose, J.M.: User engagement in online news: under the scope of sentiment, interest, affect, and gaze. J. Assoc. Inf. Sci. Technol. **65**(10), 1988–2005 (2014)
3. Bannon, L.: A human-centred perspective on interaction design. In: Pirhonen, A., Isomäki, H., Roast, C., Saariluoma, P. (eds.) Future Interaction Design, pp. 9–30. Springer, New York (2005)
4. Battarbee, K., Koskinen, I.: Co-experience: user experience as interaction. CoDesign **1**(1), 5–18 (2005)
5. Beardsely, M.: The Aesthetic Point of View: Selected Essays. Cornell University Press, New York (1982)
6. Bödker, S.: When second wave HCI meets third wave challenges. In: Proceedings of the 4th Nordic Conference on Human-Computer Interaction (NordCHI'06), pp. 1–8. ACM, New York (2006). doi:10.1145/1182475.1182476
7. Botella, C., Riva, G., Gaggioli, A., Wiederhold, B.K., Alcaniz, M., Baños, R.M.: The present and future of positive technologies. Cyberpsychol. Behav. Soc. Netw. **15**(2), 78–84 (2012). doi:10.1089/cyber.2011.0140
8. Brandtzaeg, P.B., Folstad, A., Heim, J.: Enjoyment: lessons from Karasek. In: Blythe, M.A., Monk, A.F., Overbeeke, K., Wright, P.C. (eds.) Funology: From Usability to Enjoyment, pp. 55–65. Kluwer Academic Publishers, Dordrecht (2003)
9. Brockmyer, J.H., Fox, C.M., Curtiss, K.A., McBroom, E., Burkhart, K.M., Pidruzny, J.N.: The development of the game engagement questionnaire: a measure of engagement in video game-playing. J. Exp. Soc. Psychol. **45**(4), 624–634 (2009). doi:10.1016/j.jesp.2009.02.016
10. Cairns, P., Cox, A., Nordin, A.I.: Immersion in digital games: review of gaming experience research. In: Angelides, M.C., Agius, H. (eds.) Handbook of Digital Games, pp. 339–361. IEEE/Wiley, New York (2014)

11. Calvo, R.A., Peters, D.: Positive Computing: Technology for Wellbeing and Human Potential. MIT Press, Cambridge (2014)
12. Chapman, P.M.: Models of engagement: intrinsically motivated interaction with multimedia learning software. Unpublished Masters of Applied Science, University of Waterloo, Waterloo (1997)
13. Cocciolo, A., Rabina, D.: Does place affect user engagement and understanding? Mobile learner perceptions on the streets of New York. J. Doc. **69**(1), 98–120 (2013)
14. Colbert, M., Boodoo, A.: Does 'letting go of the words' increase engagement: a traffic study. In: Proceedings of the Extended Abstracts on Human Factors in Computing Systems, pp. 655–667. ACM, New York (2011). doi:10.1145/1979742.1979663
15. Csikszentmihalyi, M.: Flow: The Psychology of Optimal Experience. Harper & Row, New York (1990)
16. Deci, E.: Intrinsic motivation inventory. http://www.psych.rochester.edu/SDT/measures/intrins_scl.html (2009). Retrieved 20 Apr 2015
17. Dewey, J.: Experience and Education, 1st Touchstone edition 1997. Simon & Schuster, New York (1938)
18. Dobrian, F., Sekar, V., Awan, A., Stoica, I., Joseph, D., Ganjam, A., Zhan, J., Zhang, H.: Understanding the impact of video quality on user engagement. In: Proceedings of the ACM SIGCOMM 2011 Conference, pp. 362–373. ACM, Toronto (2011). doi:10.1145/2018436.2018478
19. Downey, L. L.: *Well-being technologies: Meditation using virtual worlds.* (Doctoral thesis). Available from ProQuest Dissertations and Theses database (UMI 3721692) (2015)
20. Finneran, C.M., Zhang, P.: A person-artefact-task (PAT) model of Flow antecedents in computer-mediated environments. Int. J. Hum. Comput. Stud. **59**, 475–496 (2003)
21. Ghani, J.A., Deshpande, S.P.: Task characteristics and the experience of optimal Flow in human-computer interaction. J. Psychol. **128**(4), 381–391 (1994)
22. Halbert, H., Nathan, L.: Designing for discomfort: supporting critical reflection through interactive tools. In: Proceedings of the Conference on Computer Supported Cooperative Work & Social Computing, pp. 349–360. ACM, New York (2015). doi:10.1145/2675133.2675162
23. Harrison, S., Tatar, D., Sengers, P.: The three paradigms of HCI. In: Proceedings of alt.chi Conference Human Factors in Computing Systems. ACM, New York (2007)
24. Hart, S., Staveland, L.: Development of NASA-TLX (task load index): results of empirical and theoretical research. In: Hancock, P., Meshkati, N. (eds.) Human Mental Workload, pp. 139–183. North Holland, Amsterdam (1988)
25. Hassenzahl, M.: User experience (UX): towards an experiential perspective on product quality. In: Proceedings of the 20th International Conference of the Association Francophone d'Interaction Homme-Machine, pp. 11–15. ACM, New York (2008). doi:10.1145/1512714.1512717
26. Hyder, J.A.: Proposal of a website engagement scale and research model: analysis of the influence of intra-website comparative behavior. Unpublished Doctoral Dissertation, University of Valencia, Valencia (2010)
27. Jacques, R.D.: The nature of engagement and its role in hypermedia evaluation and design. Unpublished Doctoral Dissertation, South Bank University, London (1996)
28. Jacques, R., Preece, J., Carey, T.: Engagement as a design concept for multimedia. Can. J. Educ. Commun. **24**(1), 49–59 (1995)
29. Jones, M. (n.d.): Creating engagement in computer-based learning environments. ITFORUM, Paper 30. http://itech1.coe.uga.edu/itforum/paper30/paper30.html. Cited 5 Mar 2005
30. Konradt, U., Sulz, K.: The experience of Flow in interacting with a hypermedia learning environment. J. Educ. Multimed. Hypermed. **10**(1), 69–84 (2001)
31. Laurel, B.: Computers as Theatre. Addison-Wesley, Reading (1993)
32. Law, E.L-C., van Schaik, P., Roto, V.: Attitudes towards user experience (UX) measurement. Int. J. Hum. Comput. Stud. **72**(6), 526–541 (2014)
33. McCarthy, J., Wright, P.: Technology as Experience. MIT Press, Cambridge (2004)

34. McCay-Peet, L., Lalmas, M., Navalpakkam, V.: On salience, affect and focused attention. In: Proceedings of the SIGCHI Conference on Human Factors in Computing Systems, pp. 541–550. ACM, New York (2012). doi:10.1145/2207676.2207751
35. Merton, R.K.: Social Theory and Social Structure. The Free Press, London (1968)
36. Moran, T.P.: The command language grammar: a representation for the user interface of interactive computer systems. Int. J. Man Mach. Stud. **15**(1), 3–50 (1981)
37. Norman, D.A.: Cognitive engineering. In: Norman, D.A., Draper, S.W. (eds.) User Centred System Design, pp. 31–61. Lawrence Erlbaum, Mahwah (1986)
38. O'Brien, H.: Defining and measuring user experiences with technology. Unpublished Doctoral Dissertation, Dalhousie University (2008)
39. O'Brien, H.: The influence of hedonic and utilitarian motivations on user engagement: the case of online shopping experiences. Interact. Comput. **22**(5), 344–352 (2010)
40. O'Brien, H.: Exploring engagement in online news interaction. In: Proceedings of the Annual Meeting of the Association for Information Science and Technology. Association for Information Science and Technology, New Orleans (2011). doi:10.1002/meet.2011.14504801088
41. O'Brien, H., Lebow, M.: A mixed methods approach to measuring user experience in online news interactions. J. Assoc. Inf. Sci. Technol. **64**(8), 1543–1556 (2013)
42. O'Brien, H., Toms, E.G.: What is user engagement? A conceptual framework for defining user engagement with technology. J. Am. Soc. Inf. Sci. Technol. **59**(6), 938–955 (2008)
43. O'Brien, H., Toms, E.G.: Measuring interactive information retrieval: the case of the user engagement scale. In: Proceedings of Information Interaction in Context (IIiX), pp. 335–340. ACM, Rutgers, NJ (2010). doi:10.1145/1840784.1840835
44. O'Brien, H., Toms, E.G.: The development and evaluation of a survey to measure user engagement in e-commerce environments. J. Am. Soc. Inf. Sci. Technol. **61**(1), 50–69 (2010)
45. O'Brien, H., Toms, E.G.: Measuring engagement in search systems using the user engagement scale (UES). Inf. Process. Manag. **49**(5), 1092–1107 (2013)
46. Oliphant, T.: User engagement with mental health videos on YouTube. J. Can. Health Library Assoc. **34**(3), 153–158 (2013)
47. Patel, N., Clawson, J., Voida, A., Lyons, K.: Mobiphos: a study of user engagement with a mobile collocated–synchronous photo sharing application. Int. J. Hum. Comput. Stud. **67**(12), 1048–1059 (2009)
48. Peters, C., Castellano, G., de Freitas, S.: An exploration of user engagement in HCI. In: Proceedings of the International Workshop on Affective-Aware Virtual Agents and Social Robots, pp. 9:1–9:3. ACM, New York (2009). doi:10.1145/1655260.1655269
49. Quesenbery, W.: Dimensions of usability. In: Albers, M., Mazur, B. (eds.) Content and Complexity: Information Design in Technical Communications, pp. 81–102. Lawrence Erlbaum, Mahwah (2003)
50. Reavley, N., Pallant, J.F.: Development of a scale to assess the meditation experience. Personal. Individ. Differ. **47**(6), 547–552 (2009). doi:0.1016/j.paid.2009.05.007
51. Rice, R.E.: Media appropriateness: using social presence theory to compare traditional and new organizational media. Hum. Commun. Res. **19**(4), 451–484 (1993)
52. Rieber, L.P.: Seriously considering play: designing interactive learning environments based on the blending of microworlds, simulations, and games. Educ. Technol. Res. Dev. **44**(2), 45–58 (1996)
53. Rieh, S.Y., Danielson, D.R.: Credibility: a multidisciplinary framework. Ann. Rev. Inform. Sci. Technol. **41**, 307–364 (2007)
54. Riva, G., Baños, R.M., Botella, C., Wiederhold, B.K., Gaggioli, A.: Positive technology: using interactive technologies to promote positive functioning. Cyberpsychol. Behav. Soc. Netw. **15**(2), 69–77 (2012). doi:10.1089/cyber.2011.0139
55. Romero, P., Calvillo-Gáamez, E.: An embodied view of Flow. Interact. Comput. **26**(6), 513–527 (2013). doi:10.1093/iwc/iwt051

56. Schneiderman, B.: Direct manipulation for comprehensible, predictable and controllable user interfaces. In: Designing the User Interface, 3rd edn., pp. 33–39. Addison-Wesley, Reading (1997)
57. Sharek, D.J.: Investigating real-time predictors of engagement: implications for adaptive video games and online training. Unpublished Doctoral Dissertation, North Carolina State University, Raleigh (2012)
58. Shedroff, N.: Information interaction design: a unified field theory of design. http://www.nathan.com/thoughts/unified/ (1994). Cited 29 Jan 2015
59. Stephenson, W.: Play theory. In: The Play Theory of Mass Communication, pp. 45–65. University of Chicago Press, Chicago (1967)
60. Sundar, S.S.: Exploring receivers? Criteria for perception of print and online news. J. Mass Commun. Q. **76**(2), 373–386 (1999)
61. Sundar, S.S., Xu, Q., Bellur, S., Oh, J., Jia, H.: Beyond pointing and clicking: how do newer interaction modalities affect user engagement? In: Extended Abstracts on Human Factors in Computing Systems, pp. 1477–1482. ACM, New York (2011). doi:10.1145/1979742.1979794
62. Sutcliffe, A.: Designing for User Engagement: Aesthetic and Attractive User Interfaces. Morgan & Claypool Publishers, San Rafael (2010)
63. Szafir, D., Mutlu, B.: Pay attention! Designing adaptive agents that monitor and improve user engagement. In: Proceedings of the SIGCHI Conference on Human Factors in Computing Systems, pp. 11–20. ACM, New York (2012). doi:10.1145/2207676.2207679
64. van der Steen, W.J.: A Practical Philosophy for the Life Sciences. State University of New York Press, New York (1993)
65. Webster, J., Ahuja, J.S.: Enhancing the design of web navigation systems: the influence of user disorientation on engagement and performance. Manag. Inf. Syst. Q. **30**(3), 661–678 (2006)
66. Webster, J., Ho, H.: Audience engagement in multimedia presentations. Data Base Adv. Inf. Syst. **28**(2), 63–77 (1997)
67. Webster, J., Martocchio, J.J.: Microcomputer playfulness: development of a measure with workplace implications. Manag. Inf. Syst. Q. **16**(2), 201–226 (1992)
68. Wiebe, E.N., Lamb, A., Hardy, M., Sharek, D.: Measuring engagement in video game-based environments: investigation of the user engagement scale. Comput. Educ. **32**, 123–132 (2014)
69. Woszczynski, A.B., Roth, P.L., Segars, A.H.: Exploring the theoretical foundations of playfulness in computer interactions. Comput. Hum. Behav. **18**, 369–388 (2002)

# Translating Theory into Methodological Practice

Heather O'Brien

## 1   Introduction

Despite a decade of devoted research, user engagement (UE) remains a difficult concept to define. Many of us have used various theories and frameworks to guide our understanding of UE and, while there is certainly overlap and congruence amongst our perspectives, key differences are apparent. In the preceding chapter, varied definitions of user engagement were analysed to articulate several challenges: *clarity*, in terms of the unit of analysis (e.g. user, system, content) and level of interaction (e.g. micro or macro); *scope*, the temporal, contextual, and conceptual boundaries of UE; and the defining attributes and accompanying antecedents and outcomes of UE that give the concept *meaning*. An assessment of existing definitions gave rise to a number of emerging propositions and questions to guide future inquiry, yet also an acknowledgement that a unified definition—given the varied applications, settings, and variables of interest in UE research—is difficult to achieve. At the same time, it is this lack of a shared definition of UE that makes the question of how to measure it so arduous.

There are a variety of methodological approaches in human-computer interaction (HCI) that are utilized in user engagement research. These range from self-report methods, such as questionnaires, interviews, focus groups, and verbal elicitations, to neurophysiological methods, including eye tracking, brain imaging, facial expressions, and muscle movements, and observational methods of user behaviour as measured through embodied and on-screen actions, for example, mouse clicks, navigation patterns, etc. [27]. As we will see in this chapter, many researchers are using and combining various methods and measures in innovative ways to further our understanding of user experience. However, we may be putting the "cart before

H. O'Brien (✉)
iSchool, The University of British Columbia, Vancouver, BC, Canada
e-mail: h.obrien@ubc.ca

© Springer International Publishing Switzerland 2016                                        27
H. O'Brien, P. Cairns (eds.), *Why Engagement Matters*,
DOI 10.1007/978-3-319-27446-1_2

the horse," so to speak. Research studies are typically focused on a phenomenon of interest; for example: Is online shopping platform A more engaging than B? Do the behavioural patterns of "engaged" searchers differ from those of the "unengaged"? Seldom do we evaluate the methods and measures themselves in terms of their reliability, validity, and generalizability. The question of whether we are measuring what we *think* we are measuring has serious implications for the conclusions we draw about users' experiences (engaged or unengaged) and what precipitated or deterred their engagement.

The purpose of this chapter is to focus on the measurement of UE with respect to two intersecting and fundamental challenges: (1) How do we operationalize UE, a multidimensional, complex quality of subjective user experience with technology? And (2) How do we evaluate the robustness of UE methods and measures?

The chapter is organized as follows. First, I will elaborate on the aforementioned challenges by exploring what is meant by operationalization and robustness in the context of this chapter. Subsequently, I will draw upon the user engagement scale (UES), a multidimensional experiential rating scale, as a case study for illustrating these challenges. The case study will trace the origins of the UES and its adoption and adaptation in a variety of studies, with emphasis on findings related to its reliability, validity, dimensionality, and generalizability. This chapter will conclude with an assessment of the UES as a measurement tool for UE, but will also touch upon the broader challenges that have inspired this chapter with recommendations that UE researchers conduct concurrent research on methods and measures as they continue to investigate UE, and that we articulate the *what* and *why* behind our measurement practices, as well as the *how*, in a more systematic way. Good research is not only about the effective execution of methods and measures, but fostering a reciprocal relationship between theory and practice.

## 2   Challenges in the Measurement of User Engagement

The chapter "Theoretical Perspectives on User Engagement" of this book explores definitions of user engagement and demonstrates a mixture of overlap as well as a lack of consensus amongst researchers. As such, when we operationalize user engagement in the form of a measurement instrument, we encounter problems. If engagement comprises affective, cognitive, and behavioural elements, then what are these and are they the same in each situation? If our definition of UE is guided by defining features or attributes, then do we agree that these adequately capture the concept and should form the basis of measurement? Furthermore, research design is informed by and informs theory. In the case of quantitative research, experiments are intended to test or verify theory, while qualitative researchers may employ theory to explain observations of the world or to guide inquiry [15]. Many studies of UE incorporate established theories from other disciplines, yet an actual theory of UE is in its infancy. Thus, we do not yet have a theoretical "anchor" for our methodological practices.

Any discussion of measurement must acknowledge the tension between observable and latent variables. Latent variables are "hidden" and must be inferred, since there are phenomena we cannot directly observe. In the case of UE we are trying to account for subjective experiences, how people felt or thought about an HCI, and we must use tools, such as self-report questionnaires, to measure these latent variables. UE research does include variables that can be directly observed and measured, such as behavioural interaction patterns on a website and physiological data based on bodily responses or facial expressions. While more objective, each of these measures still requires a certain level of interpretation: how do we know that specific patterns of muscle movement, behaviours, or electrodermal activity are indicative of UE and not something else?

Kelly [25], in her discussion of the measurement challenges inherent in interactive information retrieval (IIR), emphasized that the dynamic nature of searching and the influence of different contextual factors can mean that the user experience at any one moment is different from the next. One of the key concepts underlying IIR studies is that of relevance, the measures of which "assume [relevance] is stable, independent, binary" (p. 198). This argument could be extended to user engagement—and indeed many other areas of interest in HCI—where we are interested in not only the outcome of interaction but also the trajectory. In Chap. 1 of this book, I discussed user engagement as both a process (journey) and product (outcome) of an interaction. It is difficult to design measures that address both of these aspects simultaneously or that capture definitive shifts in engagement levels over time. This also makes it extremely difficult to examine test-retest reliability, since the dynamism of UE means that no experience—even with the same person using the same system—may be the same.

Lastly, the study of user engagement occurs in numerous settings that vary in location (field or laboratory) and scale, which refers to the number of participants. Scale may range from a qualitative study with 12 people to a log analysis of millions of users' Web interactions [27]. We cannot employ the same methods in each of these settings. It is not feasible to gather dependable data about user's emotions, for example, in a large-scale study, or to calculate effect sizes for small-scale studies; field and laboratory-based research represents trade-offs between internal and external validity, and each study must deal with potential confounds and constraints. Thus, a "one-size-fits-all" methodological approach or measure does not exist for UE.

Given the challenges that we face in the operationalization of user engagement, what then constitutes a useful measure of UE? Ideally, measures of user engagement would be relatively easy to administer and interpret, making replication of research designs and findings possible. Ultimately, however, researchers need to know that the measures they are using are robust, and this involves evaluating a measure in terms of its reliability, whether it produces similar results under similar conditions, and validity, its ability to capture what it is intended to measure. Reliability and validity are the cornerstones of effective measures and can help strengthen and expand theory.

In the following section, robustness will be explored using the specific example of the UES. The UES is a 31-item self-report instrument designed to capture six dimensions of user engagement: perceived usability, aesthetic appeal, focused attention, felt involvement, novelty, and endurability, or the overall evaluation of the experience [34, 35, 40]. This case study is not an argument that the UES is the best or only way to measure UE. Rather the UES is used here, in part, because, as its developer, I have a keen interest in its evaluation for the purposes of improving its composition and administration. In addition, it has seen a fair amount of uptake within the research community over the past 5 years. Analysing its multidisciplinary use provides insights regarding its robustness and utility in different computer-mediated contexts.

## 3   Operationalizing User Engagement with the User Engagement Scale

The UES is one of a handful of self-report questionnaires developed over the past 30 years to measure user engagement.[1] The UES was created during my doctoral work, and I have continued to examine its effectiveness as an experiential rating scale for measuring UE since that time in a range of settings.

When I began my research in the area of user engagement a decade ago, a common reaction was, "Ah, engagement. That's very interesting, but how are you going to measure it?" This was a concern I shared. UE is, after all, not easy to delineate in terms of the user, system, and contextual elements at play; the multi-disciplinary literature in which I engaged—from marketing to hypertext systems to games and educational technologies—highlighted different considerations for and attributes of engagement. I unified these varied literatures and examined different theoretical perspectives and their characteristics in an attempt to anchor the concept, and to identify what engagement is and is not. With a theoretical basis in place, I attempted to operationalize UE in the form of a self-report instrument on the basis of its attributes.

I built on the substantial work of Webster [53] and Jacques [23] and their colleagues, who had both constructed self-report instruments of UE in the domain of multimedia education technologies. Both had been developed in the mid-1990s and were domain specific. I cast my net wider than had Webster and Jacques, articulating a range of attributes and attempting to build and test a rating scale using a combination of existing instruments and interview data. I intended for theory to inform the selection of attributes, and that the attributes would shape the content of the self-report measure; the evaluation of the resulting measure would then feed back into the definition and theoretical framework of UE.

---

[1]For description of some of these and other self-report questionnaires, please see "Chapter 2: Approaches Based on Self-Report Methods" in [27].

The scale development and evaluation process were guided by the literature in terms of the steps and statistical practices employed [18, 45].[2] Peterson [45], for example, outlines several distinct steps, including (1) reviewing the information requirements necessitating a questionnaire; (2) developing and prioritizing potential questions; (3) assessing potential questions in terms of the types of questions to be asked and how these will be worded; (4) determining the structure of the questionnaire, for example the number of categories and their labels; and, finally, (5) evaluating the design and usefulness of the resulting scale.

My process mirrored these steps. First, I generated a list of over 400 potential items derived from the theoretical and applied research literature and a qualitative study. I and another independent researcher assessed this list for the purposes of screening and prioritizing the potential items. These activities led in steps three and four (above), the outcome of which was further screening and pretesting. For step five, the UES was employed in two large-scale studies in the online shopping environment. These two studies allowed me to make the UES more parsimonious, explore its factor structure, and examine the reliability and validity of these resulting factors. The result was a 31-item instrument with six distinct sub-scales, which were arrived at through factor analysis, interpreted, and labelled as perceived usability, focused attention, felt involvement, novelty, aesthetic appeal, and endurability. The UES was published in its entirety in two academic papers [35, 40] and my doctoral dissertation [34].

Subsequently, I have continued to evaluate the UES in information search [41, 42] and online news [36–38]. In addition, the UES has been adopted and, in many cases, adapted by other researchers for use in different settings. Based on data provided by Google Scholar, publications of the UES have been cited 84 [35], 180 [40], and 16 [34] times as of the writing of this chapter.

For the purposes of looking here at how the work has been drawn upon, I specifically isolated the 180 works citing [40]. These comprised journal articles, conference proceedings, book chapters, Master's theses, and Doctoral dissertations published in 2010–2015. These works were first surveyed to determine whether or not the UES was used and, if so, whether the nature of the use was clear. In screening the articles, I also took into account works by the same author or group of authors and whether they were reporting on the same study across multiple papers. If this was the case, then only one paper was retained for this review to avoid redundancy. Lastly, there were some works that were not written in English that I was unable to read. After examining all works according to relevance, overlap, and language, there were approximately 44 remaining works; these were thoroughly read and annotated.

The papers represented a broad range of applications and studies in the areas of information search, online news, online video, educational applications, haptic interfaces, consumer applications, social networking systems, and video games. Overall, there were three categories of implementation of the UES: (1) use of

---

[2]For an in-depth description of the UES development and evaluation process, please see [34] or [40].

individual items or a combination of items unrelated to the original sub-scales; (2) use of specific sub-scales of the UES; and (3) use of the UES in its entirety. In the following sections, I will investigate the various implementations of the UES in greater detail, with particular emphasis on the instrument's reliability, validity, dimensionality, and generalizability.

## 3.1 Evaluation of the User Engagement Scale

The evaluation of an experiential scale involves assessing its usefulness through four distinct procedures: dimensionality, reliability, validity, and generalizability [45, p. 81]. *Dimensionality* refers to the number of underlying constructs being measured with the scale. This is typically assessed using principal components analysis (PCA) or factor analysis (FA), which are "statistical techniques applied to a single set of variables when the researcher is interested in discovering which variables in the set form coherent subsets that are relatively independent of one another" [50, p. 612]. The UES is a multidimensional tool and, as such, should produce a six-factor structure, according to its original configuration [34, 40].

The *reliability* of a measurement scale may be assessed along two lines: internal consistency and longitudinal stability. Internal consistency refers to how well scale items are measuring the same construct and can be assessed statistically using techniques such as Cronbach's alpha. Devellis [18] suggests that the ideal range for Cronbach's alpha is 0.7–0.9; this range represents good reliability without redundancy. Longitudinal stability, or test-retest reliability, examines the results of administering the instrument over time to the same participants and comparing the responses [45].

There are many forms of *validity*, and this evaluation will look specifically at criterion-related validity and construct validity [18]. Criterion-related validity is demonstrated when measures that should be associated with each other are, indeed, related. Construct validity is "the extent to which a measure 'behaves' the way that the construct it purports to measure should behave with regard to established measures of other constructs" [18]. In this chapter, validity is operationalized according to how well the UES can help differentiate between different experimental conditions or systems and its relationship to established measures, including other self-report scales.

Lastly, *generalizability* refers to "the administrative viability [of the scale] and interpretation in different research situations" [45, pp. 79–80]. To examine the generalizability of the UES, I will provide an overview of its success within the variety of technology domains represented in the reviewed articles.

The case study will conclude with an overall assessment of the UES according to its use and usefulness in measuring engagement in different studies and an examination of the limitations of both the tool and its administration.

### 3.1.1 Dimensionality

The original UES purported that user engagement comprises six dimensions: perceived usability, aesthetic appeal, focused attention, novelty, felt involvement, and endurability. These six dimensions emerged from exploratory factor analysis (EFA) in the first online study of online shoppers; structural equation modelling (SEM) was used in the second study to confirm the factor structure and test a hypothesized path model of the relationship amongst these factors [34, 40]. Subsequently, only a small number of studies have examined the dimensionality of the UES.

Banhawi and Ali [7] surveyed over 100 Facebook users to examine the generalizability of the UES in a social networking system (SNS) setting. Using EFA, they determined that there were four distinct UES factors: focused attention, perceived usability, aesthetics, and novelty-endurability; furthermore, the number of items retained from the original 31-item scales was 28. Wiebe et al. [55] arrived at a similar outcome in their exploration of the UES in gaming environments. Using principle axis factoring (PAF) with promax rotation, the researchers reported that the "UESz" consisted of four factors: focused attention, which included focused attention items and one felt involvement item; perceived usability, which included the perceived usability items and one endurability item; aesthetics; and "satisfaction", which was comprised of items from the novelty, endurability, and felt involvement sub-scales. 28 items were retained in the analysis.

In my own work, I have also observed this four-factor structure with one exception. In studies of exploratory search [42] and online news [37], perceived usability, aesthetic appeal, and focused attention have been "stable" sub-scales, while endurability, felt involvement, and novelty items have combined to form one factor or component, which we have labelled as "hedonic engagement". When we looked at the internal consistency of these four factors post-FA or PCS, we find support for their reliability. The exception to this four-factor finding was a study of educational webcast users [41]. This study found a six-factor UES, but one that differed from the original. The aesthetic appeal, focused attention, novelty, and endurability sub-scales were retained through factor analysis, though some items were eliminated from each sub-scale. The felt involvement sub-scale was eliminated and the perceived usability sub-scale loaded on two factors: one that contained affective items ("frustrated", "discouraged") and the other comprised cognitive items ("taxing").

This handful of studies that have both used the UES in its entirety and examined its factor structure strongly suggest that the instrument is comprised of four dimensions rather than six, but more studies are needed to confirm this finding. All of the aforementioned studies indicated good reliability of post-factor analysis sub-scales, but only two have commented on the relationship between factors. Wiebe et al. [55] conducted regression analysis with the maximum difficulty achieved by players in the game as the outcome variable and the flow state scale (FSS) and the newly derived UESz as predictors. FSS and UESz explained more of the variance in player performance than either scale individually (though the variance explained was still quite low). They noted that all of the post-PAF sub-scales were significantly correlated with each other but that there appeared to be "hedonic/utilitarian divide in the sub-scales" (p. 130), with perceived usability being least correlated with the other factors.

In our study of exploratory search [42], we noted a non-significant correlation between focused attention and perceived usability and a significant but low correlation between focused attention and aesthetic appeal. Thus our divide seemed to be not utilitarian/hedonic but system/user. Nonetheless, when we used multiple regression with focused attention, perceived usability, and aesthetic appeal as predictors and the combined endurability/novelty/felt involvement factor as the criterion variable, we found that the strongest model contained all three predictors, which accounted for 55 % of the variance. One way to interpret this is that these empirical findings are in line with the Process Model of User Engagement [34, 39] and that the attributes (or factors) of engagement are varying in intensity, depending on how salient they are in a given context.

The only other study that has utilized SEM in the study of UE is that of Seedorf et al. [47]. They conducted an Amazon Mechanical Turk study where MTurk workers interacted with a shopping website alone or with another remote person; in the collaborative conditions, participants could either communicate via a text chat window or could co-browse the site, view each others' mouse movements, and communicate via the chat feature. Social presence and collaboration usefulness were measured for the participants shopping in pairs, and all MTurkers completed 14 items from the focused attention, endurability, novelty and felt involvement sub-scales, which had good reliability.

Two different path models were examined for those searching alone (control group) and the participants browsing in the social conditions. For the control group, novelty increased focused attention and involvement, focused attention increased felt involvement, and involvement increased endurability; this model reproduced the relationships we identified between engagement factors in our original work [40]. The path model was similar for the paired searchers, except that there was no relationship between focused attention and felt involvement in this model. However, the path model also took into account new variables, namely social presence and collaboration, which increased the overall explained variance of the basic path model. Social presence increased both endurability and felt involvement, and collaboration usefulness led to higher levels of novelty and social presence. When the two paired conditions were compared, social presence, induced through co-browsing, led to stronger ratings of the endurability of interacting with the shopping website. Although this study did not indicate how they selected the 14 UES items, it replicated and enhanced elements of the original SEM results, confirming focused attention, felt involvement, novelty, and endurability as distinct dimensions and their interrelationships.

These findings are interesting in light of the four-factor structure that emerges in other studies where felt involvement, novelty, and endurability are combining into one factor. One explanation is that EFA, a data reduction technique, is best suited for scale development when the underlying latent constructs of a scale are unknown, whereas confirmatory analysis is more appropriate for testing an existing measurement model with another data set.

### 3.1.2 Reliability

Reliability, in terms of internal consistency, is related to the above discussion about dimensionality. Studies that have used PCA or FA to examine the factor or component structure of the UES have also examined the reliability of the sub-scales before PCA/FA and the resulting factors/components. Others have calculated Cronbach's alpha even though PCA and FA were not part of their analysis. For example, Arguello et al. [5] used 11 items from the focused attention, felt involvement, perceived usability, and endurability sub-scales and found good reliability with Cronbach's alpha values of 0.714–0.94. In some cases, items were removed during data screening to improve internal consistency, either due to redundancy amongst items or when an item did not correlate well with other items of the same sub-scale [37, 42].

Fewer studies have examined the test-retest reliability of the UES, though there are some noteworthy studies. Bustillo and Garaizar [12] examined the engagement of student teachers with Scratch, an application that combines programming and online community to teach computational thinking and digital literacy. They tested perceived engagement with Scratch in two different academic years and reported no differences; they anticipated higher engagement in year two. However, a focus group conducted with a subset of participants emphasized contextual factors, such as participants' inexperience with programming and limited programming training practices in schools, that may have affected the findings.

Another study in the education domain was conducted by Vail et al. [51], who were interested in whether male and female students might respond to different types of support: cognitive (e.g. problem solving) or affective (e.g. motivation, self-confidence) support offered by intelligent tutoring systems. The researchers tested four versions of a text-based adventure game; the baseline system scaffolded introductory computer programming tasks, and the other three versions were augmented with affective, cognitive, or cognitive-affective support. In all versions, the students completed the learning tasks in five separate but iterative sessions. Some students interacted with a human tutor (human–human), while others received support via the intelligent tutoring system (human–ITS); participants in both groups achieved significant learning gains, according to pre- and post-test scores for each tutorial session. Students rated their level of engagement according to the sum of three UES sub-scales, focused attention, felt involvement, and endurability, and their frustration using the NASA-TLX workload survey after each tutorial session; average engagement, frustration, and learning gain scores were computed for each student across the five sessions [51]. In addition to insightful findings regarding gender differences in preferences for affective or cognitive feedback and human or computer feedback, the authors took consistent measures over five sessions with the same students and examined the relationship between self-reported engagement, frustration, and learning gains. Males and females made similar learning gains, but females preferred affective, system feedback.

Lastly, Bangcuyo et al. [6] compared the user experience of sampling coffee in a traditional sensory environment with a "virtual coffee house" featuring visual, auditory, and olfactory cues; they were interested in contrasting user preferences in these settings and the stability of these preferences over time. Participants rated samples of four different coffees brewed at different strengths on a 9-point hedonic scale and completed an engagement questionnaire (21 items derived from the UES and Witmer and Singer's Presence Questionnaire [56]); total engagement scores were calculated for the virtual and traditional coffee tasting environments. The experiment was repeated twice, with a 1-month lapse between the first and second replications. In the first part of the experiment, there were significant differences in engagement between the traditional and virtual tasting environments, and these findings were stable 1 month later. Based on this finding, the authors concluded that the virtual coffee house remained hedonically appealing to participants over the two trials and that the engagement questionnaire used in the study, of which the UES was a part, was "both a reliable and valid testing instrument" (p. 93).

### 3.1.3 Validity

Validity, here operationalized according to how the UES functions in relation to other constructs, will also be discussed in the following section on generalizability that looks at the scale's performance in each domain more broadly. This section targets specific examples that support or refute the validity of the instrument.

The UES has been shown to correlate with other self-report instruments, including the FSS [55], system usability scale (SUS) [10], and cognitive absorption scale (CAS) [1, 38]. Flow Theory has informed UE research (see chapter "Theoretical Perspectives on User Engagement"), and the SUS and CAS are akin to the perceived usability and focused attention/felt involvement dimensions of the UES; thus, these measures should and have found to be correlated. Other studies have used elements of the UES and NASA-TLX concurrently to examine the interplay of engagement and its logical opposite, frustration [20, 49].

There have been mixed results concerning the relationship between the UES and objective measures. We found no significant relationship between UES scores and browsing behaviours (time, pages visited, and use of recommended links) or physiological measures (heart rate, electrodermal activity, electromyogram) [38]. However, those who rated their engagement as low spent almost twice as long reading during the session as highly engaged participants and visited more links on average (16 compared to 9.5), suggesting some level of disorientation or inability to engage with the task. Although the lack of statistically significant congruence with the objective measures was disappointing, the study questioned the validity of using some behavioural metrics in isolation, since more time on task was indicative of both low and high engagement. Further, Warnock and Lalmas [52] found no relationship between cursor behaviours and the UES, while [3] discovered a negative correlation between cursor movements and focused attention and affect (PANAS). In other words, "negative emotions [were] more influential on cursor behaviour than positive ones" (p. 1447).

Parra and Brusilovsky [44] looked specifically as users' interactions with two different interfaces of a novel conference navigation system. Subjective metrics included UES items that corresponded to the focused attention, perceived usability, novelty, and endurability, as well as objective information retrieval metrics, such as average rating of users in particular conditions, precision, mean average precision (MAP), mean reciprocal rank, and normalized discounted cumulative gain. Participants interacted with both versions of the conference navigation system: a baseline system and one that included additional features (e.g. sliders and Venn diagrams) to enhance the controllability of the interface and to assist users in locating relevant papers amongst recommended results. The results of a regression analysis showed that the effects of engagement on usage metrics were dependent upon the order in which people interacted with the baseline or experimental interface. The researchers also demonstrated a relationship between UE and MAP and participants' understandability of the interface in the task performed with the controllable interface; using the controllable interface after the baseline system also resulted in significant positive effects for subjective impressions of the endurability of the system. In addition, specific user characteristics, namely, experience with Conference Navigator and recommender systems, trust propensity, trust in recommender systems, and expertise in the research domain significantly influenced user engagement.

Grafsgaard [20] conducted a series of studies to investigate the relationship between affect and nonverbal behaviours in tutoring systems. Facial action units were recorded as students interacted with JavaTutor and coded across seven tutoring sessions. Significant facial movement patterns were observed between focused attention, involvement and endurability (UES), frustration (NASA-TLX), and learning. Brow lowering intensity, for example, was associated with higher levels of frustration and lower endurability, namely a reluctance to return to future tutoring sessions; average intensity of inner brow raising was associated with students' rating of the session as worthwhile. Postural shifts were also used to examine disengagement. Specifically, body position during student questioning, tutor responses, and positive feedback from the tutor mapped to higher self-reported engagement. Based on the findings, Grafsgaard [20] devised a predictive model of user engagement whereby students' initial computer science self-efficacy scores, one-hand-to-face gestures after successful compile (i.e. a programming subtask), and brow lowering after sending a student dialogue message led to higher post-session engagement; more facial movements (and perhaps more intense affective reactions) were associated with lower engagement.

In a portion of the studies, the UES has been shown to distinguish between conditions or experimental systems. We manipulated news source familiarity [37] and news media [36] and detected differences in users' experience, showing the UES to be sensitive to different study conditions. Moshfeghi et al. [33] developed a news search system with blog and news entries and associated images to determine whether enhanced visual search features would improve user engagement. Log files collected queries, mouse clicks for the distinct components of the user interface, overall time spent interacting with the news system, and time spent reading articles. All MTurk participants ($n = 63$) interacted with both versions (baseline and enriched) in counterbalanced order and were asked about their system preference and level of engagement. Findings indicated a clear preference for the enriched system, and participants found it more engaging than the baseline system on most of the UES dimensions; there was, however, no difference in the perceived usability of the systems.

However, other researchers have found less support for the UES's validity. Kajalainen [24] reported no significant differences in perceived engagement across five experimental conditions that altered the presentation of a satirical news show; the engagement questionnaire was derived from various instruments, including the UES.

Sharek [48] tested three types of game designs with Amazon Mechanical Turk (AMT) workers: static, based on a linear progression of difficulty; user controlled, where users selected a difficulty level at the beginning of the game; and adaptive, which manipulated the level of difficulty algorithmically. MTurk workers described their experience using the UES, the NASA-TLX cognitive load sub-scale, and items pertaining to interest and enjoyment ("personal affect") from the Intrinsic Motivation Inventory based on Self-Determination Theory [17]. He did not find any significant differences for any of the self-report measures across the three gameplay conditions, though there were performance differences. For example, those in the adaptive conditions played fewer levels of the game yet achieved greater difficulty, and those in the linear condition took more time to complete each level and react to the secondary task. Sharek speculated about the lack of significance for the self-report measures, reasoning that MTurkers are paid to participate and may be therefore less intrinsically motivated and involved with the game. In addition, the game seemed to have good entertainment value, regardless of the condition of play. However, Sharek cautioned that reliance on self-reported experience is problematic and "highlights a limitation in the diagnosticity of these cumulative self-report measures and strengthens the case for including real-time measures when possible" [48, p. 85].

Warnock and Lalmas [52] also drew upon MTurkers, asking them to carry out low- and high-interest search tasks (based on pre-task assessments of topical interest) using a "normal" or "ugly" website; the websites contained the same content, but the "ugly" website was made to be unappealing with changes to the colour, font, and presence of ads. Findings most pertinent to the validity of the UES were that no differences were found in participants' aesthetic appeal ratings of the websites. The authors questioned the reliability of the user experience data, since the "ugly" website violated so many aesthetic conventions. A possible explanation is that the usability of the ugly site was not affected by the cosmetic alterations made and that the ability to carry out the tasks proficiently led to less deterrence that expected. In addition, since participants interacted with only one of the websites, they had no basis of comparison in terms of what was "normal" or "ugly". Nonetheless, the fact that aesthetic ratings were not significantly different between the two websites challenges the validity of the aesthetic appeal sub-scale.

In another AMT study, McCay-Peet et al. [32] manipulated the visual catchiness of entertainment news headlines or topics to examine the effects of task-relevant saliency on focused attention, affect, and search performance. Self-report measures included the PANAS, the focused attention sub-scale of the UES, and questions about interest in news items, confidence in search effectiveness, and task difficulty. The focused attention sub-scale was shown to be highly reliable in three pilot studies, but did not detect differences between the salient and non-salient tasks. However, the authors noted that those in the non-salient condition said they were more distracted by the non-task-relevant features of the websites. Thus, the focused attention of both groups may have been similar overall, but they were attending to different aspects of the interface.

In addition to studies that support or refute the validity of the instrument, there are those that suggest more complexity. Arapakis et al. [2], for example, found no significant differences in responses to the UES's focused attention sub-scale across article interestingness levels (as determined by participants' pre-ranking) in their online news study. However, when participants were grouped according to their perceived interest in the articles, the "interesting" group reported significantly higher levels of focused attention than the "uninteresting" group, but these groupings did not affect actual or perceived time spent on the news reading task. Overall, Arapakis et al. [2] found that interesting news content increased positive affect and led to more focused attention and longer fixations on new and popular news item comments, which demonstrated congruency between subjective self-report and objective eye tracking data. These findings revealed differences when situational interest was fostered in the experiment, but not when it was based on preconceived notions of what news articles participants thought would be interesting to read at the outset. In another study of engagement and search performance with aggregated search displays, Arguello et al. [5] demonstrated significant findings for their objective measures of search performance and task complexity. However, user perceptions of search effectiveness and engagement were not significantly different for two experimental interfaces, even though post-session interviews confirmed that the majority of participants did notice a difference between the two interfaces. Yet participants indicated clear preferences for one of the two interfaces, and, when this preference was taken into account, there was congruency between user interface preferences and their user experience ratings, especially for perceived usability and endurability.

A small number of studies have treated UE as a mediating variable, exploring antecedents and outcomes of engagement with companies' Facebook pages [46], advertisements [28], social media [21], and health information seeking [22]. Reitz [46] adopted and modified 11 UES items to measure cognitive and affective aspects of online consumer engagement, and three items from the narrative engagement scale [11] were included to measure presence. SEM was used to examine the relationship between information quality, enjoyment, interactivity, affective/cognitive engagement, behavioural engagement, loyalty, and (re)purchase intent. Results indicated that perceived information quality, enjoyment, and interactivity predicted cognitive/affective engagement and participation; these, in turn, predicted brand loyalty, which led to intention to (re)purchase. In other words, users' content-based and physical interactions with online consumer Facebook pages led to affective, cognitive, and behavioural engagement, which influenced how they thought about and intended to interact with the company in future.

Another study based in the online consumer domain manipulated the perceived authorship of an ad for the Amazon eBook reader, Kindle [28]. Some people were told the ad was created by a communications firm on behalf of Amazon, while others were led to believe the ad was made by a Kindle user, "Angela", who was either motivated by her enthusiasm for the product or the potential to win a 20,000 dollar prize. Self-report items were derived from the UES and other sources. Based on the positive correlations observed between all of the engagement dimension and ad performance, the authors concluded there was a definitive link between engagement and the effectiveness of the ad, particularly when the ad was perceived to be made by a fellow consumer rather than the communications firm.

Halpern [21] studied the relationship between user engagement, cognitive involvement, and collective efficacy, the shared belief held by individuals about the group's capabilities and skills for performing a collective action. This study collected participants' ($n = 151$) comments on the White House and other US federal agencies' Facebook and YouTube accounts over a 2-week period. Pre- and post-task questionnaires were used to look at the three primary variables of interest, as well as participants' demographic characteristics, social media use, and interest in political affairs; user engagement items and cognitive involvement were derived from some of the UES's felt involvement items and Kwak et al.'s [26] work on political engagement. The author demonstrated that social networking sites have the potential to positively affect collective efficacy, particularly when the media enables networked information access that supports the formation of an online public sphere. Further, user engagement and cognitive involvement, along with participants' preference for social media channels, helped to explain increases in cognitive efficacy. UE was related to the types of behaviours participants engaged in: those who participated in more interactive conversations and replied to others' messages were more engaged than those who did not.

Hong [22] included UES items in a multifaceted study of online health information seeking, capturing both click stream and user perception data. Participants ($n = 106$) were randomly assigned to interact with health information in one of four message conditions where motivation orientation (health promotion or prevention) or message frame (health outcome gain or loss) was manipulated. The researcher examined the content selected by participants and the extent of their search, as measured by search session length and number of pages viewed. Participants were also asked about their impressions of task engagement (three focused attention and perceived usability UES items) and message quality (two items addressing stylistic quality and interestingness). Hong [22] found that those in the promotion orientation/gain frame condition were more engaged, and this had a mediating effect on message quality. The relationship between content presentation, engagement, and content assessment has important implications for the design of online content in health and potentially other fields.

### 3.1.4 Generalizability

This section looks specifically at the generalizability of the UES according to domain areas: online shopping, online news, online video, educational applications, haptic and consumer applications, social media, and video games. The caveat in examining the generalizability of the UES is that few studies use the scale in its entirety, and this makes it difficult to draw definitive conclusions. Therefore, this section focuses more on the fit and success of the UES as it relates to the researchers' goals and outcomes of interest and varied domain-based settings.

Online Search

Studies conducted in the online search domain have used UES items to investigate subject-specific information retrieval and aggregate search systems. These studies have tended to use a selection of UES items [22] or one or more sub-scales [4, 5, 9, 44]. These studies largely support the utility of the UES. Where reliability assessments were conducted, UES sub-scales showed good internal consistency [5] and adequate validity. The UES (or components of it) helped to distinguish user experience when the motivation and message frame of the information seeking interface was were manipulated [22], and differentiated between the parallel and dependent search conditions tested by Bron et al. [9] and the fast and slow search systems introduced by Arapakis et al. [4]. However, they did not show effects of search latency [4] or discriminate search results presentation [5] or two versions of an information retrieval conference systems [44] *unless* user system preference or the order of system use was taken into account.

These latter findings question the sensitivity of the UES, but Arguello et al. [5] offer an alternative view, suggesting that user experience may be more person dependent than system/interface dependent. This idea has some support in Parra and Brusilovsky's [44] findings that certain user characteristics influenced participants' perceived usability of the conference system, at least amongst those who interacted with the baseline system first. These studies do demonstrate some validity for the UES: both Hong [22] and Parra and Brusilovsky [44] found relationships between UES items and performance measures or other self-report variables (e.g. message quality and understandability). In the case of Hong [22], UE was shown to be a mediating variable between message frame and motivation and perceived message quality.

None of the search studies profiled used the UES in its entirety. However, aspects of the scale that were used demonstrate utility in helping researchers explore variables of interest, differentiate experimental conditions or interfaces, and gain an understanding of user search behaviour, user characteristics, and system order and preferences on subjective experiences and search behaviour.

Online News

Many of the studies conducted in the online news domain have focused intensely on the relationship between focused attention, emotion, and user behaviour [2, 3, 32, 52]. Arapakis et al. [2, 3] and McCay-Peet et al. [32] did not find differences in focused attention across different levels of article interestingness, and Warnock and Lalmas [52] found that aesthetic appeal items failed to differentiate an obvious manipulation of a news website's aesthetic conventions. Further, while Warnock and Lalmas [52] did not report a connection between self-reported focused attention and cursor behaviours as measured by mouse clicks, Arapakis et al. [2] successfully linked focused attention and eye movements: self-reported focused attention and eye gaze movements should be and indeed were related in their study. This collection of studies also underscored important connections between interest and user engagement, which we have also observed [38]. They specifically emphasized the relationship between interest, negative affect, and cursor behaviour [3] and interest, emotion, and focused attention [2].

Additional work in the online news domain has used more of the UES sub-scales beyond focused attention and has looked at user experience in relation to the presentation of news search results [33] or how people might "think" about news content [43]. Moshfeghi et al. [33] were able to distinguish a baseline and enriched news system on every dimension of the UES except perceived usability. Further, they showed that user characteristics, previous search experience, and performance data collected during the study were able to predict UE (with the exception of focused attention). Okoro [43] did not reveal significant differences in user engagement when performing a news selection task in freeform, timeline, or argumentation conditions with a news corpus; however, there were also no performance differences across the three interaction modes, and this may indicate that the manipulation was not successful overall.

Online Video

Online video may be part of online searching and news reading, but several studies have isolated video interaction. Lee et al. [29] and Zhu et al. [57] explored the social dimensions of online video viewing; Kajalainen [24] investigated the effects of different amounts and types of interactivity; and De Moor et al. [16] compared self-report and physiological data in this domain.

Lee et al. [29] observed different UE levels between a baseline (static) and dynamic version of a video system that featured affective and social commentary. Although they did not look at UE, learning, and social interaction in concert, the individual analyses of these pairs of variables suggested that content-related comments provided learning benefits, as well as social interaction and engagement. Similar to findings in online news, De Moor et al. [16] showed a clear relationship between interest and UE, and intuitively that engagement is higher when video viewing is error-free and contributes to perceived video quality. Interestingly, Zhu et al. [57] did not find differences in users' evaluation of their experience when they manipulated perceived usability through bitrate speed, but did find a connection between perceived endurability of the experience, genre (e.g. comedy), and viewing videos with friends.

None of the online video studies used the UES in its entirety. It is also not clear what items were used in Kajalainen's [24] study, and this makes it challenging to determine if the lack of differences between conditions in this study is due to the quality of the UES. In the case of the other studies, UES components utilized by De Moor et al. [16], Zhu et al. [57], and Lee et al. [29] were useful for understanding the video experience, particularly illuminating the role of socialization in engagement.

Educational Applications

Studies that have used the UES in the education realm have been technology centered and in the classroom. Studies reviewed here examine engagement, and its antithesis, frustration, with tutoring systems, as well as applications and workshops designed to be more novel than traditional classroom lessons.

The dichotomous relationship between user engagement and frustration, measured with the established NASA-TLX, provides evidence of the UES's validity in this setting. Two studies [51, 54] focused on an especially salient outcome— learning. Vail et al. [51] found that although students had higher learning gains with human tutors, they found them less engaging; there were also no differences in learning when students interacted with the baseline and enhanced systems, which provided cognitive, affective, or cognitive/affective feedback. However, they observed gender differences in students' responses to the type of feedback and mode of feedback delivery. Since learning was not affected, but engagement was, this implies that tutoring systems can be personalized to the preferences of groups of learners to provide an enjoyable experience without compromising learning. Whitman [54] had similar revelations when learning gains were made for students interacting with a baseline or interactive tutorial, even though the latter was more engaging. In this case, however, the interactive tutorial allowed students to perform well on declarative and procedural knowledge tests and to do so faster than the baseline condition while still enjoying the experience. Thus, while there were no differences in learning outcomes for the static and interactive system, the students performed more efficiently and experienced greater enjoyment with the interactive system. The author did not look at long-term retention of the information gleaned from the tutorials, and this would be an interesting and informative investigation of the longitudinal effects of engagement and interactivity on learning.

In sum, the UES was effective for helping authors in this domain explore UE in different settings and therefore showed utility. However, the findings highlight the complexity of learning environments, where more engagement does not necessarily equate with increased learning and where previous experience in the domain area or contextual factors influences learners' motivations and ability to learn [12]. Grafsgaard's [20] work, highly innovative and robust in its own right, isolated specific facial units gathered during the learning process and related these to self-reported frustration and engagement. The relationship between summative and formative and objective and subjective measures is an exciting finding related to the validity of the UES and self-report methods more generally.

## Haptic Applications

Haptic applications, technologies that use vibrations or motion to convey tactile feedback to users, are featured in two of the reviewed studies that employed the UES. Levesque et al. [30] did not use the UES in its entirety, but did draw items from each of the six sub-scales. They showed that haptic versus non-haptic interactions resulted in no performance differences but did impact users' perceptions of the four widgets they tested (alarm clock, text editor, game, and file manager), with higher perceived engagement when the widgets featured friction. Shirzad [49] also used an assortment of UES items, along with the self-assessment manikin (SAM), NASA-TLX, and Godspeed questionnaire (user responsiveness to the robot), to explore performance differences in a robotic reaching task. The UES was related to various dimensions of NASA-TLX, in that the experimental group were less frustrated, exerted less perceived effort, and achieved higher task performance than the control group; the UES was also associated with the SAM, which examined task satisfaction and attentiveness. The coupling of UES, NASA-TLX, and SAM showed good criterion validity for the UES. For this haptic application, which could be employed in a clinical setting as part of rehabilitation therapy, there is a real impetus to increase people's willingness to use it. Therefore, the performance itself may be less relevant to actual and continued use than engagement.

## Consumer Engagement

The range of applications of the UES and related measures in consumer research is quite fascinating. In addition to studying how people interact with companies in a social networking or online shopping setting, researchers have focused on company logos, ads, and virtual tasting environments.

In consumer engagement, UE has been explored along with presence [6, 46], a pairing that may not be suitable in all domains. However, UES items and sub-scales have assisted researchers in testing diverse research questions, such as the dynamism conveyed in brand logos [14] and how the creator of an ad (corporate versus fellow consumer) influenced users' perceptions of trust and overall engagement [28]. Along with the source of the information, studies have looked at the perceived quality of the information [46]. Both Reitz [46] and Seedorf et al.

[47] constructed and validated path models featuring engagement. In the case of the former, engagement was a mediating variable: information quality, along with level of interactivity and enjoyment experiences, predicted engagement, which in turn influenced company loyalty and intention to (re)purchase. Seedorf et al. [47] confirmed the path model we originally tested between some of the UES sub-scales [40] and added to this "social presence" in their study of collaborative online shopping. The inclusion of the UES in these structural equation models is a boost for the scale's validity, and Bangcuyo et al.'s [6] finding that users' experiences with the virtual coffee house were stable after a 1-month period supports the longitudinal stability of the UES.

## Social Networking Applications

Although some of the studies included in other sections of this chapter feature social networking sites (SNS), the three studies discussed here focus specifically on personal relationships through technology (as opposed to responding to a company through SNS).

Banhawi and Ali [7] tested the factorization of the UES and indicated a four-factor structure for the scale (discussed further in Sect. 3.1.1) and also found that interactions with Facebook using mobile devices were more engaging than those using a computer. Other SNS studies reviewed did not test the entire UES, but did show that self-reported engagement was linked with online behaviours [21] and that UE was one element (along with SNS preference and cognitive involvement) that predicted cognitive efficacy. This is a particularly salient finding given the plethora of research investigating crowdsourcing applications and provides additional insights into work using analytic data to study such phenomenon. Fuchsberger et al.'s [19] finding that user engagement persisted despite poor perceived system usability and lack of computer skills amongst older adults is interesting. In previous research, I made a case that a minimum amount of usability is necessary for engagement to occur [40], but, in this case, the desire to connect socially puts this hypothesis into question and warrants further examination of the trade-off between usability and perceived social gains in predicting UE.

## Video Games

Findings in the area of video games are mixed. Neither Choi [13] nor Sharek [48] found significant differences in perceived engagement for participants in their studies across experimental manipulations. However, Choi [13] also did not see hypothesized performance differences for participants training to do maze tasks using other different video games; thus, if all conditions were equally enjoyable or arduous, then there may have been no procedural or perceived engagement differences. None of the self-report measures tested by Sharek [48] were significantly different across the linear, user-controlled, and adaptive gameplay systems tested.

Wiebe et al. [55] lend further evidence to a four-factor UES with their study and did show the reliability of the six UES sub-scales (pre-PAF) and factors (post-PAF). Further, they demonstrated a relationship between the UES and FSS, but their regression analysis with game level as the criterion variable did not include focused attention and resulted in a small amount of variance explained. This raises the questions of what else should be measured and examined in conjunction with engagement and flow to account for the outcome variable, and whether the outcome variable chosen for this study was the most suitable for looking at UE.

In summary, in the video game domain, the UES failed to be a sensitive measure for [13, 48] and weakly predicted the criterion variable in Wiebe's [55] study. However, it did correlate well with the FSS and presented a four-factor structure similar to other studies subsequent to the original publication of the UES [37, 42].

## 3.2  Discussion of the User Engagement Scale

HCI rating scales have been aptly called a "tricky landscape" to traverse [31]. The case study of the UES reinforces this statement.

UES items, sub-scales, and the instrument as a whole have been used by researchers exploring UE with a range of applications and outcomes, including behavioural intentions for continued use, brand loyalty, learning, and system preferences. On a positive note, the adoption and adaptation of the UES in various domains implies that others have found the tool to be a useful instrument that resonates with their notion of engagement. Components of the UES have been combined with other self-report and objective measures (e.g. eye tracking, user behaviours) to generate interesting research questions, examine differences between experimental systems or conditions, and understand the relationship between user characteristics, engagement, and perceptions of hedonic and utilitarian technologies. Those authors who tested antecedents and outcomes of UE in specific contexts allow us to understand what predicts and is predicted by user engagement in these contexts. Overall, the literature reviewed in this chapter suggests that the UES is flexible, appropriate, and useful in terms of helping researchers achieve their goals and objectives. When reliability (i.e. internal consistency) was specifically tested, the UES passed the test. It demonstrated reasonable validity in most cases, correlating with other measures, such as the NASA-TLX, and helping to distinguish conditions or systems.

The UES also demonstrated its limitations across this set of studies. It was not always able to distinguish between experimental systems or conditions and did not correlate with cursor behaviour in some studies; person-dependent characteristics, such as preferences, seemed to factor heavily into perceived engagement, sometimes independent of the system or construct of interest in the research study. Studies that have examined the dimensionality of the UES support a four-factor structure with distinct focused attention, aesthetic appeal, and perceived usability sub-scales and items from the remaining three sub-scales (felt involvement, novelty, and endurability) loading on one factor. While we need more research to ascertain whether this reduction of factors is due to the underlying concept of engagement, the use of exploratory versus confirmatory factor/components analysis or a signal of a problem with the UES items [42], these findings do indicate that researchers who cannot perform factor/component analysis in their own studies and want to use the UES should adopt the four-factor structure.

The UES operationalized UE according to a set of attributes, a challenge since the definition of the concept is still maturing. The same range of biases and demand effects that affect all self-report instruments limits the UES, although no method is immune to shortcomings. Yet these limitations must be tempered with the fact that few researchers have used the instrument as a whole, and this leaves an incomplete picture of the UES's robustness. Some of the researchers do not address why they selected particular items or sub-scales, that is, what, in terms of their system, context, objectives, or theoretical orientation, motivated their choices. Therefore, we are unable to link theory and application in these cases. The use of one sub-scale cannot necessarily be equated with studying overall engagement. Studies could recognize formally that they are exploring one of several dimensions of UE.

Another challenge is the summation of engagement items to create an overall engagement "score". While this may be useful and appropriate in some cases, authors should do this with the understanding that the UES is multidimensional and its gradations may be lost by looking at the scale in a summative manner. This is reinforced by Devellis [18] who writes, "items must share one and only one underlying variable if they are to be combined into a scale... If a set of items is multidimensional (as a factor analysis might reveal), then the separate, unidimensional item groupings must be dealt with individually" (p. 159). In other words, aesthetic appeal, focused attention, perceived usability, etc., should be examined discretely with other variables of interest in the study. This reinforces the Process Model of User Engagement [34, 39] that proposes that UE attributes vary in intensity and significance depending on the context of use, yet all are necessary for examining UE holistically.

Pragmatically speaking, the 31-item UES may be cumbersome for researchers to use, particularly those testing multiple systems or asking participants to complete multiple trials. Participants are often asked to complete several questionnaires during an experiment, with the UES being one of many, and only so much can be included in user studies without running the risk of fatiguing users and compromising their responses. This is the reason why questionnaires such as the "quick and dirty", time-tested, and easy-to-use ten-item SUS [10] remain so appealing. Based on this review and the number of studies utilizing the UES in some capacity over the past 5 years, it is apparent that there is a need for a questionnaire that measures UE (as opposed to usability or other subjective experiences), but we must ensure that this instrument is robust and measures what it is supposed to be measuring. Increasing the number of studies that use the whole scale may provide insights into how we can create a brief version of the UES without compromising its reliability, validity, or dimensionality.

## 4 User Engagement Research: A Measurement Agenda

Methods and measures are growing in response to the complex phenomena of "third wave" HCI [8]. In the case of user engagement, for example, Grafsgaard's [20] work with patterns of facial expressions demonstrates the potential to capture objective data over the course of an interaction and to disambiguate positive (engagement) and negative (frustration) user experiences. Increasingly, studies are employing mixed methods and sophisticated analyses to examine the relationship between performance (cursor movements), physiology (eye tracking), and self-reports [3]. As many of the technologies used to capture physiology and user behaviour become more commercially available, and large data sets increase in accessibility, development of UE measurement practices is sure to be rapid.

The studies reviewed in this chapter and those on the measurement of UE more broadly suggest that researchers are working to address some of the challenges identified earlier in this chapter. Process-based measures, such as eye tracking, facial expression analysis, and other neurophysiological observations, are attempting to capture engagement as a dynamic concept that changes over time. Rather than looking at individual measures, researchers are instead identifying patterns that are more reliable indicators of user experience. Furthermore, there is also an attempt to bridge the issue of scale. The work of Arapakis et al. [3] shows great potential in this regard. Mouse clicks are relatively easy to collect in large-scale studies, whereas it is not feasible to collect self-report or individual physiological data in these environments. If mouse movements can be used as a reliable proxy of attention, both observed and latent, then this increases the potential for more in-depth analyses of attention across millions of users and would allow comparisons across Web domain areas at scale.

While existing and emerging work is promising, a challenge we continue to face is to demonstrate the construct validity of our measures: do they measure what they were designed to measure? The only way we will tackle this challenge is to ground our research studies theoretically and to use the findings of our work to inform theory. Looking within and beyond our own research domains, as this book attempts to do, opens up the conversation of what engagement is and how it can adequately be captured methodologically.

As the case study of the UES has shown, it is difficult to create a cohesive picture of measurement when instruments are used only in part or studies lack a rationale for why specific measures were chosen. As we forge ahead to look at the role of user engagement as a predictor, mediator, or outcome of other variables of interest, we must be mindful that the quality of this work and the ability to draw accurate conclusions depend upon the robustness of our measures.

In conclusion, a measurement agenda for UE would include support for the exciting and emerging work that is attempting to capture the dynamic nature of UE, the concurrent use of subjective and objective measures, and the interpretation of patterns rather than individual actions. However, this agenda would be furthered through the development of a parallel stream of research that looks intentionally at

UE methods and measures. This stream would focus on the reliability and validity of measures, replication of research findings with different populations or domain areas, and the assessment of methodological "fit" given the location, scale, and context in which the research takes place. Further research in this direction would provide researchers with a basis for comparison for their own work and the ability to make predictions about user engagement on the basis of others' findings. It would provide a solid basis upon which to conduct UE research, allow for the incorporation and assessment of new techniques and technologies into measurement practices as advances occur, and contribute to the evolution of user engagement theory.

**Acknowledgements** I wish to express appreciation to the Social Science and Humanities Research Council of Canada and the Networks of Centres of Excellence in Graphics, Animation and New Media Project for funding support.

# References

1. Agarwal, R., Karahanna, E.: Time flies when you're having fun: cognitive absorption and beliefs about information technology usage. Manag. Inf. Syst. Q. **24**(4), 665–694 (2000)
2. Arapakis, I., Lalmas, M., Cambazoglu, B., Marcos, M., Jose, J.M.: User engagement in online news: under the scope of sentiment, interest, affect, and gaze. J. Assoc. Inf. Sci. Technol. **65**(10), 1988–2005 (2014)
3. Arapakis, I., Lalmas, M., Valkanas, G.: Understanding within-content engagement through pattern analysis of mouse gestures. In: Proceedings of the 23rd ACM International Conference on Conference on Information and Knowledge Management, pp. 1439–1448. ACM, New York (2014)
4. Arapakis, I., Bai, X., Cambazoglu, B.B.: Impact of response latency on user behavior in web search. In: Proceedings of the 37th International ACM SIGIR Conference on Research & Development in Information Retrieval, pp. 103–112. ACM, New York (2014)
5. Arguello, J., Wu, W.-C., Kelly, D., Edwards, A.: Task complexity, vertical display and user interaction in aggregated search. In: Proceedings of the 35th International ACM SIGIR Conference on Research and Development in Information Retrieval, pp. 435–444. ACM, New York (2012)
6. Bangcuyo, R.G., Smith, K.J., Zumach, J.L., Pierce, A.M., Guttman, G.A., Simons, C.T.: The use of immersive technologies to improve consumer testing: the role of ecological validity, context and engagement in evaluating coffee. Food Qual. Prefer. **41**, 84–95 (2015)
7. Banhawi, F., Ali, N.M.: Measuring user engagement attributes in social networking application. In: Proceedings of the 2011 International Conference on Semantic Technology and Information Retrieval (STAIR), pp. 297–301. IEEE, New York (2011)
8. Bödker, S.: When second wave HCI meets third wave challenges. In: Proceedings of the 4th Nordic Conference on Human-Computer Interaction (NordCHI '06), pp. 1–8. ACM, New York (2006). doi:10.1145/1182475.1182476
9. Bron, M., van Gorp, J., Nack, F., Baltussen, L.B., de Rijke, M.: Aggregated search interface preferences in multi-session search tasks. In: Proceedings of the 36th International ACM SIGIR Conference on Research & Development in Information Retrieval, pp. 123–132. ACM, New York (2013)
10. Brooke, J.: SUS-A quick and dirty usability scale. In: Jordan, P.W., Thomas, B., Weerdmeester, B.A., McClelland, A.L. (eds.) Usability Evaluation in Industry, pp. 4–7. Taylor and Francis, London (1996)

11. Busselle, R., Bilandzic, H.: Measuring narrative engagement. Media Psychol. **12**(4), 321–347 (2009)
12. Bustillo, J., Garaizar, P.: Scratching the surface of digital literacy...but we need to go deeper. In: 2014 IEEE Frontiers in Education Conference Proceedings, pp. 1440–1443. IEEE, New York (2014)
13. Choi, H.S.: The impact of visuospatial characteristics of video games on improvements in cognitive abilities. Unpublished Doctoral Dissertation, North Carolina State University (2013)
14. Cian, L., Krishna, A., Elder, R.S.: This logo moves me: dynamic imagery from static image. J. Mark. Res. **51**(2), 184–197 (2013)
15. Creswell, J.W.: Research Design: Qualitative, Quantitative, and Mixed Methods Approaches. Sage, Los Angeles (2003)
16. De Moor, K., Mazza, F., Hupont, I., Ríos Quintero, M., Mäki, T., Varela, M.: Chamber QoE: a multi-instrumental approach to explore affective aspects in relation to quality of experience. In: Proceedings of SPIE 9014, Human Vision and Electronic Imaging XIX, 90140U (2014). doi:10.1117/12.2042243
17. Deci, E.L., Ryan, R.M.: Handbook of Self-Determination Research. University Rochester Press, New York (2012)
18. Devellis, R.F.: Scale Development: Theory and Applications, 2nd edn. Sage, Thousand Oaks (2003)
19. Fuchsberger, V., Sellner, W., Moser, C., Tscheligi, M.: Benefits and hurdles for older adults in intergenerational online interactions. In: Miesenberger, K., Karshmer, A., Penaz, P., Zagler, W. (eds.) Computers Helping People with Special Needs. Lecture Notes in Computer Science, vol. 7382, pp. 697–704. Springer, Berlin/Heidelberg (2012)
20. Grafsgaard, J.F.: Multimodal affect modeling in task-oriented tutorial dialogue. Unpublished Doctoral Dissertation, North Carolina State University (2014)
21. Halpern, D.: Towards a networked public sphere: how social media triggers civic engagement through news consumption and political discussion. Unpublished Doctoral Dissertation, Rutgers University (2013)
22. Hong, T.: Internet health search: when process complements goals. J. Am. Soc. Inf. Sci. Technol. **63**(11), 2283–2293 (2012)
23. Jacques, R.D.: The nature of engagement and its role in hypermedia evaluation and design. Unpublished Doctoral Dissertation, South Bank University (1996)
24. Kajalainen, K.: Increasing the enjoyment of online video increasing the enjoyment of online video content with topical interactivity. Unpublished Doctoral Dissertation, Aalto University (2015)
25. Kelly, D.: Methods for evaluating interactive information retrieval systems with users. Found. Trends Inf. Retr. **3**(1–2), 1–224 (2009)
26. Kwak, N., Williams, A.E., Wang, X., Lee, H.: Talking politics and engaging politics: an examination of the interactive relationships between structural features of political talk and discussion engagement. Commun. Res. **32**(1), 87–111 (2005)
27. Lalmas, M. O'Brien, H., Yom-Tov, E.: Measuring user engagement. Synth. Lect. Inf. Concepts Retr. Serv. **6**(4), 1–132 (2014)
28. Lawrence, B., Fournier, S., Brunel, F.: When companies don't make the ad: a multimethod inquiry into the differential effectiveness of consumer-generated advertising. J. Advert. **42**(4), 292–307 (2013)
29. Lee, Y.-C., Lin, W.-C., Cherng, F.-Y., Wang, H.-C., Sung, C.-Y., King, J.-T.: Using time-anchored peer comments to enhance social interaction in online educational videos. In: Proceedings of the 33rd Annual ACM Conference on Human Factors in Computing Systems, pp. 689–698. ACM, New York (2015)
30. Levesque, V., Oram, L., MacLean, K., Cockburn, A., Marchuk, N.D., Johnson, D., Colgate, J.E., Peshkin, M.A.: Enhancing physicality in touch interaction with programmable friction. In: Proceedings of the SIGCHI Conference on Human Factors in Computing Systems, pp. 2481–2490. ACM, New York (2011)

31. Lindgaard, G., Kirakowski, J.: Introduction to the special issue: the tricky landscape of developing rating scales in HCI. Interact. Comput. **25**(4), 271–277 (2013)
32. McCay-Peet, L., Lalmas, M., Navalpakkam, V.: On salience, affect and focused attention. In: Proceedings of the SIGCHI Conference on Human Factors in Computing Systems, pp. 541–550. ACM, New York (2012). doi:10.1145/2207676.2207751
33. Moshfeghi, Y., Matthews, M., Blanco, R., Jose, J.M.: Influence of timeline and named-entity components on user engagement. In: Serdyukov, P., Braslavski, P., Kuznetsov, S., Kamps, J., Rüger, S., Agichtein, E., Segalovich, I., Yilmaz, E. (eds.) Advances in Information Retrieval. Lecture Notes in Computer Science, vol. 7814, pp. 305–317. Springer, Berlin/Heidelberg (2013)
34. O'Brien, H.: Defining and measuring user experiences with technology. Unpublished Doctoral Dissertation, Dalhousie University (2008)
35. O'Brien, H.: The influence of hedonic and utilitarian motivations on user engagement: the case of online shopping experiences. Interact. Comput. **22**(5), 344–352 (2010)
36. O'Brien, H.: The role of story and media in user engagement with online news. In: Proceedings of the Annual Conference of Canadian Association of Information Science (CAIS), CAIS, Victoria (2013)
37. O'Brien, H., Cairns, P.: An empirical evaluation of the user engagement scale (UES) in online news environments. Inf. Process. Manag. **51**(4), 413–427 (2015)
38. O'Brien, H., Lebow, M.: A mixed methods approach to measuring user experience in online news interactions. J. Assoc. Inf. Sci. Technol. **64**(8), 1543–1556 (2013)
39. O'Brien, H., Toms, E.G.: What is user engagement? A conceptual framework for defining user engagement with technology. J. Am. Soc. Inf. Sci. Technol. **59**(6), 938–955 (2008)
40. O'Brien, H., Toms, E.G.: The development and evaluation of a survey to measure user engagement in e-commerce environments. J. Am. Soc. Inf. Sci. Technol. **61**(1), 50–69 (2010)
41. O'Brien, H., Toms, E.G.: Is there a universal instrument for measuring interactive information retrieval? The case of the user engagement scale. In: Proceedings of Information Interaction in Context (IIiX), pp. 335–340. ACM, Rutgers (2010). doi:10.1145/1840784.1840835
42. O'Brien, H., Toms, E.G.: Examining the generalizability of the user engagement scale (UES) in exploratory search. Inf. Process. Manag. **49**(5), 1092–1107 (2013)
43. Okoro, E.M.: A study of different representation conventions during investigatory sensemaking. Unpublished Masters Thesis, Middlesex University (2014)
44. Parra, D., Brusilovsky, P.: User-controllable personalization: a case study with SetFusion. Int. J. Hum. Comput. Stud. **77**, 43–67 (2014)
45. Peterson, R.A.: Constructing Effective Questionnaires. Sage Publications, Thousand Oaks (2000)
46. Reitz, A.R.: Online consumer engagement: understanding the antecedents and outcomes. Unpublished Doctoral Dissertation, Colorado State University (2012)
47. Seedorf, S., Thum, C., Schulze, T., Pfrogner, L.: Social co-browsing in online shopping: the impact of real-time collaboration on user engagement. In: Proceedings of the Twenty Second European Conference on Information Systems, Tel Aviv 2014. AIS Electronic Library (2014)
48. Sharek, D.J.: Investigating real-time predictors of engagement: implications for adaptive video games and online training. Unpublished Doctoral Dissertation, North Carolina State University (2012)
49. Shirzad, N.: The use of physiological signals and motor performance metrics in task difficulty adaptation: improving engagement in robot-assisted movement therapy. Unpublished Doctoral Dissertation, The University of British Columbia (2013)
50. Tabachnick, B.G., Fidell, L.S.: Using Multivariate Statistics, 6th International edition (cover) edn. Sage Publications, Thousand Oaks (2013)
51. Vail, A.K., Boyer, K.E., Wiebe, E.N., Lester, J.C.: The Mars and Venus effect: the influence of user gender on the effectiveness of adaptive task support. In: Ricci, F., Bontcheva, K., Conlan, O., Lawless, S. (eds.) User Modeling, Adaptation and Personalization. Lecture Notes in Computer Science, vol. 9146, pp. 265–276. Springer, Berlin/Heidelberg (2015)

52. Warnock, D., Lalmas, M.: An exploration of cursor tracking data. arXiv preprint (2015). arXiv:1502.00317

53. Webster, J., Ho, H.: Audience engagement in multimedia presentations. Data Base Adv. Inf. Syst. **28**(2), 63–77 (1997)

54. Whitman, L.: The effectiveness of interactivity in multimedia software tutorials. Unpublished Doctoral Dissertation, North Carolina State University (2013)

55. Wiebe, E.N., Lamb, A., Hardy, M., Sharek, D.: Measuring engagement in video game-based environments: investigation of the user engagement scale. Comput. Educ. **32**, 123–132 (2014)

56. Witmer, B.G., Singer, M.J.: Measuring presence in virtual environments: a presence questionnaire. Presence: Teleoper. Virtual Environ. **7**(3), 225–240 (1998)

57. Zhu., Y., Heynderick, I., Redi, J.A.: Alone or together: measuring users' viewing experience in different social contexts. In: Proceedings of SPIE 9014, Human Vision and Electronic Imaging XIX, 90140W (2014). doi:10.1117/12.2042867

# eLearning

Eric Wiebe and David Sharek

## 1 Why Do We Care About Engagement in eLearning?

It might be worth taking a moment to set the stage of why engagement is a worthwhile construct to study when looking at learning in general and eLearning in particular. It's important to remind ourselves that the reason so many researchers and educational designers are interested in engagement is not because they simply want to engage people, but it is because they want to change people's behavior. In eLearning contexts, behaviors such as clicking on video links more frequently, revisiting an online course more often, or even spending more time with learning materials are not the goals in and of themselves. Rather, instructional designers want to create learning environments to shape behavior that leads to enhanced learning outcomes; they wish to encourage learners to put forth time and effort toward thinking and experiencing learning content and activities that are deemed to be central to schema (i.e., mental concept) development and skill acquisition.

In order to understand what kinds of observed behaviors exhibited by an individual are indicative of engagement that leads to learning, educational researchers such as ourselves need to consider not only *what* is learned but also *why* we saw the outcomes we did. For example, if we looked at an engineering student taking an undergraduate course as part of their curriculum, we would want to be able to both understand the mechanisms at work that shape the student's learning outcomes in the course and also hopefully use the same general model to drill down and look at specific elements of the course while also being able to pull back and take a broader

E. Wiebe (✉)
North Carolina State University, Raleigh, NC, USA
e-mail: eric_wiebe@ncsu.edu

D. Sharek
Playgraph LLC, Cary, NC, USA
e-mail: dsharek@playgraph.com

© Springer International Publishing Switzerland 2016
H. O'Brien, P. Cairns (eds.), *Why Engagement Matters*,
DOI 10.1007/978-3-319-27446-1_3

look at this student's educational arc of experience. One such model we could apply at all these levels is a *cascading goal hierarchy*, of which engagement is a central driving component.

To better understand this concept of a cascading goal hierarchy, let's take a closer look at our student. She is a sophomore mechanical engineering student who has set a goal of graduating near the top of her class and going to work for an aerospace firm. Right now, however, she has to do well in her classes this semester, including an introductory statics course for which she has a goal of getting an "A". The class has a number of learning components online, including the homework problem sets that are due each week. Since the homework sets are worth 30 % of the grade and form the basis of what is on the quizzes and tests, she has set a goal of completing every homework set, understanding the concepts being utilized, and solving most of the problems correctly. Coupled with each of the stated goals is a requisite mode of engagement. She wants a mechanical engineering degree; therefore she has engaged with this goal by enrolling in a set of classes. Successful completion of the statics course requires going to class, taking notes, reading the textbook, and completing the online homework—all of which leverage behavioral and cognitive engagement. The homework problems will require focused, cognitive engagement in reading, comprehension, and problem-solving. For each of these goals in which she has engaged in, there is a set of explicit and implicit outcomes against which she will measure herself. In both the long and short term, she will reflect on the outcomes against her engaged effort and how far these outcomes get her toward her goals. She will then formulate at varying levels of complexity her next set of goals and strategies for engagement.

As you see, engagement sits dead center in this model between goals and outcomes. It effectively represents where "the rubber hits the road" for learning. Learning happens because she has decided to engage in the instructional tasks. If learning is the goal of our engineering student, our instructor, and the instructional designer of the curriculum, then each one of them has some level of responsibility for creating positive engagement with learning. That is, the goal is to shape both psychological states and behaviors that result in productive engagement. As educational researchers informing both instructors and instructional designers, we want to create learning environments that shape behavior by encouraging learners to put forth time and effort toward thinking and experiencing learning content and activities that instructors have deemed central to conceptual or skill development.

In both the small- and the large-scale learning contexts, one of the most important goals instructional designers are interested in are schema development on the part of the student that links new information with existing knowledge, forming more robust cognitive structures. These cognitive and physical skills may also be rehearsed in a variety of settings to the point of expert use and application. In addition, metacognitive skills may be developed to help our engineering student decide when, where, and how knowledge should be applied. Understanding these goals will help designers and instructors decide what productive behaviors they want our engineering student to engage in and, just importantly, how to create a learning environment that motivates our student to put forth effortful engagement in her learning. Our instructional designers may have rightfully concluded that they will have little influence over a student's larger goals—for example, the desire to obtain an engineering degree and work for an aerospace firm. However, instructional designers understand that they have the potential to significantly influence these overarching goals through the design of engaging day-to-day interactions such as coursework and in-class skill development.

Historically, the design of learning materials and environments was commonly made on assumptions about a learner's engagement. Take, for instance, our engineering student example. One such common assumption was that our student was not only motivated to become an engineer but that she was willing and able to positively engage with instructional content day in and day out. For instructional designers and class instructors, the goal for curriculum development has typically been to create a linear sequence of content in an optimal order of increasingly complex content. As computer-based (eLearning) instructional environments became more prevalent, there arose more interest in the flexibility and the usability of instructional content and its delivery mechanisms. For example, instructional designers began questioning whether the delivery of key elements could be manipulated such that they could be perceived and processed with the least amount of cognitive effort (e.g., [65]). There was a similar, parallel movement that also explored alternative pedagogies in presenting and supporting learning activities [42, 59]. However, much of this effort worked under an implicit assumption that learners would motivate themselves to positively engage in the instructional materials.

Today, a growing line of research recognizes that both the affective and cognitive dimensions of learner engagement must be attended to. While it is necessary that instructional environments need to be designed so that they are usable and comprehensible, it is now known that this is not sufficient. Learners need to engage with instructional content as a necessary precondition to learning, and for this, they typically need to be motivated to do so. While instructional designers can leave it to chance that this motivated engagement will happen, it is better to create instructional environments conducive to both engagement and learning.

## 2 What Underlies Our Willingness to Engage?

Working from the assumption that learning can be a positive enjoyable experience, educational researchers and the designers of eLearning environments have tapped the literature of positive psychology (e.g., [15]) to better understand how computer-based environments can be designed that are fun, enjoyable, and productive to the end goals (learning or otherwise) [44, 54].

The rise of powerful, interactive computing interfaces has understandably led to interest into how these interfaces can be designed to result in both positive affective and cognitive outcomes [39]. Researchers have begun to look to activities outside of the traditional educational world—sports, games, theater, and movies—as inspiration for behaviors, activities, and environmental stimulations that both give rise to positive affect and motivate individuals to engage in these activities.

Appropriately, with both the emergent technologies and social phenomena of computer-based entertainment, parallel developments in the art and science of video game development have also provided impetus to look more deeply at the links between gameplay, learning, and engagement [57]. In fact, since the very first computer-based training programs emerged in the 1960s and 1970s, instructional designers have explored ways to make learning a more engaging experience by adding game-like elements in their learning material. It stood to reason that if a game could engage players, then why couldn't aspects of game design be integrated into training and used to engage learners? After all, through simple observation, it was clear that most people experienced high levels of engagement and delight while playing games. Through these observations, early instructional designers developed computer-based training materials with a heavy emphasis on fun, yet the designs lacked the deeper insights into what mechanisms within a game were appropriate to use in learning contexts. As researchers continued to explore game design in the context of learning, a common theme emerged from social psychology in the form of Csikszentmihalyi's Flow Theory [2, 15].

Instructional designers noticed that concepts described in Flow Theory were commonly observable in game players. For example, players in flow often report being in an optimal experience with feelings of exhilaration and deep enjoyment. They are almost always intrinsically motivated and commonly report states such as focused concentration, feelings of control, and a lack of awareness of time. These are also the types of appealing experiences that instructional designers seek to create in online learning environments. But just how can instructional designers leverage game design mechanics to create these types of captivating experiences? After all, it is not as simple as "making learning fun" as was once thought. Insights from Flow Theory led to the recognition that a critical strategy for designing learning environments was to include elements of both work and play [71]. Understanding that learners, like other humans, have both work and play as a goal provides a starting point for unpacking the motivations that drive engagement.

One way of framing the motivation that resides behind engagement is the willingness to undertake future learning as a goal. Applying this lens raises the importance of the temporal dimension in understanding engagement. That is, our engineering student's willingness to engage in a learning activity at some point in the future is heavily influenced by both her current psychological state and her prior experience in similar activities. By extension, her perception of a current task or challenge will be shaped by what she believes the outcome will be which, in turn, is shaped by her past experience in similar situations [5, 61]. As pointed out earlier, goal-setting is often very hierarchical in nature. It follows that what is motivating our student to engage with a statics homework set is likely to be a combination of immediate goals concerning this specific homework set and longer-term goals for the semester or her academic career. Similarly, shorter-term goals may be artificially linked to goals somewhat extraneous to the task at hand; for example, our student may link going out for an ice cream as a reward after completing her homework set.

By doing so, she has created a temporal contingency as part of a personal strategy to motivate herself through a possibly not-so-exciting homework set with another shorter-term goal that will provide immediate pleasure.

Finally, the social dimension is critical to understanding the mechanisms of engagement. The reward for engaging in a learning task may not only be ice cream at the other end but the opportunity to work with other students. Social interaction, either direct or mediated by technology, is a very powerful force in shaping the motivation to engage. The relationship between the learner and those they are interacting with can be quite varied in terms of both their social relationship, the resulting nature of their interaction, and the degree to which the student finds these interactions motivating and engaging. Our engineering student may choose to do the homework set as part of a group activity in a library meeting room where she and her peers are all (hopefully) equally engaged in working through the problem set. This social interaction both mediates the cognitive aspects of learning and the affective dimensions driving the motivation to engage in this learning task. Just as easily, our engineering student may be engaged in the homework set by setting up a Google Hangout with her fellow students and virtually connecting with them [17, 28]. Instead of her peers, the student may be engaged by her teacher in a classroom setting [27] or an online setting where one-on-one tutoring may be taking place. For younger students, other adults besides a teacher (including parents) may be the motivating force [10]. Clearly, the social dynamic and the resulting engagement may be very different between peers and parents.

In this section, we have provided a simple scenario of our undergraduate engineering student to contextualize how engagement relates to learning. We have situated engagement as a central pivot point as to the quality of learning that occurs. Instructors and instructional designers not only need to design quality instructional content and present it in an efficacious manner, but the overall learning environment needs to be designed in a way that motivates learners to engage in effortful learning. A successful learning environment will attend to both the cognitive and affective needs of learners. Such design strategies recognize that learning can also be a psychologically positive experience. Because of this, the designers of eLearning environments have borrowed from social psychology research on other positive contexts such as gameplay and social interaction to design effective, engaging learning environments. These environments also recognize that engagement is deeply rooted in the temporal dimension of learning, the ever-changing state of the learner over time. Finally, emerging technologies and advanced learning theories have helped unlock a range of innovations that maximize engagement for learning.

# 3 Models of Engagement

This section explores a number of well-established and interrelated psychological models that help form an understanding of engagement. As is the case with many important constructs in the psychological sciences, there is no one unified model of

# Motivation > Engagement > Learning

**Fig. 1** General model of engagement—Step 1

engagement that we can make use of. Instead, we will use multiple lenses to create an integrative understanding of engagement in different learning contexts, resulting in different behaviors and outcomes. All of these models will link to a high-level connected sequential model (Fig. 1).

Let's start by exploring this model's end goal of learning through the lens of information processing models of cognition as they provide very useful insights into this facet of engagement [79]. Such models provide a structured way of looking at cognition in a task-oriented environment, assessing cognitive aspects of task demand and resources required to meet cognitive processing needs. At the heart of information processing models is the notion of resource allocation. That is, the human cognitive system functions in a constant stream of information from both the natural and human-built world. From this fire hose of information, decisions are constantly being made with regard to which streams of information should be attended to and processed. While some of these streams are automatically processed to some degree, only a limited amount of this information can be processed at a conscious, cognitive level. To do so requires attention to, and engagement with, these information streams. Executive functions in the cognitive system make decisions as to what to attend to and, therefore, what (limited) cognitive resources should be directed to these information streams for further processing [78, 80].

A relevant framework built from this general model is Cognitive Load Theory [52, 75]. This theory is predicated on the basic information processing model of limited working memory and (effectively) unlimited long-term memory. This theory was developed specifically to better understand both how students learn and what learning environments are best suited for which kinds of learning tasks. Allied theories developed from the same general information processing model have come to similar conclusions concerning underlying cognitive mechanisms and outcomes [45]. These models work under the assumption that a primary goal is schema formation and the activation and modification of existing schemas for learning [73]. While entire books have been devoted to this concept, the relevant idea here is that Cognitive Load Theory posits that our limited short-term memory is central to the accessing, formation, and modification of schemas, which reside in long-term memory. Our metacognitive and attentional resources determine how short-term memory is going to be allocated. While the learner has made the higher-level decision to engage in a learning task, the design of the learning environment will heavily influence what specifically is attended to over the arc of a learning session.

Cognitive Load Theory posits three primary types of load that are applied to our limited short-term memory system. Intrinsic load is determined by the relationship of the characteristics of the learning task relative to the knowledge and abilities of the learner. This construct predicts that, generally, experts will experience lower cognitive load than novices with the same material. Extraneous load is dependent on the nature of the learning environment and the degree to which it creates cognitive load on the learner that is not directly related to the learning task at hand. Much research has gone into development of empirically derived design heuristics based on this construct [46, 53]. Perhaps the most relevant line of work, and also the one that has been of considerable research interest in recent years, has been on the third construct: germane cognitive load [47, 64]. This load is the voluntary cognitive effort the learner commits to schema formation above and beyond the other forms of load. At the risk of oversimplification, for a given learning task in a given learning environment, if intrinsic load is the given load and extraneous load is the bad load, then germane load is the good load necessary for maximizing the learning opportunities. The goal therefore is to have the learner maximize germane load within the capacity limits of short-term memory. Given the voluntary nature of germane load, how do we get learners to commit this effort? It is here that we now bridge from the purely cognitive domain to the affective domain.

For our engineering student, a novice at solving many of the kinds of problems she will eventually be asked to do as a professional engineer, the learning environment needs to be designed with a recognition of the intrinsic cognitive load on novices for such homework problem sets. In addition, this learning environment should be designed in a way that maximizes support for engaging in the cognitive task at hand and minimizes extraneous load. More of a challenge is figuring out how to maximize the germane load our student is willing to put into the learning task. In summary, information processing models help us better understand the learning component of our overarching sequence (Fig. 2).

Now it is time to move upstream and better understand what created the decision to engage in the learning task at a level appropriate for learning. Self-determination theory [61] takes us back to the beginning of the sequence and explores why, and under what conditions, individuals in learning contexts and elsewhere are willing to engage in effortful tasks. Based on a fundamental understanding of human need for self-fulfillment, this theory explores the conditions for self-motivation around specific goals and states. In this case, we're particularly interested in what makes individuals motivated to learn, both the existing traits and experiences an individual brings to a learning context, but also under what conditions within the learning task psychological states will be created that continue to motivate the learner. These motivations can come both from external (extrinsic or instrumental) influences and factors and internal (intrinsic) ones. Intrinsic motivation is a fundamental manifestation of the human tendency toward learning and creativity [15]. Here, we can see the interaction of an individual learner's traits with the current learning conditions to either motivate or de-motivate the individual to engage in learning. Extrinsic motivation recognizes that most individuals function a good part of their

**Motivation > Engagement >** [Cognitive effort towards schema formation in a learning context] **> Learning**

Fig. 2 General model of engagement—Step 2

lives in a social context that has requirements or pressures to engage in activities that we otherwise might not be intrinsically motivated to pursue. Though research has consistently shown that extrinsic or instrumental motivating factors do not have the power of intrinsic factors for long-term motivation, they are a recognizable influence, both positive and negative, for our current state of motivation [86].

Self-determination theory and cognitive evaluation theory (a related sub-theory) posit that self-motivation is our natural state and will flourish if provided with the right conditions [21]. However, individuals will only be intrinsically motivated to do things that hold intrinsic interest to them, activities that have the appeal of novelty, challenge, and aesthetic value. More distally, these activities need to be related to either longer- or shorter-term goals and help to reinforce one's autonomy and competence. Collectively, this broad framework provides many avenues for learning environments that either motivate or de-motivate an individual. It is important to realize that factors driving extrinsic motivation are not wholly separate from intrinsic ones. Quite often, immediate tasks may be driven extrinsically with the knowledge that, in the larger picture, the tasks that will provide fulfillment of goals are intrinsically motivating. It will be, in part, the degree to which an individual has the self-regulation to motivate through these otherwise extrinsically driven tasks by linking them to longer-term goals.

Linking intrinsic and extrinsic motivation can perhaps best be done by thinking how temporally framed goals are a primary driver of these motivations. Let's return to our engineering student. Her long-term goal of being an engineer is intrinsically motivating to her because she believes this career will help her demonstrate socially desirable competencies (for which she will be well compensated for) and express creativity through self-volition. However, first she has to get through this homework set. There may be a combination of both extrinsically driven motivations (her instructor has told her this homework set is due tomorrow or it will be assessed a late penalty) and other intrinsic motivations (she truly enjoys the ice cream she will reward herself with at the completion of the assignment) that she will use to move herself closer to that long-term goal.

Expectancy-value theory [24, 82] takes the fundamental notions of self-determination theory and sets it within a task-driven environment where learners are setting goals at varying temporal scales. In a sense, while this is a very robust theory that generalizes into many contexts, it also is extremely helpful in operationalizing the particulars of engagement. For example, by understanding what the learner believes to be the mechanism(s) and strategies for the desired goal or outcome, we are able to discover the critical elements used for goal-setting as a driver for motivation. Our student will need to assess what is the likely cognitive effort (load) based both on the material to be learned and the context in which the learning will take place. Similarly, she may weigh the risk-rewards of multiple possible pathways or strategies. Central to this decision-making are considerations of both general self-efficacy and specific self-efficacy around the task at hand [8]. That is, how capable does our student feel she is at learning and problem-solving in general, and how capable does she feel at solving this specific homework set? Similarly, control beliefs will drive decision-making by assessing how much the individual feels the outcome(s) is under their own control. Collectively, self-efficacy and control beliefs help form the degree of agency the learner feels they have in determining the outcomes for specific goals they have set.

We can see how these factors will drive the multitude of ways in which a learner may engage in the material. Generally, students are more likely to become engaged when academic work intellectually involves them in active processes they find meaningful. Such activity enhances one's perception of competence and autonomy, contributing to students' engagement, likely by increasing self-efficacy and perceptions of self-worth as suggested by these models of motivation [24, 55, 71]. For example, they may feel that they are good at problem-solving in general, but don't feel very confident in the kinds of problems presented in this homework set. They may also feel that they are capable of solving this homework set, but the learning management system has been acting up all day and they do not trust the system will stay up long enough to allow them to complete the homework set. More broadly, they may be weighing strategies of seeking help from the course teaching assistant versus trying to tackle the homework set on their own, based on the time and effort required and the likelihood of getting an acceptable grade on the assignment. Implicit in this decision-making with how and where to engage in learning is the student's self-regulatory ability to make good decisions [66]. Another central driver to this decision-making is going to be the value that the individual places on the various goals and alternative outcomes. These, of course, can be driven both by a positive desire for a particular outcome and the negative desire to avoid other ones. In addition, there almost inevitably will be conflicting goals— often short-term goals pitted against long-term ones—which need to be weighed based on their intrinsic and extrinsic value.

Theory has now fleshed out the sequence on both sides of engagement (Fig. 3). These broad cognitive and social psychological theories have been applied in many contexts and used to address many theoretical and practical questions. Here, we have brought these theories together to understand the antecedents and outcomes of engagement in a learning context. Now the task will be to see what are the specific strategies that are likely to lead to positive, productive engagement. In addition, we need to understand what engagement looks like, so that it can be recognized and facilitated.

[Goals, values and the expected outcomes ]
[Extrinsic and Intrinsic] Motivation > Engagement > [Cognitive effort towards schema formation in a learning context] > Learning

Fig. 3 General model of engagement—Step 3

## 4  Elements of Engaging eLearning Environments

At the broadest level, engaging learning environments will need to both engender and support motivation to learn, limit barriers to engagement, provide feedback as to a student's progress toward their learning goals, and provide a robust environment that adapts and supports learning based on a student's current affective and cognitive state. Fundamental to this is an understanding that this process proceeds cyclically over time as a hierarchy of goal states unfold. Additionally, a student's perceptions based on how they have cognitively and affectively responded to the task will ultimately drive the engagement process.

A student will engage initially with an eLearning environment with a set of shorter- and longer-term goals in mind. The environment will hopefully provide a clear set of information that facilitates this goal formulation and strategies to meet these goals. Our engineering student, at the beginning of the semester, has signed up for the statics course based on information she has received from her advisor. More immediately, she is now on the learning management system formulating goals for successfully completing this homework set. The environment needs to help her quickly assess what needs to be done, what is the likely effort required, and what are the risks and rewards of different strategies to achieving these goal states. This information feeds into setting both extrinsic and intrinsic motivational factors. Incorrectly assessing these factors means surprise and possibly maladaptive responses to negative affective states such as disappointment and frustration [7]. These negative states can be de-motivators that feed disengagement. If this happens often enough, a student may question their agency in achieving their goals: do they have control over their ability to successfully complete this course and reach this important longer-term goal? This crisis of faith will put considerable downward pressure on engagement.

Once the decision is made to engage with the learning environment, the goal of the instructional designer is to make sure that the experience engenders those positive psychological states that lead to both continued (short term) and returning (long term) engagement. A number of positive factors can help propel engagement forward. The best learning environments will strike the appropriate level of both challenge and immediate enjoyment. The challenge needs to come in forms that allow learners to demonstrate the mastery, continue to build on it, and know that they are in a supportive environment that will help them achieve their goals. Immediate enjoyment can come from many forms; while it may be derived from achieving short-term goals ("I got that problem right!"), it may also derive from more universal positive experiences, such as an aesthetically pleasing learning context, positive social interactions with peers and instructors, or other elements that create a fundamentally positive physiological experience [77]. Perhaps this is worth expanding on. As noted earlier, humans naturally seek out positive psychological and physiological experiences—either simply for the sake of it or because it represents achieving some other goal [15, 71].

In learning environments, this often takes the form of seeking out achievable challenges tied to goals a student might have. The resulting state, flow, is both what is sought and the result of engaging in these activities. This state of flow is complex and researchers are still a long way from fully unraveling this construct. It is clear that it is related to the concept of immersion, or telepresence, which is characterized by many of the same psychological states as flow, including loss of awareness of time and place. Gameplay [12] and narrative-driven environments [22, 72], supported by perceptual experiences that dominate the senses (i.e., virtual reality), are designed to create these types of positive experiences. A compelling story can quickly sustain a person's engagement for hours on end. This can be so influential that it can induce a parasocial interaction where people intrinsically desire to interact with story characters [16]. This aspect of "computers as theater" induces a willing suspension of disbelief just as when a person becomes enthralled while watching a film [40]. When a person engages with a story, they typically report feelings of flow, enjoyment, persuasion, and telepresence [23]. A good narrative should facilitate the ease of which a person experiences learning over time. Hazari et al. [32] call this ease of cognitive access, and it is directly related to the more general goal of creating a highly usable eLearning interface. In sum, quite often the most engaging learning environments are those that manage to find a balance between (achievable) challenge and play and can be situated in immersive, narrative-driven contexts—too rarely seen in current learning environments [71].

Throughout history, people have created communities of practice that provide environments where collective learning can be achieved [70]. The introduction of electronic social media and user-contributed content on the Internet lends itself extremely well to these types of communities of practice. It should be no surprise that social media is considered highly engaging, and sometimes addicting, as it dominates many people's online activities. The lines between work and play are increasingly becoming blurred as students are commonly integrating their use of social media with their scholastic activities [16]. This provides an opportunity for researchers and educators to carefully examine which elements of social media are engaging and can be used to thoughtfully facilitate learning.

One such engaging aspect of social media is simply the act of interacting with others. This can profoundly influence what and how much people learn [70]. Collaborative wikis and shared blogs are common and simple approaches for providing these types of opportunities for learners to collaborate and share in the learning experience [32]. However, simply creating environments where collaboration may occur does not always ensure high levels of engagement and, more importantly, higher learning outcomes compared to traditional educational approaches. In order to design engaging collaborative environments where it is more likely for learning to take place, a thorough understanding of the mechanisms required to encourage engagement must be identified.

One aspect of social media that has been shown to impact learning by encouraging engagement and behavior change is simply the number of people in a social network, otherwise known as a network's social influence [56]. One reason behavior change may be affected by interacting in larger groups is due to the power of normative social influence where people often mirror what they see others do in order to fit in and be accepted. Furthermore, people generally collaborate in the context of learning when they feel that the people they are collaborating with can provide them with information more efficiently compared to learning solo [52].

It's also important to be aware of the potential obstacles that online learning environments may produce. For example, the group as a whole may be engaged in learning, while some individuals disengage yet still benefit from the outcomes produced by the group. This problem is known as the freerider problem [43] and must be monitored by any educator who leverages social collaborative learning tools. Additionally, it's important to make sure that students are not simply socially engaged, but rather that they are intellectually engaged, because simply collaborating and interacting in an online shared environment does not necessarily guarantee that a person will learn [43]. Interacting in an online learning environment does not mean a person is engaged in actively learning new and increasingly challenging content. Research has demonstrated that people may elect to engage in a task yet purposefully maintain a low level of challenge as long as the environment remains fun and continues to produce a degree of positive affect [67].

Central to the application of these engagement strategies is communication back to the learner. The art of good instructional design often hinges on how performance feedback is provided to the learner. When does our engineering student want feedback? After every problem or only at the end of the set? Do they only want positive feedback when they get a question right or also encouragement when they get one wrong? When do they feel pandered to with false praise, and when does the environment feel unfeeling and cold? Not surprisingly, feedback needs to be carefully tuned to factors that reinforce intrinsic motivation and the mastery goals associated with them [1]. Appropriate feedback sends the message to the learner that they properly assessed their ability and strategies for achieving the goals they set out to tackle. It supports them affectively and helps them cognitively calculate strategies for moving forward toward the next set of goals. A recent trend has been to provide this feedback in the form of "badges." However, it is important to consider whether the feedback is private and targeting intrinsic motivational factors or more public acknowledgement of one's successes. This latter form tends to support extrinsic, instrumental factors and may not be as successful for longer-term engagement [1, 3].

Not surprisingly, many of the factors that detract from engagement are foils for those that enhance it. Usability of the learning environment is a necessary but not sufficient factor for engagement. Poor usability creates unnecessary extraneous cognitive load, saps agency from the learner, and leaves a negative aesthetic impression. Poor instructional design can present educational challenges to learners that are either perceived as too hard to achieve or unrelated to their intrinsic goals. Finally, insufficient or the wrong kind of information can detract from a learners ability to assess their progress toward goals or present unwanted or inappropriate feedback. Usability can also be seen at the center of many information failures. While performance information may be available to the learner, usability issues may make it hard to access or interpret this information.

While there are both positive and negative factors that contribute to engagement, it is important to note that engagement followed by disengagement is not only expected but necessary. Embedded within the cascading goal structure is a natural hierarchy of engagement-disengagement cycles. In the short term, it is simply too cognitively demanding for an individual to stay at a high level of cognitive performance on any single task for any considerable length of time. While some level of cognition, affect, and its accompanying physiological arousal is necessary for productive engagement, optimal levels of arousal in the short run will result in fatigue, stress, and accompanying performance decline in the long run [79]. Natural physiological needs for sleep, food, etc., will also invariably interrupt many learning tasks, whether the student likes it or not. For that reason, well-designed learning environments are created to engage students, but only for lengths of time considered manageable. While an online synchronous class may run for 2 h, an attentive instructor knows to break this time up into cognitively and physiologically manageable chunks and to give students breaks to get up, change focus momentarily, stretch, and take care of other needs. Our engineering student working on her homework assignment is given more freedom to decide how to regulate her time. However, good instructional design will not only sustain engagement in the assignment but will create appropriate breakpoints or changes in activity. Again, the video game industry has developed highly evolved design heuristics that maximize the effort of players while also recognizing their cognitive and physiological limitations. These designs work to find ways to increase a level of psychological momentum that encourages the game player/learner to continue despite natural cyclic disengagement effects [69]. Finally, there is a sound cognitive basis for this engagement/disengagement cycle in that limited cognitive resources effectively demand disengagement from external stimuli to give the brain time to process, organize, and consolidate newly acquired information into new and existing schema. There needs to be "time for reflection" in all learning situations [63, 74].

## 5 Operationalizing the Study of Engagement in eLearning

Both the broader theory presented here and general strategies for creating engaging learning environments provide insight into how instructional designers and instructors might create environments that leverage engagement strategies. However, as with all design problems, they must be created, tested, and modified to serve specific learning contexts and learner audiences. For that reason, it is necessary to operationalize these more broad-brush concepts and heuristics into tools that can be used by designers and researchers trying to understand and measure engagement in learning environments. Returning to Shernoff and colleagues [71], a very useful heuristic is that high-quality learning environments should contain elements of both work and play, and one can design instruments that measure both of these aspects. Similarly, given the nature of how instructional tools are designed, utilized, and studied in educational settings, it is also useful to consider factors that load primarily on the interaction between an individual and the instructional content and those interactions primarily driven by social (multi-individual) contexts. Both of these educational contexts are, in many cases, mediated in some way by technology. While we need to acknowledge the impact of many demographic and other individual differences on engagement, we are going to focus on operationalized models that apply broadly to educational environments utilized across the age range. That said, many measures of engagement allow you to apply individual differences as a lens to understand why differences emerge.

## 5.1 Self-report Measures

In many ways, self-report measures provide the most proximal measure of engagement. That is, we simply ask how engaged a student is in their task. Since whole books have been written on the methodological strengths and weaknesses of self-report, suffice it to say that self-report of engagement parallels the challenges of most other psychological constructs. Perhaps most important to note is the challenges of near-real time, interstitial reporting versus retrospective, post hoc reporting. While there is a great desire to avoid the inevitable increase in error from having individuals reconstruct past states of engagement on a post hoc instrument, there is the real concern that regular interval reporting will interrupt and, therefore, disengage individuals during their task. In general, self-report measures of engagement measure state-like constructs that are expected to be impacted by a specific activity or task. That is, they ask a learner to report on some specified past period across one or more scales that, collectively, provide insight as to their level of engagement. For that reason, they are administered post hoc with specific reference to the task/activity that the individual is to report on. Also, it is not uncommon to be paired with other instruments measuring additional constructs of interest, such as cognitive load, self-efficacy, etc.

At the individual level, a number of researchers have developed and researched self-report scales that provide post hoc measures of engagement. The user engagement scale (UES) [49–51] provides a template as to how engagement can be measured across a set of subscales that represent both the work and play aspects of engagement. As analyzed by Wiebe et al. [81], the UES can be thought of as consisting of four different subscales:

- Focused Attention. This subscale is based on Flow Theory and measures the degree to which the learner felt during the time a state of focused concentration, to the point of total absorption in the task or temporally disassociating.
- Satisfaction. This subscale asks the learner to reflect on their experience and the degree to which it is fun, interesting, endurable, and novel—essentially, whether they were satisfied with their experience.
- Perceived Usability. This subscale, as the name implies, concerns the perceived ease of use of the learning environment.

- Aesthetics. This subscale encompasses the visual appearance of the learning environment including, implicitly, its functionality and layout.

These four subscales, in turn, can be grouped based on how they load on the hedonic, play-oriented goals of the learner and the utilitarian, work-oriented goals [31, 48]. As designed, thinking about their experience from a hedonic standpoint of how enjoyable and positive their experience was, the Focused Attention and Satisfaction subscales provide an opportunity to report on that side of their experience. Conversely, they can report on the utilitarian, work-oriented experience through the Usability and Aesthetics subscales. Collectively, these four scales can provide a self-report measure of the antecedent sources of engagement with a learning context.

## 5.2  Behavioral Measurement

An alternative to self-report measures is the measurement of behaviors by a third party. The challenge of such a measure, again, parallels the general methodological literature of such approaches. In this case, a researcher must make a strong connection between observable behaviors and the psychological state of engagement. Not surprisingly, the knowledge that the observer has of the student over a longer period of time (such that a teacher might have) can help with recognizing behaviors related to cognitive engagement [4]. Traditionally, behavioral measures are often used in conjunction with other measures to provide additional evidence rather than as a stand-alone source [18, 35]. Perhaps one of the most exciting avenues for the behavioral measurement is within online eLearning environments. Here, there is the potential to capture large quantities of real-time data across multiple dimensions (including learning outcome and self-report measures), where statistical power and cross validation of data sources can provide robust input into statistical modeling tools [11, 34, 62]. Along with being used by the researcher, this data can also be processed and visualized for use by the learner or instructor in the form of dashboards [13]. Here, data can be used to provide insight into learner engagement to instructors or used as a form of self-motivation on the part of the student. As with other forms of analysis, usability of this data for use by researchers or instructional designers will only be as strong as the psychological models that underlie the interpretation of the data.

As a special case of online learning environments, MOOCs (massive open online courses) provide a particularly interesting challenge for measuring user engagement through behavioral data [20]. The commonly voluntary nature of sign-ups to MOOCs would tend to point to the assumption that everyone in the MOOC is there because they are motivated to learn the material being presented in the course. However, the low penalty for engagement or disengagement at differing points of time means that users are allowed to formulate widely differing sets of goals for their engagement with the course. Unless the researcher has the ability to directly elicit what these goals are (and assuming students are able to articulate them), it can be a formidable challenge to attempt to model positive engagement outcomes based on their behavior and academic outcomes within the course. One element that many MOOCs have that provides a powerful mechanism both to engender engagement and to provide a method of measurement is online discussion forums. These forums provide rich communication streams between students and with instructors that can provide insight into the level and quality of engagement [3, 60].

## 5.3  Physiological Measurement

Another emergent area of measurement is the use of physiological measures. The rapid increase in the ratio of quality to price of biometric sensors that capture data plus the increased capacity for computational tools to process, visualize, and model this data has opened the door to inclusion of a wide range of measures by both researchers and developers [25]. One way of organizing physiological measurement methods is to distinguish between remote and direct measurement techniques. Those measures that can be collected remotely via cameras and image processing equipment include facial expression, body posture, and eye movement [29, 80]. More direct measures include sensors applied directly to the body to collect heart rate, brain activity (including EEG), and electrodermal (skin conductance) data [30, 76].

In general, remote collection is more scalable since it does not require "wiring up" individuals with sensors. Since so many computing devices now have built-in cameras, there is the potential of leveraging this data stream to help measure engagement. Even measures that require immediate proximity to the human body have become easier to leverage. The general movement toward self-measurement (i.e., the Quantified Self) means that many individuals are willing to wear multipurpose wireless sensors connected to cloud-based data analytics tools [41]. Physiological measurement, as is the case with almost all real-time trace data sources, embodies the paradox of having a wealth of data yet lacking the tools and techniques to meaningfully interpret it [6, 11]. Increased sophistication of computer modeling algorithms and power has meant a rapid increase in the utility to leverage these data streams. With physiological data streams, as with all data streams that can be collected without the individual's knowledge, it is particularly important that the proper safeguards are in place to acquire meaningful, active consent before it is leveraged as part of eLearning research activities.

In summary, we have discussed how we can use expectancy-value theory [24, 82] to take the fundamental notions of self-determination theory and set it within a task-driven, goal-oriented learning environment. These goals work within the motivation engine that drives engagement with cognitively demanding, but personally meaningful, learning tasks. We went on to describe how the design of eLearning environments can engender and support motivation to learn and limit structural barriers to engagement while providing feedback on progress toward learning goals. More advanced systems can also provide a robust environment that adapts and supports learning based on a student's current affective and cognitive state. Finally, methodological approaches to the study of engagement in eLearning environments were discussed in order to better understand how this field of work and its theoretical underpinnings might be moved forward.

# 6   Case Studies

We now present two case studies that have built off this overarching framework. In the first case study, GridBlocker, we discuss an experimental game-based learning environment that was specifically designed to manipulate motivation based on Flow Theory's notion of achievable challenges in order to maximize both level of engagement and learning outcomes. In addition, it leveraged the temporal cycle of engagement/disengagement to provide an additional measure of intrinsic motivation. In the second case study, MOOC-Ed, an exploratory study to better understand engagement in a free-choice learning environment is described. Here trace data of behavioral engagement with the eLearning site over time is used in conjunction with data mining techniques to see how learners could be characterized and clustered. These cases are meant to provide a pair of examples, albeit limited, as to the breadth of study designs and entry points into the above-described theoretical, design, and methodological frameworks.

## 6.1   GridBlocker

As we have demonstrated, instructional designers often borrow insights from video game developers when seeking to develop engaging online learning environments. Such learning environments often make use of both challenge and narrative design elements from the video game genre. One of the more common challenge-based design patterns borrowed from video games is the balancing of player control for selecting new challenges as they progress throughout a game. If players are given too much freedom, they may select challenges that they are not skilled enough to overcome which could lead to disengagement. Alternatively, in narrative-driven games, selecting challenges that are too easy could also lead to disengagement due to boredom and stagnation in the storyline. In this case study, a video game called GridBlocker [68] was developed to test the feasibility of applying an adaptive algorithm to automatically control the level of difficulty a player experienced based on real-time measures of performance, cognitive load, and affect. The goal was to keep the player engaged while also promoting skill development in as little time as possible.

One of the challenges this project sought to overcome was a previous finding that players are often content with maintaining a low level of difficulty as long as the game levels they play are considered fun [67]. In those findings, players were found to be passively engaged, resulting in a state of positive affect yet low desire for challenge. When developing simple, repetitive-action video games, this may actually be desirable if the only outcome of interest is self-perception of enjoyment; however, in terms of learning, this type of noncognitive engagement rarely promotes learning and skill development. This type of passive engagement is commonly found in eLearning courses that have emphasized the fun elements of video games without taking into account the more serious aspects of leveraging video game mechanics for enhancing engagement and schema development.

In order to investigate the efficacy of an adaptive algorithm to promote learning while maintaining positive affect, GridBlocker was developed with over 100 levels of varying difficulty. These levels were carefully developed in separate studies based on performance data and self-report measures of difficulty, challenge, and frustration. Gameplay in GridBlocker is based on a rectangular block that a player must navigate around an isometric tile-based game board. The goal is to place the block vertically over a target using a combination of three main types of movements. These movements are used to change the block's physical orientation and thus the position and location of the block on the game board. During the easier initial levels, the combinations of these movements are fairly straightforward and do not require much planning or expertise. As the game progresses, more complex combinations are required as the layout of the game board configuration becomes more complex. Players gain experience by observing and recognizing that certain combinations of movements can be used to position the block in desired locations, much like in chess or in the process for solving a Rubik's cube [38].

Three design conditions were developed: linear, choice, and adaptive. The linear condition simply incremented the difficulty of each subsequent level that a player completed. This is the most straightforward approach to developing eLearning courses. Content increasingly becomes more difficult as learners progress throughout the course. Typically, the slope of the increase in difficulty is based on the ideal learner of median ability, thus not matching either slower or faster learners. In the choice condition, players chose an easier, more difficult, or similar level of difficulty to play next. Promoting user autonomy by providing these options has often been thought to produce engaging experiences for purely entertainment-based video games; however, engagement in the context of learning requires a person to not only engage with the game but also to learn new and more challenging content over time. Thus, it was unclear whether learners would choose appropriately challenging levels. The adaptive condition selected the difficulty of each level based on a player's past performance, cognitive load, and affect. Performance was measured as the length of time it took a player to complete a level compared to an ideal time based on data captured during the level-building design studies. Real-time affect was indirectly measured based on a novel game-clock that captured a player's desire to play the game when given the opportunity to stop in between game levels. Finally, cognitive load was measured as secondary task performance through an embedded monitoring task integrated within the game.

When comparing the players on all three conditions, it was found that players in the adaptive algorithm maintained high levels of positive affect while also solving more challenging levels compared to players in the linear and choice conditions. Those in the choice condition recorded equally high levels of affect, but they did not select increasingly difficult levels. The linear condition produced slightly less affect, and players in this condition required more time to reach levels of difficulty equal to those in the adaptive condition. These findings reinforced prior research that predicted level of challenge needs to be tuned to the ability of users, as seen in the linear condition. Similarly, the choice condition supported the assumption that users would seek out levels of challenge that fulfilled hedonic desires for enjoyment through challenge, but not necessarily an optimal level of challenge for learning outcomes. Finally, the adaptive condition has supported prior research that (near) real-time measures of cognitive load and affect can be paired with user profiles of prior experience to help shape an engaging experience. Further research needs to be conducted to test the reasoning that the more engaged a person is, the more likely they are to experience optimal learning conditions. These findings may have implications for the design of online programs, such as eLearning courses, which could benefit from adaptive content of varying difficulty that is automatically selected based on real-time measures of engagement. Online learning content lends itself well to this type of design because it is fairly easy to divide and chunk content based on difficulty. However, considerable more work needs to be done to translate these findings from a fairly simple game-based environment into a complex, large-scale learning environment.

## 6.2 MOOC-Ed Project

Massive online open courses (MOOCs) are a way for learners to engage with educational content through a relatively new paradigm for delivering large-scale open access to online instruction, resources, and social networks or communities [3, 20, 33]. Web 2.0 technologies, backend cloud-based processing and storage and emergent intelligent pedagogical agents, coupled with the increasing access to web-enabled devices by the global population have meant that both traditional and nontraditional forms of instruction can be delivered at scale to large numbers of individuals. This scalability situates MOOCs in an ideal position to address a number of educational issues and research questions about the nature of online learning using large-scale data mining techniques [33]. However, the distal nature of MOOC activity makes for considerable challenge when it comes to measuring engagement. While traditional classroom settings allow for direct observation/measurement of learning activities [26] and experimental studies provide a good venue for collecting self-report or direct-measure physiological data, the distant, free-choice nature of MOOCs means that studying user engagement in this eLearning environment will mean depending primarily on trace data generated by learners interacting with web-based educational resources.

MOOCs attract a diverse population of users with different motivations and goals for participation compared to a traditional course [19, 36, 83, 84]. While MOOCs are widely criticized for their low completion rates—only a fraction of participants who register for a MOOC actually complete the MOOC [58]—there is reason to believe that the motivations and goals of MOOC users are decidedly different than that of traditional students [14]. Research by Clow and others (e.g., [3]) points to the importance of better understanding how learner goals and expectations for success may be very different for MOOCs than for traditional courses (online or not). In addition, the interplay between goals, effort, and cues used to gauge outcomes may lead to dynamic patterns of engagement that look different than traditional educational settings. Revealingly, for a MOOC offered by Google, only half of the participants indicated that they intended to complete the whole course [83]. Low completion rates may represent a reasonable outcome for many participants and typifies the great diversity of MOOC user goals, making it necessary to reframe and possibly restructure typical analyses relating to student dropout, participation patterns, and learning outcomes.

The nature of MOOCs enables this new platform for online education to provide exceptionally low barriers to participation in high-quality educational opportunities and, thus, has the potential to radically alter the educational enterprise [33]. However, it poses the need to re-operationalize and broaden what participation and success means within a MOOC [20, 85]. Similarly, the large numbers of diverse students who have voluntarily signed up for a MOOC provide the ideal context for theory-based quantitative modeling of students' motivations [21, 24, 61, 82] and resulting behavioral patterns of engagement [5, 26]. Using these psychological models within this context also provides an opportunity to engage in person-centered analysis to better understand the characteristics of MOOC users based on their behavioral patterns [9]. Insight into user characteristics provides the opportunity to better design MOOCs to meet the needs of these nontraditional students. A study evaluating alternative data mining techniques to understand student engagement through interactions with course content was conducted using trace data from an 8-week course designed specifically for educators (MOOC-Ed). This course engaged students in an online curriculum designed to provide critical professional development to educators through self-directed, peer-supported, and projected-based learning [37]. Students were professionals from all levels of an institution, including district planning teams, teachers, and students of education. Of the 1322 individuals who registered for the course, 1086 engaged in curriculum activities for either lesson content or forum discussions. Of these students, 68 % had master's degrees, 18 % had bachelor's degrees, 10 % had doctoral degrees, and 4 % had high school, 2-year, or professional degrees.

Based on prior data mining work with MOOCs and statistical principles of cluster analysis, three clustering techniques that use alternative distance metrics were implemented to cluster individuals based on their participation for each week in the MOOC: hierarchical agglomerative cluster analysis, two-step cluster analysis, and latent class growth analysis.

Overall, the clusters from each of the models reveal distinct patterns of MOOC usage and interaction across the 8 weeks of the course. However, the hierarchical clusters tended to overlap with one another more than either the two-step or LCGA clusters for the lesson interaction data. The pairs of clusters (one and four and two and three) were not distinguishable from each other for most of the weeks. In contrast, both the two-step and LCGA techniques produced clusters that were readily distinguishable from each other in terms of lesson interaction over time. LCGA cluster values only crossed each other once over all the weeks of the course, while two-step only had one cluster with more than one crossover. Therefore, for this data, the hierarchical technique did not provide results that were as interpretable as the fairly separate clusters produced by the other two methods.

Cluster agreement between the hierarchical technique and other methods was generally poor for lesson interaction, meaning that the class assignment was not comparable between methods. In contrast, LCGA and two-step cluster assignment for lesson interaction was quite good. The fairly strong agreement between the hierarchical model and the LCGA model for the forum data could be due to the fact that the forum data was more sparse with more people not participating at all, and the hierarchical model was better able to partition this data compared to the lesson data where a greater number of people participated at various weeks. On the other hand, LCGA and two-step clustering for forum data were not as strong. In examining the class trajectories, the two-step clustering model seems to be more sensitive to picking up dropout after initial participation in week one or two in the lesson data. Though not as sensitive, LCGA picks up the same trend while offering the added benefit of being able to assign a probability that an individual is in a specific cluster. Because of this probabilistic approach, cluster results from LCGA could be better situated to be used in an adaptive learning system as this analysis can be modified to predict cluster transitions.

This study provided additional insight to the research team as to how they might use student interaction with MOOC online content as one measure of engagement. Rather than use single, summative outcome measure of completion or dropout, this clustering technique provides a richer view of engagement with the educational resources over time. This data and the resulting cluster classifications can be integrated with other self-report and outcome data to better understand how to design engaging online experiences for a diversity of learners. Initial cluster models based on patterns of participation can be enriched with further data to better understand learner goals and whether their interactions with the MOOC have met these goals. Expectations that have not been met are likely to lead to either lower levels of engagement or discontinuation of participation altogether. Modeling approaches such as these may provide the groundwork for real-time monitoring tools for instructors or adaptive tools that provide guidance or recommendations for MOOC participants that help them find useful resources that align with their goals. The massive data sets generated by such courses open new statistical approaches for applying and refining psychological models of engagement, where researchers

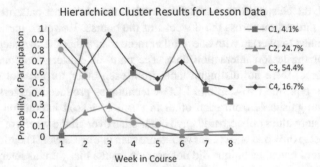

**Fig. 4** Hierarchical (*top*) and latent class growth (*bottom*) models of learner cluster assignment

have typically relied on self-report data from smaller numbers of more homogenous groups of participants (Fig. 4).

# 7   Conclusion

The study of engagement in eLearning parallels the increased interest in developing models of learning that integrate both affective and cognitive elements of the human experience. This chapter began developing this model on a foundation of a cascading goal hierarchy. Exemplified by our model engineering student, there will be a set of interrelated goals that provide motivation to engage productively with an eLearning environment. Within this model, engagement sits at the center between the goals that trigger the motivation to engage in the eLearning environment and the outcomes that result from this engagement.

A model of engagement is developed by first exploring the underlying cognitive models of schema development that help both predict learning outcomes and also provide guidance for the design of eLearning environments that optimizes the application of cognitive effort toward learning. Moving to the antecedents of engagement, affective models that link goal-driven behavior to individual characteristics such as self-efficacy and agency are used to better understand what leads to behavioral and cognitive engagement in the first place. Central to this model is an understanding of the critical role of the temporal dimension. This model of engagement is heavily influenced by prior experience, and the outcomes, immediate and longer term, of engagement are constantly fed back into the model. Similarly, goal direction at the beginning of the cycle can be targeted to both long- and short-term goals that are varying degrees of relationship to the target engagement of interest to the researcher.

Finally, these basic, high-level models of engagement in eLearning are operationalized to some degree through a discussion of how instructional design elements such as game-based learning, narrative, and social can help productively engage learners. Conversely, these same heuristics, when inappropriately applied, have also been found to be detrimental to learning outcomes. Again, individual differences in learners need to be considered and accommodated within the application of these instructional design heuristics. The chapter closes with two case studies of how the authors team has applied these theoretical frameworks and design heuristics to the study of eLearning. In the first case study, experimental research driven by these theoretical frames is used to explore ways that game-based principles can be built into adaptive eLearning environments to maximize the cognitive effort and outcomes of learners while still providing an affectively positive experience. In the second case study, data mining techniques are used to investigate large-scale trace data from a MOOC to better understand how measures of engagement can be used to classify eLearning participants.

Both case studies point to the broad set of experimental and applied eLearning contexts in which these cognitive and affective models of engagement can be applied. Future work will continue to push along both of these fronts to continue to explore how eLearning contexts can be designed to dynamically respond to diverse learner populations and the evolving goal, motivation, and engagement states of learners.

# References

1. Abramovich, S., Schunn, C., Higashi, R.: Are badges useful in education? It depends upon the type of badge and expertise of learner. Educ. Technol. Res. Dev. **61**(2), 217–232 (2013). doi:10.1007/s11423-013-9289-2
2. Admiraal, W., Huizenga, J., Akkerman, S., Dam, G.: The concept of flow in collaborative game-based learning. Comput. Hum. Behav. **27**(3), 1185–1194 (2011). doi:10.1016/j.chb.2010.12.013
3. Anderson, A., Huttenlocher, D., Kleinberg, J., Leskovec, J.: Engaging with massive online courses. Paper presented at the WWW '14, Seoul (2014)
4. Appleton, J.J., Lawrenz, F.: Student and teacher perspectives across mathematics and science classrooms: the importance of engaging contexts. Sch. Sci. Math. **111**(4), 143–155 (2011). doi:10.1111/j.1949-8594.2011.00072.x
5. Appleton, J.J., Christenson, S.L., Kim, D., Reschly, A.L.: Measuring cognitive and psychological engagement: validation of the student engagement instrument. J. Sch. Psychol. **44**(5), 427–445 (2006)
6. Baker, R., Yacef, K.: The state of educational data mining in 2009: a review and future visions. J. Educ. Data Min. **1**(1), 3–17 (2009)
7. Baker, R.S.J.d., D'Mello, S.K., Rodrigo, M.M.T., Graesser, A.C.: Better to be frustrated than bored: the incidence, persistence, and impact of learners' cognitive-affective states during interactions with three different computer-based learning environments. Int. J. Hum. Comput. Stud. **68**(4), 223–241 (2010). doi:10.1016/j.ijhcs.2009.12.003
8. Bandura, A.: Social Foundations of Thought and Action: A Social Cognitive Theory. Prentice-Hall, Englewood Cliffs (1986)
9. Bauer, D.J., Shanahan, M.J.: Modeling complex interactions: person-centered and variable-centered approaches. Mod. Context Eff. Longitud Stud. **42**(4), 255–283 (2007)
10. Bempechat, J., Shernoff, D.: Parental influences on achievement motivation and student engagement. In: Christenson, S.L., Reschly, A.L., Wylie, C. (eds.) Handbook of Research on Student Engagement, pp. 315–342. Springer, New York (2012)

11. Bienkowski, M., Feng, M., Means, B.: Enhancing Teaching and Learning Through Educational Data Mining and Learning Analytics: An Issue Brief. U.S. Department of Education, Office of Educational Technology, Washington, DC (2012)
12. Boyle, E., Connolly, T.M., Hainey, T.: The role of psychology in understanding the impact of computer games. Entertain. Comput. **2**(2), 69–74 (2011). doi:10.1016/j.entcom.2010.12.002
13. Charleer, S., Klerkx, J., Duval, E.: Learning dashboards. J. Learn. Anal. **1**(3), 199–202 (2014)
14. Clow, D.: MOOCs and the funnel of participation. Paper presented at the Third International Conference on Learning Analytics (2013)
15. Csikszentmihalyi, M.: Flow: The Psychology of Optimal Experience. Harper-Row, New York (1990)
16. Dabbagh, N., Kitsantas, A.: Personal learning environments, social media, and self-regulated learning: a natural formula for connecting formal and informal learning. Internet High. Educ. **15**(1), 3–8 (2012). doi:http://dx.doi.org/10.1016/j.iheduc.2011.06.002
17. de Kort, Y., Ijsselsteijn, W., Poels, K.: Digital games as social presence technology: development of the social presence in gaming questionnaire (SPGQ). Paper presented at the presence (2007)
18. Deater-Deckard, K., Chang, M., Evans, M.A.: Engagement states and learning from educational games. New Dir. Child Adolesc. Dev. **139**, 21–30 (2013). doi:10.1002/cad.20028
19. DeBoer, J., Stump, G., Seaton, D., Breslow, L.: Diversity in MOOC students' backgrounds and behaviors in relationship to performance in 6.002x. In: Proceedings of the Sixth Learning International Networks Consortium Conference. http://tll.mit.edu/sites/default/files/library/LINC'13.pdf (2013). Cited 15 Feb 2015
20. DeBoer, J., Ho, A.D., Stump, G.S., Breslow, L.: Changing "course": reconceptualizing educational variables for massive open online courses. Educ. Res. **43**(2), 74–84 (2014). doi:10.3102/0013189x14523038
21. Deci, E.L., Ryan, R.M.: Intrinsic Motivation and Self-determination in Human Behavior. Plenum, New York (1985)
22. Dede, C.: Immersive interfaces for engagement and learning. Science **323**(66), 66–69 (2009). doi:10.1126/science.1167311
23. Delgado, A.R., Picking, R., Grout, V.: Remote-controlled home automation systems with different network technologies. In: Proceedings of the 6th International Network Conference, pp. 357–366 (2006)
24. Eccles, J.S., Wigfield, A.: Motivational beliefs, values, and goals. Annu. Rev. Psychol. **53**, 109–132 (2002)
25. Fairclough, S.H.: Fundamentals of physiological computing. Interact. Comput. **21**(1–2), 133–145 (2009). doi:10.1016/j.intcom.2008.10.011
26. Fredricks, J.A., Blumenfeld, P.C., Paris, A.H.: School engagement: potential of the concept, state of the evidence. Rev. Educ. Res. **74**(1), 59–109 (2004)
27. Fredricks, J.A., McColskey, W., Meli, J., Montrosse, B., Mordica, J., Mooney, K.: Measuring Student Engagement in Upper Elementary Through High School: A Description of 21 Instruments. SERVE Center, Greensboro (2011)
28. Gosling, S., Augustine, A., Vazire, S., Holtzman, N., Gaddis, S.: Manifestations of personality in online social networks: self-reported Facebook-related behaviors and observable profile information. Cyberpsychol. Behav. Soc. Netw. **14**(9), 483–488 (2011). doi:10.1089/cyber.2010.0087
29. Grafsgaard, J.F., Wiggins, J.B., Boyer, K.E., Wiebe, E.N., Lester, J.C.: Predicting learning and affect from multimodal data streams in task-oriented tutorial dialogue. Paper presented at the EDM2014 (2014)
30. Hardy, M., Wiebe, E.N., Grafsgaard, J.F., Boyer, K.E., Lester, J.C.: Physiological responses to events during training: use of skin conductance to design adaptive learning systems. Paper presented at the Human Factors and Ergonomic Society 57th Annual Meeting (2013)
31. Hassenzahl, M., Diefenbach, S., Göritz, A.: Needs, affect, and interactive products—facets of user experience. Interact. Comput. **22**(5), 353–362 (2010). doi:10.1016/j.intcom.2010.04.002

32. Hazari, S., North, A., Moreland, D.: Investigating pedagogical value of wiki technology. J. Inf. Syst. Educ. **20**(2), 187–198 (2009)
33. Hollands, F.M., Tirthali, D.: MOOCs: expectations and reality. Report from Center or Benefit-Cost Studies of Education: Center for Benefit-Cost Studies of Education, Teachers College, Columbia University (2014)
34. Honey, M.A., Hilton, M. (eds.): Learning Science: Computer Games, Simulations, and Education. Committee on Science Learning: Computer Games, Simulations, and Education. National Research Council, Washington, DC (2011)
35. Jimerson, S.R., Campos, E., Greif, J.L.: Toward an understanding of definitions and measures of school engagement and related terms. Calif. Sch. Psychol. **8**, 7–27 (2003)
36. Kizilcec, R.F., Piech, C., Schneider, E.: Deconstructing disengagement: analyzing learner sub-populations in massive open online courses categories and subject descriptors. In: Proceedings of the Third International Conference on Learning Analytics and Knowledge, pp. 170–179 (2013)
37. Kleiman, B.G.M., Wolf, M.A., Frye, D.: The Digital Learning Transition MOOC for Educators: Exploring a Scalable Approach to Professional Development, pp. 1–8. Friday Institute, Raleigh (2013)
38. Kunkle, D., Cooperman, G.: Twenty-six moves suffice for Rubik's cube. In: Proceedings of the 2007 International Symposium on Symbolic and Algebraic Computation, pp. 235–242 (2007)
39. Laurel, B. (ed.): The Art of Human-Computer Interface Design. Addison-Wesley, Reading (1990)
40. Laurel, B.: Computers as Theatre. Addison-Wesley, Reading (1993)
41. Lee, V., Drake, J.: Digital physical activity data collection and use by endurance runners and distance cyclists. Technol. Knowl. Learn. **18**(1–2), 39–63 (2013). doi:10.1007/s10758-013-9203-3
42. Lin, Q.: Student views of hybrid learning: a one-year exploratory study. J. Comput. Teach. Educ. **25**(2), 57–66 (2009)
43. Macy, M.W.: Learning theory and the logic of critical mass. Am. Sociol. Rev. **55**(6), 809–826 (1990). doi:10.2307/2095747
44. Malone, T.W, Lepper, M.R.: Making learning fun: a taxonomy of intrinsic motivations for learning. In: Snow, R.E., Farr, M.J. (eds.) Aptitude Learning and Instruction, vol. 3, pp. 223–253. Erlbaum, Mahwah (1987)
45. Mayer, R.E.: Multimedia Learning. Cambridge University Press, Cambridge (2001)
46. Mayer, R.E.: Elements of a science of e-learning. J. Educ. Comput. Res. **29**(3), 297–313 (2003)
47. Mayer, R.E., Johnson, C.: Adding instructional features that promote learning in a game-like environment. J. Educ. Comput. Res. **42**(3), 241–265 (2010)
48. O'Brien, H.: The influence of hedonic and utilitarian motivations on user engagement: the case of online shopping experiences. Interact. Comput. **22**(5), 344–352 (2010). doi:http://dx.doi.org/10.1016/j.intcom.2010.04.001
49. O'Brien, H., Toms, E.G.: What is user engagement? A conceptual framework for defining user engagement with technology. J. Am. Soc. Inf. Sci. Technol. **59**(6), 938–955 (2008)
50. O'Brien, H., Toms, E.G.: The development and evaluation of a survey to measure user engagement. J. Am. Soc. Inf. Sci. Technol. **61**(1), 50–69 (2010). doi:10.1002/asi.21229
51. O'Brien, H., Toms, E.G.: Examining the generalizability of the user engagement scale (UES) in exploratory search. Inf. Process. Manag. **49**(5), 1092–1107 (2012). doi:10.1016/j.ipm.2012.08.005
52. Paas, F., Sweller, J.: An evolutionary upgrade of cognitive load theory: using the human motor system and collaboration to support the learning of complex cognitive tasks. Educ. Psychol. Rev. **24**(1), 27–45 (2012). doi:10.1007/s10648-011-9179-2
53. Paas, F., Renkl, A., Sweller, J.: Cognitive load theory and instructional design: recent developments. Educ. Psychol. **38**(1), 1–4 (2003)
54. Picard, R.W.: Affective computing: from laughter to IEEE. IEEE Trans. Affect. Comput. **1**(1), 11–17 (2010). doi:10.1109/t-affc.2010.10

55. Pintrich, P.R., Schunk, D.H.: Motivation in Education: Theory, Research, and Applications. Prentice Hall, Englewood Cliffs (1996)
56. Poirier, J., Cobb, K.N.: Social influence as a driver of engagement in a web-based health intervention. J. Med. Internet Res. **14**(1), e36 (2012)
57. Przybylski, A.K., Rigby, C.S., Ryan, R.M.: A motivational model of video game engagement. Rev. Gen. Psychol. **14**(2), 154–166 (2010). doi:10.1037/a0019440
58. Ramesh, A., Goldwasser, D., Huang, B., Daum, H., Getoor, L.: Modeling learner engagement in MOOCs using probabilistic soft logic. In: NIPS Workshop on Data Driven Education, pp. 1–7 (2013)
59. Reasons, S., Valadares, K., Slavkin, M.: Questioning the hybrid model: student outcomes in different course formats. J. Asynch. Learn Netw. **9**(1), 83–94 (2005)
60. Rosé, C., Wang, Y.-C., Cui, Y., Arguello, J., Stegmann, K., Weinberger, A., Fischer, F.: Analyzing collaborative learning processes automatically: exploiting the advances of computational linguistics in computer-supported collaborative learning. Int. J. Comput. Support. Collab. Learn. **3**(3), 237–271 (2008)
61. Ryan, R.M., Deci, E.L.: Self-determination theory and the facilitation of intrinsic motivation, social development, and well-being. Am. Psychol. **55**(1), 68–78 (2000)
62. Sabourin, J.L., Rowe, J.P., Mott, B.W., Lester, J.C.: Considering alternate futures to classify off-task behavior as emotion self-regulation: a supervised learning approach. J. Educ. Data Min. **5**(1), 9–38 (2013)
63. Scardamalia, M., Bereiter, C.: Knowledge building: theory, pedagogy, and technology. In: Sawyer, R.K. (ed.) The Cambridge Handbook of the Learning Sciences, pp. 97–118. Cambridge University Press, Cambridge (2006)
64. Schnotz, W., Kürschner, C.: A reconsideration of cognitive load theory. Educ. Psychol. Rev. **19**, 469–508 (2007)
65. Schwamborn, A., Thillmann, H., Opfermann, M., Leutner, D.: Cognitive load and instructionally supported learning with provided and learner-generated visualizations. Comput. Hum. Behav. **27**(1), 89–93 (2011). doi:10.1016/j.chb.2010.05.028
66. Shane, J., Heckhausen, J., Lessard, J., Chen, C.S., Greenberger, E.: Career-related goal pursuit among post-high school youth: relations between personal control beliefs and control strivings. Motiv. Emot. **36**(2), 159–169 (2012). doi:10.1007/s11031-011-9245-6
67. Sharek, D.: The influence of flow in the measure of engagement. M.S. Master's thesis, North Carolina State University. http://catalog.lib.ncsu.edu/record/NCSU2257724 (2010). Cited 15 Feb 2015
68. Sharek, D.: GridBlocker (Version 1.0) [Computer Game]. North Carolina State University, Raleigh (2011)
69. Sharek, D.: Investigating real-time predictors of engagement: implications for adaptive video games and online training. Ph.D. dissertation, North Carolina State University. http://catalog.lib.ncsu.edu/record/NCSU2700850 (2012). Cited 15 Feb 2015
70. Sheridan, T.B., Parasuraman, R.: Human-automation interaction. Rev. Hum. Factors Ergon. **1**(1), 89–129 (2005). doi:10.1518/155723405783703082
71. Shernoff, D.F., Abdi, B., Anderson, B., Csikszentmihalyi, M.: Flow in schools revisited: cultivating engaged learners and optimal learning environments. In: Furlong, M.J., Gilman, R., Huebner, E.S. (eds.) Handbook of Positive Psychology in Schools, 2nd edn. Taylor and Francis, Florence (2014)
72. Sherry, J.L.: Flow and media enjoyment. Commun. Theory **14**(4), 328–347 (2004). doi:10.1111/j.1468-2885.2004.tb00318.x
73. Shuell, T.J.: The role of the student in the learning from instruction. Contemp. Educ. Psychol. **13**, 276–295 (1988)
74. Smetana, L.K., Bell, R.L.: Computer simulations to support science instruction and learning: a critical review of the literature. Int. J. Sci. Educ. **34**(9), 1337–1370 (2011). doi:10.1080/09500693.2011.605182
75. Sweller, J., Merrienboer, J., Paas, F.: Cognitive architecture and instructional design. Educ. Psychol. Rev. **10**, 251–296 (1998)

76. Tops, M., Boksem, M., Wester, A.E., Lorist, M.M., Meijman, T.F.: Task engagement and the relationships between the error-related negativity, agreeableness, behavioral shame proneness and cortisol. Psychoneuroendocrinology **31**(7), 847–858 (2006). doi:10.1016/j.psyneuen.2006.04.001

77. Vorderer, P., Klimmt, C., Ritterfeld, U.: Enjoyment: at the heart of media entertainment. Commun. Theory **14**(4), 388–408 (2004). doi:10.1111/j.1468-2885.2004.tb00321.x

78. Wickens, C.D.: Multiple resources and performance prediction. Theor. Issues Ergon. Sci. **3**(2), 159–177 (2002)

79. Wickens, C.D., Hollands, J.G.: Engineering Psychology and Human Performance, 3rd edn. Prentice-Hall, Upper Saddle River (2000)

80. Wiebe, E.N., Annetta, L.A.: Influences on visual attentional distribution in multimedia instruction. J. Educ. Multimed. Hypermedia **17**(2), 259–277 (2008)

81. Wiebe, E.N., Lamb, A., Hardy, M., Sharek, D.: Measuring engagement in video game-based environments: investigation of the user engagement scale. Comput. Hum. Behav. **32**(3), 123–132 (2014). doi:10.1016/j.chb.2013.12.001

82. Wigfield, A., Tonks, S., Klauda, S.L.: Expectancy-value theory. In: Wentzel, K., Miele, D. (eds.) Handbook of Motivation at School, pp. 55–75. Routledge, London (2009)

83. Wilkowski, J., Deutsch, A., Russell, D.: Student skill and goal achievement in the mapping with Google MOOC. In: Proceedings of the First ACM Conference on Learning @ Scale Conference, pp. 3–10. http://dl.acm.org/citation.cfm?id=2566240 (2014). Cited 15 Feb 2015

84. Winne, P.H., Baker, R.S.J.d.: The potentials of educational data mining for researching metacognition, motivation, and self-regulated learning. J. Educ. Data Min. **5**(1), 1–8 (2013)

85. Wise, A.F., Speer, J., Marbouti, F., Hsiao, Y.-T.: Broadening the notion of participation in online discussions: examining patterns in learners' online listening behaviors. Instr. Sci. **41**(2), 323–343 (2012). doi:10.1007/s11251-012-9230-9

86. Wrzesniewski, A., Schwartz, B.: The secret of effective motivation. New York Times. http://nyti.ms/1qG0jiO7/14 (2014). Cited 15 Feb 2015

# Engagement in Digital Games

**Paul Cairns**

## 1 Playing and Engaging

There is substantial debate around many aspects of digital games. Which games are actually games [65]? For example, is *The Sims* a game, a toy, a simulator or something else entirely? Secondly, what are the basic genres of games, for example, are they platform, role-playing, first-person shooters or more? [2]. Lastly, why do people play games? Despite differing views on what games are and people's motivations to play, what is clear is that games are hugely popular and an increasing part of everyday life [25]. And even when games are uncontroversially games, they can be very different from each other, for example, *Candy Crush* and *Heavy Rain*. These two games have very little in common in terms of gameplay, controls, platform, aesthetics, fun and so on. Nonetheless, in order to play these games, the player must be engaged with the game. In that sense, engagement is one of the more fundamental attributes of digital games. Indeed, the notion of engagement comes out in many studies of digital game experience (GX) and is expressed in various forms such as immersion [12], flow [19], as well as engagement itself [11]. It should be noted that despite engagement being widely acknowledged as central to GX, it is not always referred to as such. There is a pluralistic approach to engagement, reflecting a pluralistic approach to the research of GX: different words for engagement are used interchangeably by some people, the same words being used by different people to mean different things and in other cases, to reflect subtle nuances of meaning in different contexts.

The goal here is not to dictate which is the "correct" way to think of engagement in digital games. Indeed, the conceptual debates around the nature of digital games [65] do rather suggest that there is not a one-size-fits-all approach. Instead,

P. Cairns (✉)
University of York, York, UK
e-mail: paul.cairns@york.ac.uk

© Springer International Publishing Switzerland 2016
H. O'Brien, P. Cairns (eds.), *Why Engagement Matters*,
DOI 10.1007/978-3-319-27446-1_4

this chapter aims to think about games in terms of the process of engagement as modelled by [55]. In order to facilitate this, the next section describes the elements of the model and illustrates with reference to a particular (idiosyncratic) experience of playing a digital game. The example shows that, even with a single player engaging with digital games on a single platform, the unit of analysis for engagement needs to be carefully considered. For instance, engagement in a digital game can be a part of a single play session or a whole play session or protracted across a large number of playing sessions. Depending on which unit of analysis is intended, the process of engagement differs. The remainder of the chapter then reviews our current understandings of engagement of digital games in the context of this model. However, understandably, a great deal has been written on what it means to play digital games and therefore what engagement is in this domain. In order to constrain the focus of this chapter, the emphasis is on empirical work that is supported either through qualitative or quantitative studies that go beyond anecdotal or individuated experiences. While many game designers and game players have valid views on the nature of playing digital games based on their own experiences, such claims for generic relevance are inherently limited. Through focussing on empirical work, the goal here is to provide a view on engagement in digital games that has more general relevance as a result of being based on more objective evidence.

Before proceeding, it is also perhaps worth declaring a personal perspective. My own work in digital games has looked extensively at the concept of immersion and uses a definition of immersion that I was heavily involved in developing [12]. However, for this chapter (and generally), I view my understanding of immersion as just one way of thinking about engagement in digital games. Elsewhere I have aimed to position immersion conceptually among the variety of related concepts [15]. Here, immersion is just one concept among many similar concepts that are of equal relevance and equal merit, objectively speaking at least. Immersion just happens to be the one that I have a particular preference for!

## 2 Illustrating the Process Model of Engagement

The process model of engagement [55] has four stages: point of engagement, period of sustained engagement, disengagement and (possibly) re-engagement. Each of these is associated with or even characterised by a set of attributes. As a process of engagement, players who are engaged with digital games cycle through these stages and at different levels. They may experience cycles of engagement within a single playing session or their engagement may occur over several sessions. To see this more clearly, I will illustrate this with my experience of playing the game *Infinity Blade II* (IB2). In using my own experiences of engagement, the aim is to make it easier to describe the process model rather than speaking in generalities or hypotheticals.

IB2 was released in December 2011 by Chair Entertainment and Epic Games and is for the iOS mobile platform [75]. It is primarily a third-person sword fighting game with role-playing game (RPG) elements. That is, the player sees themselves as a character, something like a medieval knight, in a virtual world, and the main action of the game is to fight with swords, or similar weapons, against other characters to gain experience (XP) and gold. As a result of gaining XP, the player is able to improve their character with statistics, for example, for their magical power or shield strengths. With gold, they can buy equipment which also enhances statistics. As a result, the player's character is able to take on increasingly difficult enemies. Eventually (and I don't think this is a spoiler as it is self-evident how this kind of game plays out), the player faces three key opponents and then gets to face one final terrible opponent and win out overall. I assume this is self-evident as at the time of writing, I have not completed the game (or even got close). I may be in for a big surprise!

I am a regular game player of the style that is often called a casual gamer [40]. That is, I don't spend large periods of time playing in any particular session nor do I tend to play Triple A titles, that is, high-price-tag games from big studios for the popular consoles like Microsoft Xbox and Sony PlayStation. Indeed, I don't have a game console but play on my iPhone or web-based games on my PC. Like many gamers when faced with the plethora of games to choose from, I rely on reviews and recommendations of games. I particularly use the jayisgames.com website as it has daily updates, and I often agree with its assessment of the games which makes me feel I can trust their recommendations. IB2 was a little different from my usual sort of games as I am not particularly into fighting games, but it looked (visually) amazing for an iPhone game and, better yet, it was recently offered for free on iTunes presumably as IB3 is due out. So I had little to lose if I didn't like it. Thus the concerns of aesthetics, my regular motivation to play games, the novelty of the game (for me) and my interest based on reviews were all relevant to my point of engagement. These are precisely the attributes specified in the process model.

As with any game that I like playing, when playing, I exemplify well the period of engagement described in the model. That is, the game holds my attention (much to the frustration of my wife, at times!) and the fights within the game are very challenging. I do not always win but I do get a sense of progress, steadily, which is clearly indicated by the feedback of the game which shows my stats and my goal and the equipment that I have bought. Also, IB2 is structured so that novelty is essential: you cannot beat the successively difficult enemies unless you buy new weapons, armour and the like. But these have different characteristics that need to be learned and understood to make the most of them. In addition, there are areas of the game world that "unlock", some in relation to the stage of the game but some in relation to the equipment that I have bought or found. So there is lots to engage with in the game itself. These attributes of novelty, attention, feedback and so on characterise sustained engagement in the process model.

Also, I have periods of disengagement and re-engagement with the game, which is an important part of the process model. Sometimes I get beaten several times by the same opponent so I stop playing partly out of boredom and partly out of frustration. Sometimes I stop when I reach a natural break in the game as I am doing well and enjoying it but it is time to do something else. And even within a single play session, sometimes I stop the fighting part to focus on my strategy to buy equipment or to manage my stats, which can be desultory flicking through stuff I may never buy or more focused engagement in what I might buy/upgrade next. And this can be disengaged from in order to go back to hacking at opponents with my latest bit of kit. So challenge, my affective state, time and interruptions are all components of my disengagement with parts of the game within a particular session or with a particular playing session.

This model therefore captures well many aspects of the experience of engagement in digital games. However, I would also note two things that are not explicit in the process model in this particular context as these are relevant to the work that is done in understanding research into gaming experience.

First, people who play games have a disposition to play games. This could be in part represented as the motivation to play within the process model, but what exactly is that motivation? In my case, I did not have a motive to play IB2 specifically. I wanted to play something simply because I like to play generally and a combination of circumstances suggested IB2 to me, but if it had not been IB2, then it would have been something else. That it continues to be IB2 is part of the process of engagement with that particular game but there was, before that process started, a disposition to be engaged, an openness to the opportunity for engagement. This was not influenced in any way by IB2 or any other game and so must stand apart somewhat from the experience of interacting with IB2.

Secondly, within my account of the process model, which I hope faithfully reflects O'Brien and Toms account [55], there is a blurring of what might be called the unit of analysis. In the point of engagement, I was drawn to engage with IB2. But in any particular session of playing the game, I am engaged in that play session. However, outside of that play session, it is possible to still describe me as engaged with the game. Arguably, while I am not actually playing the game, I should be described as not being engaged with it, but I would disagree with this perspective. I am currently starting to find IB2 very hard. I am finding myself cash-poor (in the game) which is impairing my ability to progress, and the fights themselves are becoming more challenging. So when not actually playing, I am wondering in idler moments (e.g. walking my dog) if I need to restart my character and make some wiser decisions about how to spend my gold and how to upgrade my stats. I also checked out some websites to see if there were elements of strategy that I had overlooked. There were. This is all part of my sustained engagement with the game. However, in terms of the process model, it is tricky to characterise this aspect of my engagement: it is not related to particular challenges or feedback that the interaction is giving me. Rather, it is merely my sustained interest and desire to play games and, now that I've started it, this game.

This blurring is also seen in terms of disengagement. I stop playing on any particular session for reasons discussed, but I know that at some point, I will stop playing IB2. This may be because I complete it or the challenge is finally too much for me, which would fit with the process of disengagement. But there is another effect related to the first point which is that I may simply drop it in preference to another game. My disposition to play games means that I may simply find another game and on occasion decide to play that over IB2, and if I repeatedly make many of those decisions, I may never play IB2 again. This is not so much active disengagement but more of a drifting off.

Of course, having stated that I would be motivated by empirically based research, I seem to have lapsed into anecdotal reflection. The intention though is to both illustrate the process model of engagement and to highlight places where the unit of analysis for engagement is unclear. This requires more careful consideration in this particular context. This variation in unit of analysis is sometimes reflected in GX research but not always or not always explicitly.

# 3   Starting to Play

The popularity of digital games alone indicates that many people have a strong inclination to play games. Since the early days of digital games research, the question has been into why do (so many) people play games. Philosophically, play has been held to be something inherent in human nature [34], indeed existing before humans, and therefore the desire to play is nothing to belittle nor even to be surprised by. However, digital games have always been marked out for the avidity with which they are played [76]. The recent proliferation of digital technology both in terms of devices and connectivity has also made it even easier for digital games to be played almost anywhere, at anytime and with anyone [32].

So if engaging with digital games is more or less expected, the question is not so much why do people engage but how do they come to be engaged with particular games. That is, what is it about specific games that makes them engaging? This has been interpreted within gaming research as understanding player styles but would also equate with player personalities, that is, the enduring individual differences between people that lead them to play some games over other games.

The earliest attempt to categorise player styles was probably Bartle's four suits [3] where he analysed the postings of players from a multi-user dungeon (MUD) and condensed their reasons for playing from their contributions to the discussion on this topic. For example, one of the types is Explorer who plays in order to find out as much as possible about the world. Bartle also called Explorers Spades after the suit from a deck of cards because they dig into the world. The four types could further be positioned on two axes: a player/world dimension and an acting/interacting dimension. Spades are driven by a desire to interact with the world in diametric contrast to Clubs (Killers) who are driven by a desire to act on players (lethally). Bartle then uses these categories to help inform what makes a good MUD.

This understanding of the motivations of players was expanded on and updated by Yee et al. [79] in the context of massively multiplayer online role-playing games (MMORPGs), specifically the paragon of the genre *World of Warcraft*. In many ways, MMORPGs are the successors to MUDs. Yee [78] developed a questionnaire of 40 items based on Bartle's original classification and found ten underlying factors that grouped naturally into three categories: achievement, doing well in the game either against the achievements in the game or against other players; social, having the opportunity to interact with others in more or less structured activities; and immersion, moving from the real world into the game world (not just in the sense of engaging with the game). With three overarching dimensions, it extends and shifts Bartle's two MUD dimensions.

In Yee's framework, players can have a complex mix of motivations, but based on their predispositions, it is possible to predict to some extent their levels of achievement in the different aspects of the game. This suggests that players' motivations not only move them to engage with the game but also shape the way in which they engage. There have also been developments of these same ideas for role-playing games not of the MMO type [74]. It should be noted though that these results are better interpreted as correlation rather than causation. It might be that players who succeed a certain way with, say, *World of Warcraft* reflect this in how they describe their motivations to play.

Necessarily with this work, the game itself has been an important factor as all players in the different studies played the same game or style of game. At the very least, all of the games addressed so far involved the opportunity for role-playing. This is something which is not particularly present in other games, say *Tetris* or *Bejewelled*. This is not to invalidate these models of motivation as determining why people engage with digital games but rather to emphasise their scope. Interestingly, there do not seem to be similar motivational models or classifications for other genres of games. This may simply be a consequence of pragmatism: players of multiplayer online games are pretty easy to find!

Moving from a player style approach to player personality, a good place to start in understanding why players engage with certain games is to see the influence of underlying personality on playing habits. The Big Five [46] is a term for a commonly accepted quantification of personality. That is, this is not a way of under-standing personality in particular contexts such as susceptibility to hypnosis [71], rather a way of understanding common sets of traits or dimensions of personality that are in some sense universal, having arisen independently from the work of many researchers [44]. The Big Five are openness to experience, conscientiousness, extroversion, agreeableness and neuroticism. A person's personality may be, to some extent, described by a set of numerical values on these five different scales and is understood to be a set of stable attributes that come into play when people act, evaluate or make decisions [44].

From this perspective, it makes sense that personality would influence the games that players choose and how they subsequently play them. Johnson and others have looked at this in a set of studies on how the Big Five relates to the genres of games that people play [37, 56]. They found some links, for instance, that extroverts prefer casual, music and party games, but that introverts prefer MMORPGs [56]. They have also found that different personalities correlate with different aspects of experiences while playing; for instance, extraversion correlates with the experience of challenge while playing [38] or with measures of competence/control [37].

Though it is appealing to think that personality leads to different gaming experiences, such results do need to be interpreted carefully for a variety of reasons. First, as the authors note, correlation is not causation, and it may be that players with different personalities experience the different genres equally or that the genres themselves are influencing their experiences. Further caution is needed because the correlations were all small, $r < 0.2$, which means that their effect size is very small, $r^2 < 4\%$, and these small effects were generally not seen in ANOVAs that tested group differences explicitly. If personality is having an effect on the motivations to play and the subsequent experiences that players have, then it is an effect that can easily be obscured by other factors.

Of course the Big Five is intended as a generic, overarching approach to personality which may be why it does not demonstrate strong effects of personality in relation to gaming behaviours. It may also be that, despite its popularity, it is not in fact an adequate description of personality [44]. More tailored measures of personality may be better suited to understanding the influences on players and why they play. To this end, the BrainHex instrument is intended to build and extend on the work of Yee and Bartle in order to produce a generic measure of player style that would have relevance for a much wider set of games, particularly beyond the RPG variants studied in earlier work [4]. The resulting model has seven distinct types of player that are further associated with underlying neurobiological responses. Some of the player types, like Socializer and Seeker, map directly to Bartle's types and Yee's motivations; some of the types like Survivor and Mastermind are specific to BrainHex (see table 15.5 in [4] for a full comparison). While this and the link to underlying neurobiology remains to be established [4], the types do seem much more likely to be relevant to understanding gamers and why they engage with digital games. Though links have been shown between BrainHex and existing personality constructs like the Big Five and the Myers-Briggs typology [51], the link to game engagement has yet to be established.

Though BrainHex is a promising development in understanding why players play particular games, I have to question the link to neurobiology. Ultimately, all experiences that we as humans are able to express boil down to neurobiology, so the need for a particular connection to particular chemicals or systems of chemicals lacks explanatory power. Some neurochemicals and some specific regions of the brain must be involved somewhere. At the same time, if, for example, the Socializer player type turns out to be completely unrelated to the oxytocin levels of players, I am not sure that this would invalidate the model. It seems to be setting the hurdle of validity rather high without any particular benefit.

Though personality types and player styles are potentially very relevant, they do not address the initial point in this section that regardless of personality or games, an awful lot of people want to play. The basic drive to play is not addressed by these models. To counter this and also to aim at general applicability like the BrainHex model, there are two approaches to understanding the desire to engage with digital games as arising from addressing basic needs of human nature.

Ryan and Rigby have drawn from extensive work in the psychology of motivation to promote the use of Self-Determination Theory (SDT) in the context of digital games [61]. SDT holds that people are strongly motivated by feelings of autonomy, that is, feeling in control of their own fate; competence, the feeling of being able to achieve things; and relatedness, making connections with others. In their analysis, they show how games offer players all three of these experiences in a way that other things do not.

To support this understanding, the relationship between SDT and player experience has been studied using the Player Experience of Need Satisfaction (PENS) questionnaire which includes scales for measuring players' experiences of autonomy, competence and presence/immersion [62]. Like many studies that have subsequently been done, for example, [37], the analysis is primarily through regression or correlation which has the same problems as mentioned above in terms of correlation and causation. Generally though, effects seen are more substantial. This is undermined though in that the studies used to promote SDT are the same ones used to validate PENS. There is a strong degree of circularity here, and I am not aware of any independent attempt to validate PENS against the usual standards of psychometry [13, 44]. One of the original studies was done to compare PENS across two different games, one of which was commercially successful and one of which was not, and though results were favourable, it obviously lacks the experimental control where only a single variable is explicitly manipulated.

My reservations notwithstanding, SDT and PENS have had a considerable impact in the study of GX. And independent of the particular issues with PENS, SDT does provide a compelling account of why people like to play digital games.

In a way similar to which SDT draws on established work in psychology, Sherry and Lucas [68] draw on media research to understand digital games as having uses and gratifications like other media. The uses and gratifications framework however, rather than immediately offering reasons why people play digital games, is a generic structure in which to understand the individual, social and cultural impact of any media. It is more like a research approach than an existing theory. Within this approach then, Sherry et al. [68] set out to develop the set of theoretical, or potential, traits for game uses and gratifications. These emerging traits are captured in a questionnaire that has six scales: competition, challenge, social interaction, diversion, fantasy and arousal. These were shown to be predictive of the time players spend playing per week.

Understandably, the uses and gratifications framework shows similarity with the previous models. Yee's achievement could map to competition and challenge and immersion to fantasy. However, Przybylski et al. [58] make an important distinction that while there is overlap, SDT is a universal set of motivators that games may or may not fulfil, whereas the uses and gratifications are derived from people's conscious explications of why they play. They note that even when these gratifications are met, people may not exhibit persistent motivations to play because their underlying needs are not being met.

Though the uses and gratifications framework may be skewed because of this, it does address something that none of the other models address, namely, why people choose to play at a particular instance. That is, the other models talk about the unit of analysis as the game and why people choose to engage with particular games. By contrast, the uses and gratifications has something to say about why people engage at a particular point in time. For instance, in the challenge item of the uses and gratifications model, there is the item "When I lose to someone, I immediately want to play again in an attempt to beat him/her." And the two items of diversion are both about playing despite having other things to do.

## 3.1 Summary and Questions

Overall then, the point of engagement in digital games is well considered in the field both in terms of reasons for engagement with particular types of games like Yee's work and with games in general through the uses and gratifications framework. However, such approaches do not step outside of the world of digital games. So, while they may describe what people get from playing, they do not indicate what draws people in the first place. Obviously a generic disposition to play is philosophically interesting but has no concrete implications: it is a background against which we need to differentiate individuals. General theories of personality are of some relevance, but both BrainHex and SDT set out to show specific elements of people's make-up that leads to the need to engage with digital games and that digital games are able to fulfil those needs.

Arising from this analysis, there are clearly open questions. Though there has been a lot of interest in the motivations to play role-playing games, particularly MMORPGs, there do not seem to be other such detailed, empirical analyses of the motivations to play other styles of games such as puzzle games, first-person shooters and so on. It may be that such games do not have enduring, and thus findable, audiences unlike MMORPG, but then what are the motivations of such players to pick up games and move on from them? Indeed, what are the driving forces behind players choosing to initiate their engagement with any particular game?

As new, game-specific theories of motivation to play develop, it is important to establish their validity, not just as measurement scales but as predictors of behaviour [44]. BrainHex seems to be ripe for testing in lots of different contexts to see how the analysis of players may lead to a richer understanding of the experiences that players have in different situations. It could be imagined that any study that examines player experience could use BrainHex as a way not only to characterise the participants of the study but also to enrich any account of the findings. There is also an entirely separate project that could link BrainHex to the underlying neurobiology, which, while potentially fascinating, I am not sure is necessary for furthering research into game engagement.

By contrast, PENS needs substantial validation particularly as it seems to be gaining wide appeal as a GX measurement scale but without convincing conceptual underpinning. In particular, is it possible to develop specific manipulations of games that influence autonomy or competence and to see these effects in PENS? Part of this problem is to produce some PENS-independent mechanism of knowing that autonomy and competence in a game are being manipulated. From my experience, players in a lab are pretty happy with almost anything they are asked to do. They seem to take even the oddest of manipulations (e.g. doing arithmetic while playing [54]) as all part of the fun. Of course, as might be expected and will be seen in the next section, relatedness in games is relatively easy to identify and manipulate.

These approaches to engagement are also essentially working at the level of the game and not at the instances of play. What are the driving forces behind why people choose to play at a particular time as opposed to doing something else? For instance, when faced with a free evening, why do sometimes people read, watch television or go out with friends and sometimes choose to play digital games? The uses and gratifications approach gives some indication of why people might choose to play as a diversion from other activities, but, outside of this, little has been done in this area. One interesting line of research has shown that playing games can act as a "destressor" for people after work, helping them to recover from the demands of the day [20]. There is much therefore to be done around this particular meaning of the point of engagement.

## 4   Engagement While Playing

It seems trivial to say that the whole point of games is to be engaged with. Games exist for the purpose of being played, that is, so that players might be engaged in playing them. Though the outcomes of games may have substantial impact, say in prize money or kudos, the actual play need have no external value whatsoever [39]. It is the act of playing and the experiences obtained from that engagement that people play for.

The incredible attraction and success of digital games as engaging activities have raised the question of whether such massive levels of engagement might be fruitfully harnessed to more productive ends such as learning, politics, crowdsourcing or other productive activities. It is this thinking that underlies serious games [47] or gamification [24] where through playing a game, something else of value outside of play is also achieved. Though these provide intriguing possibilities, it is not our concern here as such teleological approaches to gaming add a further complication to understand what it means for people to engage in the activity. Here, we consider simply what it means to be engaged in digital games for its own sake.

In this sense, engagement in gaming or indeed any experiential outcome from a game is very pure, being the end in itself of the game. It is therefore not surprising that a lot of research into gaming looks at these experiential outcomes. Unswervingly, engagement appears as a core element of GX whenever gamers talk about their experiences, for example [12, 57]. This is not to say that engagement while playing is a wholly understood concept. In their systematic review, Boyle et al. [9] demonstrate that there are several concepts that overlap around the notion of engagement, particularly flow, immersion and presence as well as engagement itself. And though there is clear overlap, there are conceptual distinctions between these different terms as detailed with particular reference to immersion in [15].

What does it mean, then, for players to be engaged while playing digital games? Turner [73] considers engagement generally as an alternative to user experience in the study of all interactive systems. In this context, engagement while playing arises when (1) games offer affordances for action to achieve goals, (2) the achievement of goals has positive emotional outcomes and (3) it has a wider meaning to the players either in terms of their identities or goals outside of the game. In other words, (1) players can play the game, (2) it makes them happy to do so and (3) it means something to them. In this formulation, goals are central to defining engagement, but what are the goals of playing digital games? With productive systems, for example, a website to buy books or book flights, activities with the system have implications outside of the activity. But with games, is the goal simply to play? If so, engagement simply collapses to the act of playing, which is not necessarily the same as being engaged in play: it is possible to be playing without particular engagement. If the goal is determined by the gameplay, for example, complete the game or win without losing a life, then it is harder to see how engagement fits with the wider meaning for players: games work because, in the magic circle of the game [63], actions have their own special meaning. There are also parallels between Turner's notion of engagement and what it means for something to be a game, for example, [39], which would also collapse engagement simply to the act of playing a game. Thus, while Turner's formulation attempts to bring an overarching structure of engagement to lots of activities, in the particular context of games, it ends up being rather simplistic.

By contrast, the process model of engagement that underpins this structure offers several attributes of engagement while playing:

- Control
- Challenge
- Feedback
- Aesthetic and sensory appeal
- Attention
- Awareness
- Interactivity
- Novelty
- Interest
- Positive affect

These are seen time and again in the operationalisation of engagement through the various questionnaires that are used to capture engagement in digital games. For example, immersion as defined by Jennett et al. [36] identifies five constitute components of immersion including cognitive involvement, emotional involvement, control, challenge and real-world dissociation. These map well onto the above attributes of engagement (if not always precisely). And where the subcomponents of a questionnaire do not so obviously map to these attributes, the individual items generally do. For example, Brockmyer et al. [11] have the subscales of the Gaming Engagement Questionnaire (GEngQ) as immersion, presence, flow and absorption (which sounds rather like engagement, engagement, engagement and engagement to me). However, the individual items of the GEngQ do map to attention, "If someone talks to me I don't hear"; control, "Things seem to happen automatically"; and so on.

Interestingly, though many people use flow with reference to engagement in digital games [19], the general view of engagement is that it is distinct from flow. This is because flow has a very clear meaning [22] and outcomes. Engagement alone does not seem to be sufficient to be called flow partly because of the lack of clear goals in some engaging tasks [55], the fact that some engaging tasks (including aspects of gameplay) do not require high skills and high challenge [73] and simply because gamers clearly identify qualitative differences in their own experiences that suggest that flow is not the norm [12]. Indeed, flow is intended as an optimal experience where players are "in the zone" [19], but in many situations, players are engaged without the all-consuming experience of flow. And simply calling this graded, less intense experience of engagement "flow" does not make it so. Thus, without this care for definitions, there is much conceptual wishy-washiness around the use of the term in the context of digital games, something which is not always addressed, for example [26, 52].

So if the process model's attributes are a reasonable starting point for engagement in digital games, the question then becomes how do they come together to form engaging experiences for players? Here, there is a very large amount of work done, and it would be practically impossible to do anything more here than give a flavour of it.

## 4.1   Playing and the Process Model Attributes

Controls, particularly with the recent innovations in controllers like Wii and Kinect and the opportunities of mobile devices, have had a lot of interest. The whole body is now a potential controller for games, and this alters not only what players can do but the social aspect of play [6]. Related to this is the notion of naturalness [70] where the actions of plays correspond to the natural actions a person might make if engaged in the real-world activity, for example, swiping a controller around like a sword or using a steering wheel for a driving game. Naturalness however is both tricky to define and does not necessarily lead to better engagement [16]. It may be that in the realm of controllers, some broader theories of interaction are needed. An important theory of interaction in mainstream HCI is instrumental interaction [5] in which any interaction between a user and a system is mediated through a set of instruments, and those instruments can be positioned across a set of dimensions that characterise how they work. This might lend the richness needed to describe game controllers and hence more easily map control in games to subsequent engagement.

Also, it is beginning to emerge that it is not necessarily that players require perfect control to play but rather that they know that, in principle, they could have an effect even if they are not skilled enough to bring that about. This is the concept of effectance and contrasts with unreliable controls where players try to do something but are unsure if their actions will have an effect [43].

Challenge is also important, but understanding what challenge is both in different games and for different players is not trivial. While many papers talk about challenge, it is not clear which aspects of a game's challenge contribute to engagement and which impair it [21] and how varying challenge over time results in the best experiences [59]. It is perhaps overly simplistic to lump the challenges that games can offer under one heading. Brandse and Tomimatsu [10] propose that challenge should be considered not so much from the perspective of difficulty to the player but from the perspective of designing for challenge. They give six characteristics of challenge, which may be distilled into saying challenges are both achievable and fair. That is, players can simply through playing learn or acquire the resources to overcome a challenge, and their ability to overcome the challenge is not artificially impaired by the game. Of course, through taking a design perspective, the question then becomes what the impact on player experience is through emphasising different aspects of the challenges in a game.

Feedback is essential in games to allow players to know how they are doing and, as such, features strongly in any heuristics around game design, for example [27], as well as being an important constituent of flow [22]. However, feedback is not widely considered in the GX literature though it does have an impact on perceived engagement [35]. This may be because feedback is simply a given in all games and there are many typical ways of presenting feedback that have established (if not proven) efficacy. However, with the move to gamification, feedback mechanisms like badges, levelling up, score and so on become very important [80]. There is much to be established in this area.

Digital games can present a visual and audio feast to the player with astonishing virtual worlds (such as drew me in to IB2) and rich musical scores that are appreciated outside of the context of the game [14]. Despite the enormous efforts put into achieving high definition and realism in certain sectors of game development, it is not clear that these increase engagement [30]. For instance, Andersen et al. [1] showed that differences in aesthetics, specifically animations, increased the length of time players played and made them more likely to return, both indicators of increased engagement. By contrast, music and sounds in the game did not show similar effects. Nonetheless, music can increase the immersion in the game [15], but only provided players like the music [64]. Sounds in a game can alter players' experiences, including their sense of engagement [50].

Attention to a game is obviously necessary for engagement to occur. But Jennett [35] has shown that the psychological sense of attention is not enough to account for immersion. Specifically, when playing a game with negative feedback outside of the players' control, players are less immersed but perform equally well, indicating comparable levels of attention to the game. Also, it is necessary to consider the level of attention that is related to engagement. With several students, I have looked at immersion in relation to inattentional blindness [69] and inattentional deafness [23] and found no link to these phenomena in perceptual attention and levels of immersion (forthcoming). This would suggest that immersion and engagement as a user experience are happening at a remove from low-level perceptual attention. So while attention is a trivial prerequisite for engagement, it is clearly not in itself a sufficient description of engagement.

Similarly, awareness of factors external to a game diminishes with engagement. Players often report less of a sense of awareness of their surroundings and of time passing [11, 12] which are characteristics of engagement more generally, for example, when in flow. This is supported by the work of Jennett [35] who showed that more immersed players are less aware of external visual and audio distractors. However, extensive studies by Nordin [53] have failed to produce any relationship between immersion and time perception, as measured through a variety of established techniques [7]. This finding is consistent with a small set of existing but less controlled studies that motivated Nordin's work [72, 77] where sometimes time perception did change and sometimes it did not.

There is therefore a poorly understood relationship between established notions of engagement like immersion and flow and the actual attentional processes involved. Whereas the idea that engaged players lose a sense of their surroundings is seen in experiments, the loss of a sense of time is not. The methods used to measure time perception are weak mostly because people have a poor sense of time, particularly over the time scale of minutes and hours used in experiments and in actual occurrences of play. But then if players are saying they are losing a sense of time, what are they then referring to? This is an established feature of flow. Is it that in flow something more intense is occurring that really does interfere with time perception that does not happen in more prosaic engagement? It may be that the way forward is to more actively seek flow experiences in games.

Turning to the remaining attributes of engagement, these are perhaps less explicitly explored in digital games research. Interaction and interest are perhaps assumed attributes of playing a game but rarely explicitly considered, except indirectly, say through controls or motivations. Novelty however is perhaps more interesting, but I am not aware of it having been studied under that name. There is both novelty within a period of engagement which may correspond to the introduction of new game elements or even new challenges. IB2, for instance, has increasingly powerful weapons and armour to buy which is definitely part of its hook to keep players invested. But some games have almost no novelty. For example, traditional Tetris has no new elements beyond the first level, and the only novelty is the increasing speed of the blocks. This is a rather paltry form of novelty, if such it is, yet the game is certainly able to be engaging.

This leaves positive affect as an attribute of engagement. In the context of games, it is tempting to equate this with enjoyment or fun. Both of these are tricky concepts though. Mekler et al. [48] have conducted a systematic review of enjoyment in digital games and it does suggest that enjoyment is not necessarily associated with cognitive involvement. And fun has the implication of aimlessness that games rarely possess [8]. It may be that pleasure is a more important concept for a positive gaming outcome, but even highly engaging games can be essentially frustrating experiences, for example, the game *Flappy Bird*!

## 4.2  Pushing the Process Model

Though the process model does offer a good account of engagement as seen widely in the GX research, it is worth considering how completely the GX research maps to the model. As noted earlier, the process model is somewhat agnostic to the unit of analysis. GX research by contrast is quite clear about what it considers to be engagement, namely, the experiential outcome of a session of play. Almost all studies involve players playing certain games for some period of time and then measuring the outcomes for the whole period. There are two ways in which this narrow view of game engagement perhaps omits important aspects of the overall process of engagement.

First, within any particular session of play, players may feel an ebb and flow of engagement [12], and this is explicitly represented in the process model. However, it is very challenging to see this when relying on questionnaires, like PENS [62] and the Immersive Experience Questionnaire [36], which, at best, only function as aggregated measures over a protracted period of play. And if administered too frequently during a session of play, questionnaires could impair the engagement they are intended to track.

Different, less obtrusive measures of engagement may offer more fine-grained analysis of engagement while playing; in particular, there is the potential in the use of objective physiological measures. Eye tracking, for instance, may be correlated to immersion, but it was found to offer only a coarse measure in relation to the reported subjective experience [36]. Psychophysiological measures have been used to see the emotional impact of specific in-game events on players, for instance, when players die [60]. However, physiological measures are far from definitive, so while they are appealing in the detail they potentially offer, they are best used with other measures like questionnaires and game logs in order to fully understand the subjective experiences that they represent [49]. In this sense, we are still a long way from seeing how engagement varies within a single session of play.

Secondly, game engagement, as seen in my illustration of playing IB2, can be protracted beyond the playing of a single session. Players not only progress through games across multiple sessions but also engage in extra-game activities like reading online tips, creating new content [45] and posting YouTube videos [14]. There are also hidden activities like players thinking about the game while not playing. Although there is some research looking at what happens in these activities, little has related this back to the experiences had by players. In particular, does engagement via these extra-game activities influence the subsequent engagement experience of playing the game? Clearly reading up "how to play" FAQs could lead to spoiling the experience (hence the term "spoilers"). But what about less broad-brush issues like when a player uses a cheat, like a mod or a hint, to surpass a single, stubborn obstacle [29]? This could lead to a much longer period of engagement that would otherwise not have occurred. This extra-game aspect of engagement seems to be wide open.

Contrasting the process model of engagement with GX research, a very notable omission is the role of social play. It arises as an important motivator to play as seen in both the SDT and the uses and gratifications approaches to digital games discussed earlier. It is also talked about by players as an important constituent of playing [57], something which comes through in studies of engagement in relation to social play. Players are more engaged when they think they are playing other people [21, 28] even if they are not co-located or able to have direct interactions except through the gameplay. When thinking more carefully about what it means to play with or against other players, it is clear that if your co-players do not engage as much as you, then it is possible that you are also unable to engage fully. Thus, there is a degree to which engagement must occur as a group, something Kaye has identified as group flow [42] (though as you might guess, I am not sure it really is flow). This may be able to account for an effect that we have observed in studying social play in team-based competitive games where players who are playing another team of real people experience increased collaborative presence with their own team (forthcoming). The engagement with the competitors may increase the engagement the team has with itself. The results so far are not definitive but are suggestive of the dependence of engagement on the collective experience of the players.

The process model then is a good starting point for exploring engagement in the context of existing (and missing) GX research. But also it is not the last word, as with any model, as it necessarily simplifies or omits details according to its focus. However, social play does seem to be an important attribute of the process of engagement that ought to be included in the model, at least in the context of digital games.

## 4.3 Summary and Questions

Much gaming experience research focuses precisely on how players engage with games through the process of actually playing. The research is wide ranging and covers many attributes of the process model but also adds to that particularly with consideration of social play. Necessarily though, with the enormous variety of games and controls that are available, there is room to revisit everything addressed so far in different games, genres, platforms and contexts.

Even though the attributes are important, it is also clear that none individually is the whole story. What then is the collection of attributes that is sufficient for engagement? Which are necessary? And are there minimal levels of both attributes and sets of attributes for engagement to be really taking place?

Alongside answering such questions, it is probably more important to move away from general meanings of these attributes to more theoretical conceptualisations of them. This would make generalising from particular studies easier while also clarifying what it is about games that lead to different experiences of engagement. For example, in control, rather than fixate on particular controllers, research might aim to develop theories of control like effectance or instrumental interaction. But then this opens up lines of research on the theories that are being offered. For instance, is instrumental interaction an appropriate way to conceptualise control in digital games [16]? Similarly, does Brandse and Tomimatsu's [10] categorisation of challenge map to meaningful differences in engagement?

Engagement while playing is still very much analysed as the outcome of a particular session of play. What about the ebb and flow of engagement within a single session? There are methodological challenges of how to access that without destroying engagement along the way. Physiological measures seem promising but are far from being definitively associated with particular experiences. Looking beyond single sessions of play, how do players sustain their interest in a game? And how do these extra-game activities influence the engagement in play experience? Though extensively studied already, engagement while playing is currently far from fully understood.

## 5 Disengagement and Re-engagement

It is generally assumed that players do, at some point, stop playing a game. There have been tragic cases where failure to stop has resulted in the death of the player, but these are extreme cases[1] and mercifully few. Aside from these, there has been the recognition that playing digital games can have many of the attributes of addiction [31]. However, there is an emerging view that to call excessive gaming "addiction" is perhaps too strong. Unlike other addictions, say with gambling, alcohol or drug use, digital gaming does not have the associate pathologies [17]. There is evidence that, in heavy gamers, scoring on addictiveness traits correlates strongly with the level of engagement that players experience [67]. In this sense, addiction might just be a consequence of high engagement, but there does seem to be further evidence of a distinction between high engagement and problematic usage [18]. And interestingly, where there is high usage suggestive of addiction, it seems that games can be playing a fulfilling role in players' lives [61]. This offers a different support to the SDT approach whereby players are playing in order to obtain satisfaction of their basic needs—games far from being the source of a problem are (at least to some extent) part of a solution.

As stated though, despite extensive playing of games by large proportions of the population and very high usage by a smaller proportion, games are not the be-all and end-all of people's lives. Games are picked up, played, enjoyed and put down. Given the emphasis on engagement in GX research as being the particular period of playing a game, it is not so surprising that little has been done to understand what brings a gaming session to an end.

O'Brien and Toms noted that frustration while playing could lead to a person finishing playing [55] because the challenge is too high or the person is simply

---

[1]For example, http://news.bbc.co.uk/2/hi/technology/4137782.stm.

making no progress. The extreme version of this is "rage-quitting" where the player quits in the middle of play because of being so angry with the game or the other players in the game.

Nordin has also found results that support those of the process model. In understanding how players perceive time, he conducted a grounded theory with players about their management of playing periods and developed a theory around self-consent [53]. It seems that players fit playing games into their lives such that normal events mark the end of session, for example, a bus comes or the oven pings that dinner is ready. Players also do not just wait for something to happen to tell them to stop playing, but rather they define the end point when they start as part of the process of giving themselves consent to play. At suitable junctures in the game, such as the end of a level or winning a race, players may plan to stop. At those planned stop points, there can be a further process of giving self-consent which may result in them stopping to play or in them playing longer than originally intended. In this theory, both disengagement and re-engagement are integral parts of the decision to play, though other events may intervene to bring about disengagement.

This theory presents quite a high-level, conscious view of engagement which perhaps fits with some of the results seen in attention earlier. There seems to be an active choice both to become engaged and to remain engaged, and this is independent of low-level processes such as attention. However, it may be that at a finer level of granularity, there are points during play at which a player will not ever choose to disengage and that these are connected to unconscious processes.

Schoenau-Fog is notable in directly addressing what brings gamers back to games. He has drawn in the idea of continuation desire, the intrinsic desire of gamers to play more, as a way to understand the re-engagement process [66]. Understandably, the process model he produces has much in common with that of O'Brien and Toms. External motives such as a novelty or social play bring a player to start a game, and they set themselves objectives, such as win a race, which they then engage with. Their activities lead them to achieve their accomplishments, or not, and the subsequent affects lead to further play or disengagement.

In continuation desire, objectives are key drivers of play. This is not entirely certain to me. Players may well report having clear objectives, but did they have them at the point of engagement or is this an a posteriori justification? And if objectives are necessary, could the inability to set new or interesting objectives be a reason (or the reason) to entirely disengage from a particular game? This may also be a summative process where the objectives of the current play session are compared with those of previous sessions (not necessarily explicitly). Players may then make decisions about continuation not just on the basis of the current session, whether successfully meeting objectives or not, but across the totality of their playing experiences, possibly even extending to similar experiences with different games.

Affect is also strongly linked to disengagement. Positive affect leads to continuation desire (and re-engagement as in the process model), but substantial negative affect leads to disengagement (though some level of frustration can be a spur to continue). So what level of negative affect is motivating? Or are there different types of negative affect that lead to differing continuation desire? For example, being fairly beaten due to lack of skill is different from being unfairly beaten due to dice that always roll against you or a trick that your opponent suddenly produces. Are such distinctions integral to continuation desire?

Even accepting a general continuation desire in players, Nordin's theory perhaps complements this by saying that even when the experience is positive and successful, players may override their desire to continue with a refusal to (self) permit further play. They prioritise other activities over playing further. How do players make such choices and when do they break down?

Thus, the theory of continuation desire has some merit in the context of digital games. It meshes well with the process model of engagement that has been used here, and it at least makes progress towards understanding disengagement and re-engagement. However, it is far from widely validated and, with Nordin's theory, opens up questions about how it plays out in the practices of individual players, individual playing sessions and across games.

# 6   Methodological Note

With a focus in this chapter on empirical studies, the results discussed here necessarily come from particular styles of studies. Most that relate to engagement while playing are lab-based studies, that is, experiments that look a lot like psychology experiments with dependent variables, an experimental manipulation and a task to do (play a game). Survey studies are also strongly represented, particularly in the motivations to play work where questionnaires are used to link personality to the experiences of play. These bring a particular slant to the study of gaming experience generally, including engagement, that should be noted.

Surveys often lack strong control as it is impossible to know the circumstances in which a person completes a questionnaire. This may simply add to the general noise of measurement or it may have particular influences that skew the results. It is hard to be sure. Furthermore, surveys are only self-reports on recollections of experiences. They are prey not only to what people recall but also to how they want to represent themselves. And in the end, at best, the analysis can only show that some measures correlate with others. It is tempting to make causal associations, "clearly personality proceeds the gaming experience", but this is false. Personality may be causally connected to gaming experiences or there may be underlying factors not measured that influence both.

Experiments offer the control that surveys lack. However, they bring with them their own problems, particularly in the context of digital games. One such problem was seen above with measuring GX through the use of questionnaires and other techniques, all of which bring their particular problems. Another major problem with experiments is the lack of ecological validity. The duration of play in experiments is typically short and rarely more than 20 min. Play takes place in a controlled environment. Here at York, we make some efforts to do our experiments in our HomeLab so people play games sitting in a room that looks like a living room with a comfy sofa, an ordinary television, bookcases of books and so on. But at the end of the day, even this is still a lab and participants are surely aware. Further, contextual features are also absent, for instance, the motive to play is that the participant signed up for a study. Overall, even with the best of efforts, playing a game in a lab is not like playing a game in everyday life. Kaye [41] calls this methodological mayhem. She also notes the problems of sampling bias where opportunity samples of undergraduates are used.

However, I think the consequences of the problems with experiments are not so severe. Yes, experiments are not ideal, but no experiment, regardless of field of study, truly captures what happens in the real world or everyday life. Nonetheless, disciplines like physics, chemistry, psychology and so on make progress through the steady accumulation of knowledge that experiments permit. An experiment is not intended to be like the real world but rather to isolate a phenomenon that would otherwise be hard to see [33]. And as a consequence of isolating it and thereby studying it, we are able to develop mastery that allows the phenomenon to be exploited even in real-world situations. To take an example from physics, until Faraday produced the first, simple electric motor as an experimental device, there was nothing in the natural world that exhibited behaviour anything like that (with the possible exception of the Earth's magnetic core which required Faraday's experiments to be understood). His experiments led directly to the theoretical understanding of electromagnetism and the daily exploitation of it in motors and dynamos which constitute fundamental technology in modern life. This is not to say that GX experiments are destined to be so profoundly important (though I live in hope) but rather that, despite experiments being unrealistic in some ways, it is only through such experiments that the important underlying relationships that drive GX can be discerned.

## 7  Conclusions

Research on engagement in digital games is thriving. This perhaps reflects the centrality of engagement to the formulation of gaming experience. The process model of engagement has helped to structure where research is currently focused. Not unsurprisingly, the process model has a good fit with existing research as it was developed based on data from players of digital games. However, it is also clear that the model is somewhat agnostic to the unit of analysis that is being considered. There is both engagement with a particular game and engagement while playing that are distinct considerations in this context. The research that addresses the point of engagement is often concerned with the former and the research on engagement while playing with the latter. Furthermore, disengagement is not extensively considered at either level of analysis. The solution may be to be clearer about which analytical level of engagement is being considered, but it may also be that, at least in the context of digital games, the process model of engagement needs to be enhanced or adapted. I would also claim that any questions that arise in the "pure" context of engagement in digital games most surely must have more complex analogues in other domains. But how such issues manifest themselves and whether there is unified solution in terms of a single process model remains to be seen. There is much work still to be done to really understand what it is about games that makes them so engaging.

**Acknowledgements** I would like to thank the many colleagues and students who have worked with me in developing my understanding of immersion in digital games over the last 10 years.

# References

1. Andersen, E., Liu, Y.-E., Snider, R., Szeto, R., Popović, Z.: Placing a value on aesthetics in online casual games. In: Proceedings of ACM CHI 2011, pp. 1275–1278 (2011)
2. Arsenault, D.: Video game genre, evolution and innovation. Eludamos **3**(2) pp. 149–176 (2009)
3. Bartle, R.: Hearts, clubs, diamonds, spades: players who suit MUDS. J. MUD Res. **1**, 19 (1996)
4. Bateman, C.: Empirical game aesthetics. In: Angelides, M.C., Agius, H. (eds.) Handbook of Digital Games, pp. 411–443. Wiley-Blackwell, Hoboken (2014)
5. Beaudouin-Lafon, M.: Instrumental interaction: an interaction model for designing post-WIMP user interfaces. In: Proceedings of the SIGCHI Conference on Human Factors in Computing Systems, pp. 446–453 (2000)
6. Bianchi-Berthouze, N.: Understanding the role of body movement in player engagement. Hum. Comput. Interact. **28**, 40–75 (2013)
7. Block, R.A., Zakay, D.: Prospective and retrospective duration judgments: a meta-analytic review. Psychon. Bull. Rev. **4**(2), 184–197 (1997)
8. Blythe, M., Hazzenzahl, M.: The semantics of fun: differentiating enjoyable experiences. In: Blythe, M., Overbeeke, K., Monk, A., Wright, P. (eds.) Funology, pp. 91–100. Springer, New York (2005)
9. Boyle, E.A., Connolly, T.M., Hainey, T., Boyle, J.M.: Engagement in digital entertainment games: a systematic review. Comput. Hum. Behav. **28**(3), 771–780 (2012)
10. Brandse, M., Tomimatsu, K.: Challenge design and categorization in video game design. In: Design, User Experience, and Usability. User Experience Design for Diverse Interaction Platforms and Environments. Springer, New York (2014)
11. Brockmyer, J.H., Fox, C.M., Curtiss, K.A., McBroom, E., Burkhart, K.M., Pidruzny, J.N.: The development of the game engagement questionnaire: a measure of engagement in video game-playing. J. Exp. Soc. Psychol. **45**(4), 624–634 (2009)
12. Brown, E., Cairns, P.: A grounded investigation of game immersion. In: CHI '04 Extended Abstracts on Human Factors in Computing Systems, pp. 1297–1300 (2004). doi:10.1145/985921.986048
13. Cairns, P.: A commentary on short questionnaires for assessing usability. Interact. Comput. **25**(4), 312 (2013)
14. Cairns, P., Blythe, M.: Research methods 2.0. In: Zaphiris, P., Ang, C.S. (eds.) Social Computing and Virtual Communities, pp. 37–67. Chapman and Hall, London (2009)
15. Cairns, P., Cox, A., Nordin, I.: Immersion in digital games: a review of gaming experience research. In: Angelides, M., Agius, H. (eds.) Handbook of Digital Games, pp. 339–361. Wiley-Blackwell, Hoboken (2014)
16. Cairns, P., Li, J., Wang, W., Nording, I.: The influence of controllers on immersion in mobile games. In: Proceedings of the 32nd Annual ACM Conference on Human Factors in Computing Systems, pp. 371–380 (2014)

17. Charlton, J., Danforth, I.: Distinguishing addiction and high engagement in the context of online game playing. Comput. Hum. Behav. **23**(3), 1531–1548 (2007)
18. Charlton, J., Danforth, I.: Validating the distinction between computer addiction and engagement: online game playing and personality. Behav. Inf. Technol. **29**(6), 601–613 (2010)
19. Chen, J.: Flow in games (and everything else). Commun. ACM **50**(4), 31–34 (2007)
20. Collins, E., Cox, A.: Switch on to games: can digital games aid post-work recovery? Int. J. Hum. Comput. Stud. **72**(8–9), 654–662 (2013)
21. Cox, A., Cairns, P., Shah, P., Carroll, M.: Not doing but thinking: the role of challenge in the gaming experience. In: Proceedings of ACM CHI 2012, pp. 79–88 (2012)
22. Csikszentmihalyi, M., Csikzentmihaly, M.: Flow: The Psychology of Optimal Experience. HarperPerennial, New York (1991)
23. Dalton, P., Fraenkel, N.: Gorillas we have missed: sustained inattentional deafness for dynamic events. Cognition **124**(3), 367–372 (2012)
24. Deterding, S., Dixon, D., Khaled, R., Nacke, L.: From game design elements to gamefulness: defining gamification. In: Proceedings of 15th MindTrek Conference, pp. 9–15 (2011)
25. Entertainment Software Association: Essential Facts About the Computer and Video Game Industry. http://www.theesa.com/facts/ (2014). Accessed 15 Feb 2015
26. Fang, X., Zhang, J., Chan, S.: Development of an instrument for studying flow in computer game play. Int. J. Hum. Comput. Interact. **29**(7), 456–470 (2013)
27. Federoff, M.A.: Heuristics and Usability Guidelines for the Creation and Evaluation of Fun in Video Games. Indiana University, Bloomington (2002)
28. Gajadhar, B., de Kort, Y., Ijsselsteijn, W.: Influence of social setting on player experience of digital games. In: CHI'08 Extended Abstracts on Human Factors in Computing Systems, pp. 3099–3104 (2008)
29. Gee, J.P.: What Video Games Have to Teach Us About Learning and Literacy. Palgrave Macmillan, Basingstoke (2004)
30. Gerling, K.M., Birk, M., Mandryk, R.L., Doucette, A.: The effects of graphical fidelity on player experience. In: MindTrek '13, pp. 229–236 (2013)
31. Grüsser, S.M., Thalemann, R., Griffiths, M.D.: Excessive computer game playing: evidence for addiction and aggression? Cyberpsychol. Behav. **10**(2), 290–292 (2006)
32. Grüter, B., Hajinejad, N., Sheptykin, I.: Mobile game play and everyday life. In: Angelides, M.C., Agius, H. (eds.) Handbook of Digital Games, pp. 444–470. Wiley-Blackwell, Hoboken (2014)
33. Hacking, I.: Representing and Intervening: Introductory Topics in the Philosophy of Natural Science. Cambridge University Press, Cambridge (1983)
34. Huizinga, J.: Homo Ludens: A Study of the Play-Element in Culture, vol. 3. Taylor & Francis, Abingdon (2003)
35. Jennett, C.I.: Is Game Immersion Just Another Form of Selective Attention? An Empirical Investigation of Real World Dissociation in Computer Game Immersion. University College London, London (2010)
36. Jennett, C., Cox, A., Cairns, P., Shoparee, S., Epps, A., Tijs, T., Walton, A.: Measuring and defining the experience of immersion in games. Int. J. Hum. Comput. Stud. **66**(9), 641–661 (2008). doi:10.1016/j.ijhcs.2008.04.004
37. Johnson, D., Gardner, J.: Personality, motivation and video games. In: Proceedings of OZCHI 2010, pp. 276–279 (2010)
38. Johnson, D., Wyeth, P., Sweetser, P., Gardner, J.: Personality, genre and videogame play experience. In: Proceedings of Fun and Games 2012, pp. 117–120 (2012)
39. Juul, J.: Half-Real: Video Games Between Real Rules and Fictional Worlds. MIT Press, Cambridge (2005)
40. Juul, J.: A Casual Revolution. MIT Press, Cambridge (2010)
41. Kaye, L.K.: The methodological mayhem of experimental videogame research. PsyPag Q **78**, 20–22 (2011)
42. Kaye, L.K., Bryce, J.: Putting the "fun factor" into gaming: the influence of social contexts on experiences of playing videogames. Int. J. Internet Sci. **7**(1), 23–37 (2012)

43. Klimmt, C., Hartmann, T., Frey, A.: Effectance and control as determinants of video game enjoyment. Cyberpsychol. Behav. **10**, 845–847 (2007)
44. Kline, P.: A Psychometrics Primer. Free Association Books, London (2000)
45. Koutsouras, P., Cairns, P.: User-generated content as cues for performance in LittleBigPlanet. In: Foundation of Digital Games 2013, pp. 372–375 (2013)
46. McCrae, R.R., Costa, P.: A five-factor theory of personality. In: Handbook of Personality: Theory and Research, 2nd edn., pp. 139–153. Guilford, New York (1999)
47. McGonigal, J.: Reality Is Broken. Jonathan Cape, London (2011)
48. Mekler, E.D., Bopp, J.A., Tuch, A.N., Opwis, K.: A systematic review of quantitative studies on the enjoyment of digital entertainment games. In: Proceedings of ACM CHI 2014, pp. 927–936 (2014)
49. Nacke, L.E.: An introduction to physiological player metrics for evaluating games. In: El-Nasr, M., Drachen, A., Canossa, A. (eds.) Game Analytics, pp. 585–619. Springer, New York (2013)
50. Nacke, L.E., Grimshaw, M.N., Lindley, C.A.: More than a feeling: measurement of sonic user experience and psychophysiology in a first-person shooter game. Interact. Comput. **22**(5), 336–343 (2010)
51. Nacke, L.E., Bateman, C., Mandryk, R.L.: BrainHex: a neurobiological gamer typology survey. Entertain. Comput. **5**(1), 55–62 (2014)
52. Nah, F., Eschenbrenner, B., Zeng, Q., Telaprolu, V., Sepehr, S.: Flow in gaming: literature synthesis and framework development. Int. J. Inf. Syst. Manag. **1**(1), 83–124 (2014)
53. Nordin, A.I.: Time Perception and Immersion in Digital Games. University of York, York (2014)
54. Nordin, A.I., Ali, J., Animashaun, A., Asch, J., Adams, J., Cairns, P.:. Attention, time perception and immersion in games. In: ACM CHI'13 Extended Abstracts, pp. 1089–1094 (2013)
55. O'Brien, H., Toms, E.G.: What is user engagement? A conceptual framework for defining user engagement with technology. J. Am. Soc. Inf. Sci. Technol. **59**(6), 938–955 (2008)
56. Peever, N., Johnson, D., Gardner, J.: Personality & video game genre preferences. In: Proceedings of Interactive Entertainment 2012, vol. 20 (2012)
57. Poels, K., de Kort, Y., Ijsselsteijn, W.: It's always a lot of fun! Exploring dimensions of digital game experience using focus group methodology. In: Proceedings of FuturePlay 2007, pp. 83–89 (2007)
58. Przybylski, A.K., Rigby, C.S., Ryan, R.M.: A motivational model of video game engagement Rev. Gen. Psychol. **14**(2), 154 (2010)
59. Qin, H., Rau, P-L., Salvendy, G.: Effects of different scenarios of game difficulty on player immersion. Interact. Comput. **22**(3), 230–239 (2010)
60. Ravaja, N., Saari, T., Salminen, M., Laarni, J., Kallinen, K.: Phasic emotional reactions to video game events: a psychophysiological investigation. Media Psychol. **8**(4), 343–367 (2006)
61. Rigby, S., Ryan, R.M.: Glued to Games: How Video Games Draw Us in and Hold Us Spellbound. ABC-CLIO, Santa Barbara (2011)
62. Ryan, R.M., Rigby, C.S., Przybylski, A.K.:. Motivational pull of video games: a self-determination theory approach. Motiv. Emot. **30**, 347–365 (2006)
63. Salen, K., Zimmerman, E.: Rules of Play: Game Design Fundamentals. MIT Press, Cambridge (2004)
64. Sanders, T., Cairns, P.: Time Perception, Immersion and Music in Videogames. In: Proceedings of BSC HCI 2010, pp. 160–167 (2010)
65. Schnell, J.: The Art of Game Design. Morgan Kaufmann, Burlington (2008)
66. Schoenau-Fog, H.: The player engagement process–an exploration of continuation desire in digital games. In: DIGRA 2011 (2011)
67. Seah, M., Cairns, P.: From immersion to addiction in videogames. In: Proceedings of BCS HCI 2008, pp. 55–63 (2008)
68. Sherry, J.L., Lucas, K., Greenberg, B.S., Lachlan, K.: Video game uses and gratifications as predictors of use and game preference. In: Vorderer, P., Bryant, J. (eds.) Playing Video Games: Motives, Responses, and Consequences, pp. 213–224. Routledge, London (2006)

69. Simons, D.J., Chabris, C.F.: Gorillas in our midst: sustained inattentional blindness for dynamic events. Perception **28**(9), 1059–1074 (1999)
70. Skalski, P., Tamborini, R., Shelton, A., Buncher, M., Lindmark, P.: Mapping the road to fun: natural video game controllers, presence, and game enjoyment. N. Media Soc. **13**, 224–242 (2011)
71. Tellegen, A., Atkinson, G.: Openness to absorbing and self-altering experiences ("absorption"), a trait related to hypnotic susceptibility. J. Abnorm. Psychol. **83**(3), 268 (1974)
72. Tobin, S., Bisson, N., Grondin, S.: An ecological approach to prospective and retrospective timing of long durations: a study involving gamers. PloS One **5**(2), e9271 (2010)
73. Turner, P.: The anatomy of engagement. In: Proceedings of European Conference on Cognitive Ergonomics, pp. 59–66 (2010)
74. Tychsen, A., Hitchens, M., Brolund, T.: Motivations for play in computer role-playing games. In: Proceedings of Future Play 2008, pp. 57–64 (2008)
75. Wikipedia: Infinity Blade II. http://en.wikipedia.org/wiki/Infinity_Blade_II. Accessed 1 Jul 2014
76. Wolf, M.: Introduction. In: Wolf, M. (ed.) The Medium of the Video Game, pp. 1–9. University of Texas Press, Austin (1997)
77. Wood, R., Griffiths, M.D., Parke, A.: Experiences of time loss among videogame players: an empirical study. Cyberpsychol. Behav. **10**(1), 38–44 (2007)
78. Yee, N.: Motivations of play in online games. Cyberpsychol. Behav. **9**(6), 772–775 (2006)
79. Yee, N., Ducheneaut, N., Nelson, L.: Online gaming motivations scale: development and validation. In: ACM CHI 2012, pp. 2803–2806 (2012)
80. Zichermann, G., Cunningham, C.: Gamification by Design: Implementing Game Mechanics in Web and Mobile Apps. O'Reilly Media, Sebastopol (2011)

# Designing for User Experience and Engagement

**Alistair Sutcliffe**

## 1 Introduction

This chapter aims to provide a design framework for user engagement design. User engagement (UE) is closely related to user experience (UX), so to set the scene, I will digress to explain my view of the difference. UE describes how people are attracted to use interactive products. It explains how and why applications attract people to use them within a session and how good UE design makes interaction exciting and fun, while UX encompasses UE but extends to the wider picture, covering why people adopt and continue to use a particular design over many sessions and even years. This view fits within O'Brien's definitions and model of UE [50].

Design needs to be based on a sound understanding of user psychology and user experience, which can be summarized as providing a product that meets the user's requirements, a product that is easy to use and learn and, last but not least, a product which is exciting and fun to use. It is this last aim which differentiates design for experience from more traditional design for utility and usability. Design is ultimately a creative process involving application of knowledge to inform context-determined trade-offs, i.e. the application domain, users and their task. This chapter is intended to provide design knowledge, i.e. ideas, concepts and heuristics, illustrated by examples to inspire innovation in UE design rather than give detailed prescriptive guidelines.

Design knowledge can be divided into foreground knowledge which can be directly applied, i.e. as guidelines, principles and examples, and background knowledge which underpins design thinking, i.e. models and theories relevant to the design problem. This chapter begins with background knowledge by explaining, first, a

A. Sutcliffe (✉)
Manchester Business School, University of Manchester, Manchester, UK
e-mail: alistair.sutcliffe@manchester.ac.uk

© Springer International Publishing Switzerland 2016
H. O'Brien, P. Cairns (eds.), *Why Engagement Matters*,
DOI 10.1007/978-3-319-27446-1_5

model of UE that helps inform the designer's understanding of what constitutes user experience and, second, the psychology of emotion, perception and cognition that can be applied to UE design. This section builds on Chapter "Theoretical Perspectives on User Engagement" which reviewed a range of UX/UE models and theories. This leads into foreground knowledge as principles and heuristics of good design drawn from the literature. Application of the design principles is illustrated by a critique of website designs used in experimental evaluations of UX [25].

## 2  Modelling User Experience

To place user engagement design in context, this section describes a model of design criteria based on a series of experiments and findings from the UX/UE literature. User experience can be considered as a process of decision making [51] and user reaction to interactive products. Initial perceptions are followed by interactive experience leading to judgements about a product's worth [13]. While most experience is ultimately about utility, i.e. is this product useful for me?, to deliver utility, a product has to be easy to operate (usability) and fun (engagement) [6]. The decision to use or reject a product depends on the interplay of several criteria, namely, utility, usability, engagement and aesthetics [27, 42]. The relative importance of these criteria depends on the users and application domain; e.g. in games, fun and engagement are prioritized, whereas in work applications, usability and utility are more important. Furthermore, the judgement process and criteria importance vary over time. Products have to first attract and engage users and then persuade them to keep interacting until the promise of utility (or fun) is delivered. From the UE perspective, the decision to use may be governed more by users' perceptions of aesthetics, novelty and their experience of in-session interaction [25, 50], while from the longer-term UX perspective goals, tasks and functional support are more important [59]. However, the decision about using products is highly contextual; e.g. in games, the goal is enjoyment, so UE is the objective.

In this chapter, I argue that "enhanced" interactivity makes a vital contribution to user experience in the form of user interfaces which afford interaction in a graphical world with active media and functionality that mediates a user presence. Enhanced interactivity goes beyond the standard interactivity present in most graphical user interfaces, i.e. menus, links, sliders and icon manipulations, and interaction to mediate communication between people, such as chat rooms, wikis and feedback forums [33]. Enhanced interactivity encompasses most virtual reality and game user interfaces (UIs) and the upper two layers of Kristof and Satran's [37] controls over objects and simulation. Examples of design features for enhanced interactivity are sliders, zoom controls and active media ranging from responsive objects to mouseover effects and pop-up features [56]. Design features which are conventional components of virtual reality design can be applied in other applications to enhance

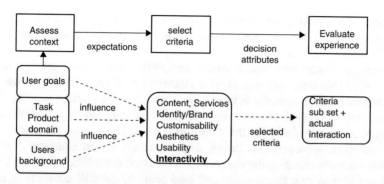

**Fig. 1** Model of users' decision-making process during UX. *Rectangles* on the *top line* represent processes, and *rounded rectangles* are input knowledge sources

user presence, e.g. avatar representations in 3D graphical worlds, view movement controls (fly-through) and interaction through avatar representations.

A summary of the UX judgement process [27] is illustrated in Fig. 1.

The first stage (assess context) specifies the UX context of the product, users' motivations, goals and tasks, which have been widely acknowledged to affect UX judgement [18, 20, 30, 52]. This is followed by select criteria, which determine the influences on the decision. Interactivity is highlighted among the other criteria (functionality/content, brand, customization, aesthetics and usability) as this makes a key contribution to user experience. The criteria and context are then applied to users' perceptions with actual experience producing judgements about the quality of the UX that eventually determine product adoption.

The product context influences criteria selection; for instance, high-value, tangible products favour aesthetics [52]. However, the criteria selected will change over time, from hedonics and aesthetics in the initial encounter [28, 42] to decisions made after interaction [16, 40, 62] and longer periods of use [35, 38]. On initial encounter (pre-use), perceptions of aesthetics and usability are determined by presentation layout. Initial judgements (50 ms) are made primarily on aesthetic appearance of products, although as exposure time increases, perceived usability and identity will be more influential [42]. Post-interaction, the relative importance of usability, interactivity and utility (functionality/content) tends to increase at the expense of aesthetics [40, 66]. Judgements after interaction are based on experience of usability, utility, aesthetics and interaction, with interactivity playing a vital role [16, 18, 61, 62]. Interactivity stimulates user arousal and emotion, thereby intensifying user experience [25].

In longer-term, multisession experience, utility probably becomes the dominant criterion for judgement and product adoption; however, this assertion requires further research. In Karapanos et al.'s [35] 5-week study on mobile phones, hedonic experience (novelty) was highly rated in the early phases of use, yet utility (goodness) and long-term usability appeared to be the main determinants for product adoption. Kujala et al. [38] reported that both pragmatic and hedonic qualities contributed to attractiveness over a 6–12-month period in mobile phone adoption, although as users overcome initial usability problems, pragmatic perceptions improve over time [46].

From the shorter-term within-session perspective, the process agrees with the point of engagement and engagement phases of O'Brien's model, which also emphasizes peaks of intensity in interactive experience when design features which enhance sensory appeal, self-awareness, feedback, novelty and challenge will select interactivity and aesthetics as the dominant criteria. Disengagement arising from poor usability, inadequate challenge, negative affect and interruption [50] is a consequence of evaluating the experience in the short term, although in the longer term, we suspect that functionality and goal achievement will dominate in many products.

The implications for designers concern which criteria to prioritize and selecting the appropriate analysis-design methods to ensure that products meet users' needs and expectations. Overall, utility and content are most important, so this view of UX is no different from conventional systems development. Interactivity may enhance perceptions of content [18, 27], but it is no substitute for appropriate content and functionality. Sound requirements analysis and user-centered design [11, 57] are essential to deliver functionality that meets users' needs. However, UX augments traditional functionality in two important ways:

i In competing products with the same functionality, better user experience may be the unique selling point. Exciting and attractive interaction could make the difference.
ii When users are not well motivated or are pressed for time, they may never discover the functionality they desire because the design does not attract them. Product exploration is supported by good usability engineering, for instance, a gradual unfolding of complexity [10]; but good usability may not be enough. UX design has to attract, excite and motivate users over the initial "hump of indifference" towards realizing the rewards of functionality.

The interaction between UX criteria and the design context is summarized in the following concerns about how the product domain, users and the task context influence the criteria in users' judgement:

1. *User characteristics:* e.g. more aesthetically sensitive users will value aesthetics over usability [26]. User predispositions such as innovation and curiosity may influence user preference [43] or attitude towards interaction and flow experience [42].
2. *Task framing effects:* more serious goal orientation favours usability and utility criteria, while more discretionary use and fun favour aesthetics and interaction [18, 31, 61]. Task or scenario framing leads people to trade off preference judgements between hedonic and pragmatically designed products [30].
3. *Product-domain framing:* games select aesthetics, enjoyment and pleasure, whereas work/goal-related products select usability and utility [32, 70]. Interaction becomes more rewarding where excitement and curiosity are stimulated

by the design, i.e. games and entertainment-oriented applications [34]. Product framing in e-commerce sites may arise via the content in e-commerce websites, e.g. high touch-and-feel goods favour expressive aesthetics [52].

4. *Usability ceiling effect:* if usability is "good enough", this criterion becomes less important in users' judgement. Furthermore, the "what is beautiful is usable" halo effect [61, 63] may reduce the salience of usability in overall judgement.

5. *Customization:* this may be important in longer-term use when applications encourage content selection [27]. Users change their preferences to favour customized designs when presented with a forced choice between customization, better aesthetics or usability [27]. Customization, e.g. through choice of mobile phone "skins", influences ratings of aesthetics and hedonic-identity aspects of judgement [28].

6. *Brand:* this is salient when the application/content has a strong, positive brand identity that matches the users' values [7, 19]. Brand can exert a considerable positive influence on judgements of content, usability and aesthetics [19].

Although there is considerable variation between models of UX, a common theme is that utility and usability, expressed as pragmatics in the inference model [29] or as effectiveness-efficiency in technology acceptance-oriented models, are dominant factors in users' overall judgement. The role of aesthetics in influencing usability and overall preference is inconclusive [18, 66] although good aesthetics promotes positive affect, i.e. pleasure in users' judgement [32]. The role of interactivity in UX is more certain since several studies [16, 25, 48, 62] show that interactivity improves satisfaction, efficiency and effectiveness. The next section investigates the psychology underpinning user experience to explain why interactivity should enhance user experience.

# 3   The Psychology of User Engagement

The term "user engagement" is used to focus on shorter-term user experience when interaction design is a key influence. Interaction is the dialogue between machine and the user which achieves a purpose (which could be just fun), and this can be seen in Clark's [12] action ladder in goal-oriented conversation set in an arena (task, product) and setting (user and interactive environment). UE is a more immediate, dialogue-driven experience, closely linked to affect and mood, whereas UX is influenced more strongly by memory and motivation. The interaction between the two in terms of Clark's theory rests in the memory of previous conversations. User engagement aims to excite and attract the user. This involves understanding how motivation and emotion may affect users' perception of experience resulting from design features that promote novelty, interest, aesthetics or the potential to fulfil a task-oriented or experiential goal [50]. Understanding perception, i.e. how a product appears to users, involves aesthetics which is then combined with experience of interaction. Both will produce an emotional reaction which the designer hopes is

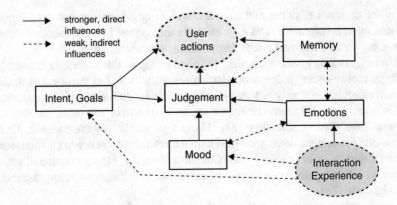

**Fig. 2** Model of cognitive factors influencing UE

positive, i.e. pleasure, joy and surprise rather than frustration, disappointment and displeasure.

The cognition underpinning UE is summarized in Fig. 2. Emotion influences judgement. A bad user experience will trigger emotions of frustration, anxiety and even anger. Since negative emotions tend to be associated with memory of the situations that gave rise to them, poor usability will be remembered and associated with the product in the future. Design qualities such as good aesthetics and stimulating interaction are likely to evoke positive emotions, such as pleasure and joy, leading to positive memories, although we tend to remember positive experiences in more general terms. Positive usability experience is not remembered in detail although poor usability is, while general impressions of good aesthetic design and interactive flow are remembered favourably [18, 25]. Usability has to avoid serious errors, while investing in aesthetics and interactivity adds value.

Emotions interact with the arousal mechanism, which can be considered as a dimension ranging from calmness to excitement [5]. Interaction, unexpected events and unusual and unpleasant stimuli all tend to increase arousal, and high arousal increases the strength of emotional experience. Our feelings are a combination of arousal and emotion that persist as a mood, which may last for hours and possibly days and affect our judgement. Pleasing and enjoyable user experience will produce a positive mood; in contrast, poor design, errors and difficulties could leave us in a bad mood, and bad moods may be reflected in future judgement of the product and related products. Arousal and excitement can be enhanced by making interaction more vivid using immersive graphical environments, avatars and novel interaction techniques [25].

High-quality aesthetic design will evoke pleasure and mild arousal; however, interaction is probably a more important influence. We have to pay attention when we act; furthermore, action, attention and concentration all increase arousal. The challenge in user engagement is to hold the user's interest and maintain arousal by interaction with optimal flow [15], which varies in difficulty and familiarity.

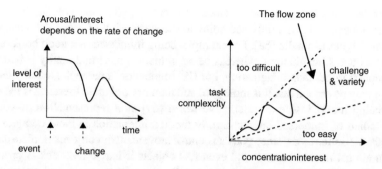

**Fig. 3** Interaction, arousal and flow

In work/goal-oriented applications, skilled operation and efficiency will be more important; hence, ease of learning and ease of use are paramount. But in entertainment and education domains, interaction that promotes arousal for engagement will be more important.

Flow is the sense of engagement and being absorbed in an interactive experience. It is a tricky concept which generally involves interaction, resulting in intense self-absorption [54]. It is closely related to presence and immersion [68] which also contribute to absorption but describe perceptual rather than action-related experience. The concept involves optimal arousal produced by a "sweet spot" trade-off between challenge and difficulty on one hand and ease of operation and achievement on the other. If operating a UI is too difficult, we will get frustrated and discouraged and may give up, leaving us with negative emotions and adverse memory of the experience. In contrast, if operating the UI is too easy, then we get bored, our excitement (or arousal) decreases and we turn our attention to more interesting things. The trick is to keep interaction in the flow zone (see Fig. 3), an intuition appreciated by game designers.

Games need to maintain the pace of change with unpredictable events while not overwhelming the user with too much change that exceeds their capabilities. Sophisticated games monitor the user's behaviour and success rate and adapt the level of difficulty to maintain flow; less sophisticated versions provide controls so the user can increase the difficulty level as required. However, engagement is also influenced by the sense of presence as well as arousal and flow in interactive experience.

## 3.1 Engagement and Presence

The origins of presence come from virtual reality (VR), in which the user is represented by an avatar or virtual character. Presence is related to immersion, and both describe the sense of "being" in an interactive world. However, presence has wider interpretations in social presence [45] versus spatial presence, and immersion can be interpreted differently according to the suspension of belief encountered in different types of media [68]. For example, being immersed in a good book or film involves one's imagination, whereas being immersed in virtual reality is bound by perception rather than imagination. For UE, immersion is perceptually oriented; for UX it may be argued that it is more goal and memory oriented. Presence is the sense of "being there" inside an interactive world [69] as a representation of yourself (embodied or immersed interaction). Embodied interaction is more complex than standard 2D interfaces, since you can control movement directly, manipulate objects in an almost natural manner and even feel objects if haptic feedback is provided. Virtual worlds become engaging because they invoke curiosity and arousal; it is clearly not reality but interaction becomes transparent, i.e. you are not aware of the computer, instead you become absorbed in the virtual graphical world. Fortunately, we do not need the experience of 3D CAVE VR technology for immersion; Desktop VR, which implements semi-3D graphical worlds on a PC with limited controls provided by a joystick, mouse or Wii device, can deliver engaging and absorbing interaction.

When the illusion of the virtual world is well designed, then you feel immersed with a strong sense of presence. When the design is flawed, e.g. if tracking is too slow so the graphical world judders as you move, cognitive dissonance intervenes and you become aware of the user interface as the illusion of the virtual world disappears, just as much as the illusion in a theatre vanishes when an actor forgets their lines.

Strange as it may seem, it takes very little to create an illusion of presence. Our powerful imaginations just need a few hints (known as priming or framing effects in psychology) to conjure up a perceived reality. The "Computers are Social Actors" (CASA) paradigm [53] explains how we treat computers as virtual people even when we are presented with limited cues, such as a photograph of a person or human voice. Indeed the image can be artificial, cartoon-like, with little correspondence to reality; and the same applies to the voice. Chatterbots, avatars on the web equipped with simple semi-intelligent scripts for responding to human conversations, are treated like real characters, and some people actually form relationships with these virtual characters [17].

An extension of presence in social presence theory [55] argues that different communication channels and representations promote a sense of social presence, i.e. awareness of the identity, location and personalities of other people. The theory does not give a formal classification or model of social presence, although it can be reinterpreted in terms of communication channels which describe degradations from the ideal of face-to-face (FTF) communication. Social presence has implications for UE in suggesting media which may enhance user engagement, as well as being an important consideration of social mediating technology, i.e. where the aim is to convey the identity and awareness of one person to a remote audience. Adding video or even still images improves presence by providing more information about the other person. Video, animation, avatars and images of people all augment presence in user engagement, as can computer-mediated social communication with features such as feedback forms and chat in e-commerce or photo-sharing, personal profiles and social awareness promoted by Facebook and other social networking sites.

## 3.2 Summary: The Psychology of Engagement

User engagement is a complex concept that synthesizes several influences to promote a sense of flow and fluid interaction leading to satisfying arousal and pleasurable emotions of curiosity, surprise and joy.

The three main components of user engagement are interaction, media and presence. Interaction concerns how human-computer communication is mediated, from simple menu-link-icon navigation in 2D graphical user interfaces to more adventurous 3D graphical worlds with fly-through controls, avatars and interactive agents. Media describes how the user and the means of interaction are represented, ranging from simple cursors to icons and interactive avatars. Representing content with "rich media" such as video, animation, speech and audio also enhances user engagement. Presence is determined by the representation of the user and how immersion is afforded by the interface on a 2D interactive surface or in a more elaborate 3D interactive world. Consideration of media in the sense of broadcast media, e.g. radio, television, blogs and books, is beyond the scope of this chapter, although media richness theory's "macro media" could have interesting implications for UX as well as UE [65, 68].

Flow is the key concept for understanding interaction in terms of the pace of action, complexity of actions and the rate of change. Flow, as explained earlier, is a finely tuned balancing act between the user's abilities and skills and responding to events within time limits and other resource constraints. Flow, presence and immersion will generally co-occur as contributions to UE, although not always. For example, riveting content on a website could stimulate users' imagination and give an immersive user experience without much interaction. How these components interact and how much they contribute to the overall sense of users' engagement and presence will depend on the interaction context, the user and other environmental factors such as time pressure and the application domain.

## 4 Designing for User Engagement

There is no single accepted process for UE design; however, most approaches advocate user-centered design of interactive products with techniques to stimulate creative design thinking. The approaches share techniques such as scenarios, mock-ups, storyboards and prototypes which provide quick realizations of designs that can be tested with users to explore their reactions [8, 14]. Scenario-based design [11] is a suitable approach for UE design since it advocates the use of scenarios, storyboards (screen mock-ups) and prototypes in an iterative cycle of requirements elicitation, design exploration, evaluation and user feedback. Scenario-based design is well suited to the challenges of UE because of its iterative approach, which facilitates user-developer dialogue by a combination of scenarios to illustrate users' experience, storyboards for design explorations and claims to record the arguments for and against a particular design.

The key component, scenarios, are specific, realistic descriptions of user experience with applications. Scenarios are similar to stories in agile methods [2], which also provide examples and narratives describing events and experiences of use, either gathered directly from real life or invented as realistic visions of future designs. Carroll articulated several different roles for scenarios in the design process including usage scenarios, which illustrate problems; initiating or envisioning scenarios, which stimulate the design of a new artefact; and projected use scenarios, which describe the future use of an artefact that has been designed [60].

Scenarios contribute realistic descriptions of desired user experience to the design process as well as contextual information for interpretation of user requirements and their priorities (see judgement criteria) for the design. Scenarios may be complemented by personae which are character sketches of typical users and user roles, presenting the designer with users' characteristics, values and feelings. Personae stimulate design exploration by providing a framework for thinking about how experiences might relate to different types of user and how individual people might react to different designs [14]. More extreme personae (extreme characters [21]) can be useful for exploring new ideas for UE to escape from more conservative descriptions of user roles.

Scenarios and personae are inputs to stimulate design exploration. Storyboards illustrate snapshots of interaction related to the users' tasks or script for the product. Storyboards may be hand-drawn or prepared as PowerPoint animations or videos which are demonstrated to users in walkthroughs, in either interviews or workshops, to get their feedback on the design and, more importantly, their contribution of ideas and participation in the design process. The walkthrough aims to elicit feedback from the users and focus discussion on critiquing and elaborating the design. Ideas relating to interaction, immersion and presence which are often important parts of UE design can be difficult to illustrate with sketches and PowerPoint presentations. Nevertheless, storyboards do allow rapid iterative exploration of design ideas and can be gradually transformed into prototypes which allow more interactive functionality to be explained. Interaction design toolkits enable 3D worlds with avatars, animated agents, interactive media, etc., to be developed rapidly with modest effort.

Figure 4 shows prototypes developed with multimedia interaction design environment (Dreamweaver) and a virtual agent toolkit (https://guile3d.com/en/product). Both of these prototypes were compared with less adventurous interaction designs, i.e. menu-based navigation, demonstrating that the enhanced interaction prototype produced better UE [24, 61]. UE can be difficult to evaluate since experience is immediate and can evaporate after a session. Flow and presence in particular are difficult to capture in session experience although post-session UE can be captured by questionnaires where the experience is salient, as in games [67]. In spite of

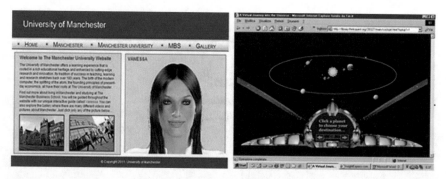

**Fig. 4** Design prototype (*left*) illustrating use of an avatar in a website-guided tour and (*right*) a planet's metaphor for accessing information in an astronomy website

these limitations, debriefing interviews, observations of facial expression, body posture and verbalization during sessions and post-session questionnaires [28, 39] are effective means of UE evaluation. If necessary, emotion and arousal can be measured by heart rate and GSR (galvanic skin resistance) monitors, although physiological measures may not always correlate with subjective reports [49], depending on the task and strength of the experiential stimulus.

UE design is initiated by creating a high-level view of interactive sequences. In work/goal-oriented applications, this will follow a task model or use cases. An alternative in entertainment, education and web applications is to start with the high-level plan for interaction, commonly identified as storylines, narratives or scripts. Sources or inspiration can come from drama, e.g. by considering:

- *Settings:* orient the audience to the purpose, location, time and context.
- *Characters:* (see personae) the actors are represented in the design as avatars and how the audience of users can engage/interact with them.
- *Plot:* how the story develops in phases composed of events, episodes and situations.
- *Movement:* the pace at which the plot unfolds, related to flow.
- *Mood:* how the emotional tone of interaction is manipulated by events and choice of media for pleasure, suspense, anxiety, fear, etc.

A good plot provides an initial setting then leads the audience through phases which build the story, leading to the denouement or climax when the moral or purpose of the story becomes clear. Progressive disclosure of facts and clues towards the denouement helps to maintain flow and engagement via suspense. Maintaining optimal flow is a key design consideration.

Storylines can be planned using informal diagrams and sketches, employing ideas from drama theory and trajectories [3] and experience planning techniques[9]. Trajectories are threads which describe journeys that actors (participants in the interaction) undergo, linking spaces, time, plot, roles and characters. Roles interact with each other or with bystanders who observe but are not directly involved, while orchestrators are power roles that control others. Storyline scripting is illustrated in

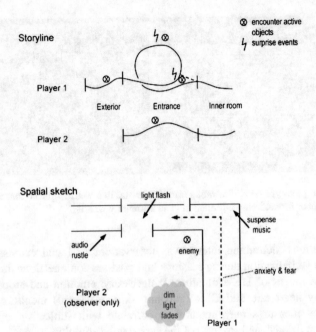

**Fig. 5** Storylines for planning interactive experience

Fig. 5, showing the planned thread for the story with sketches of the interactive space, annotated with plans for mood and emotional responses. McCarthy and Wright's [44] threads of user experience (structural composition, emotional, sensual and spatio-temporal) and Dourish's [22] concept of embodied interaction, where embodiment refers to how the interaction generates meaning and feeling in an environmental context, are further "tools for thought" in planning UE.

An exploration game is illustrated, where the first player can get advice from the second player while following a trajectory through the virtual world, encountering active objects (clues) as well as surprise events. The storyline thread is linked to sketches giving details of the graphical world and interactive effects. The extent of planning varies between designers; some may sketch ideas in detail, although the majority tend to sketch in outline then mock-up and prototype ideas.

## 5  Design Principles

UE design advice tends to be expressed as high-level and fairly general principles, accompanied by examples of good design employing the principle. This is not surprising, since design for user engagement and experience will depend on the domain and details of who the users are and their goals. There are several sources of UE design heuristics for aesthetics and user engagement which appear in the visualization, graphical and interaction design literature [37, 47]. The source of most of the following guidelines can be found in [41]; for more details, see [58, 59]. Principles are grouped first according to the high-level UE constructs, immersion/presence, flow and aesthetics, followed by principles associated with desired psychological effects on attention, mood/arousal and emotion.

*Basic Constructs: Interactive Graphical Worlds* The GUI or graphical user interface has been the norm for many years; however, interaction in a semi-3D world is more realistic and engaging since the user relates directly to the domain world rather than interacting via links, buttons and menus. Graphical worlds represent the domain directly or via metaphors. *Metaphors* provide the context in which action and functionality of components are suggested, e.g. a palette metaphor in a graphics package suggests the functionality and actions that are possible with the paintbrush, eraser, pencil, etc., icons. *Affordances* in a graphical object naturally suggest how it can be manipulated and used, including clues to its functionality. Classic affordances are the shape of door handles which suggest either turning, pushing or pulling actions to open the door. Both metaphors and affordances help "recognition rather than recall" and "natural mappings" by providing memory cues to suggest actions from common sense knowledge and analogical memory.

*Immersion and Presence* Immersion is enhanced by design of naturalistic graphical worlds, in which affordances and metaphors suggest intuitively obvious ways of interaction. Presence is promoted by creating an avatar for the user which is placed in an interactive 3D world enhancing immersion and giving a better sense of presence. Alternatively, fly-through navigation controls can be provided as the user moves through the virtual world with six degrees of freedom (NSEW, forward/backwards in z dimension), using a joystick or adaptations of mouse controls. Presence may also be enhanced by adding audio in 3D and haptic feedback, while social presence is enhanced by richer communication media (videos, avatars) and social awareness functions.

*Flow* The sense of optimal flow can be promoted by novel interaction whereby users control their own viewpoint as they move through a virtual world, i.e. fly-through navigation. Alternatively, good flow experience can be implemented by the dialogue structure in a game (see scripting in design process, Sect. 3) or guided discovery in an education application. Note that flow is closely associated with arousal, so design for mood and arousal heuristics, such as oddity, and attracting attention also apply.

*Aesthetics* Good aesthetic design sets a positive tone for user engagement and is important for all applications. Aesthetic design is a complex topic, so the following hints are just a starting point; see [37, 41, 64] for more details.

   *Colour:* Colour use should be balanced, avoiding more than 2–3 fully saturated intense colours. Yellow is salient for alerting, red/green have danger/safety positive/negative associations and blue is more effective for background. Low saturated colours (pale shades with white) have a calming effect; dayglow fully saturated colours have the converse effect.

*Gestalt effects:* There are several visual patterns, e.g. symmetry, similarity and closure (or completeness of a shape), and proximity clustering which we recognize and interpret instinctively that are collectively known as "Gestalt" effects in perceptual psychology.

*Depth of field:* Use of layers in an image stimulates interest and can attract by promoting curiosity. Use of background image with low saturated colour provides depth for foreground components. In the related, figure ground effect, the juxtaposition of visual features or grouping of shapes causes higher-order structures to emerge from the image.

*Shape:* Use of curved shapes conveys an attractive visual style, in contrast to blocks and rectangles which portray structure, categories and order in a layout.

*Attention* In goal-oriented applications, attention needs to be directed to navigation cues and important content; in contrast, for entertainment-style applications, attention is used to control the user's emotion and manipulate mood.

*Dynamic media* Video, speech and audio all attract attention. Indeed, any change in an image also stimulates attention; however, we rapidly become used to new stimuli so attention effects wane. Images of people with their gaze directed at the user are another effective choice for drawing attention since this mimics human attention in the real world.

*Salience* Within images and text, attention-grabbing stimuli in order of salience are any change (blink, move) and oddity effects using colour contrast, shape or size. Onset of audio will also direct attention.

*Mood and Arousal* Influencing mood and arousal is important for maintaining flow in experience as well as matching experience to the domain, excitement in games, managing mood in healthcare applications, etc.

*Dynamic media* (video, speech) are generally more arousing because we find stimuli which change harder to ignore than static images or text.

*Natural images* such as landscapes have calming effects and tend to reduce our arousal; in contrast, images of designed artefacts and unusual objects, e.g. space rockets, stimulate our curiosity and tend to be arousing.

*Natural sounds* (audio) have a similar effect; the sound of wind in trees and water and waves calm, while the noise of racing cars and aircraft arouses.

*Music* can set the appropriate mood, e.g. loud strident pieces will arouse and excite, romantic music calms and invokes pleasure, etc.

*Unusual or challenging images,* e.g. Dali and surrealist painters created unusual images that disobeyed normal laws of form and perspective to stimulate the users' imagination and increase attraction.

*Oddity* is when one or more elements in a large image don't fit, this invokes cognitive dissonance or our natural ability to spot the irregular among the regular. Oddity can be used to stimulate curiosity and increase arousal.

*Emotion* Designing for emotion is important not only the experience of flow but also for a wide variety of persuasive technology applications [23] which aim to influence users' decisions, e.g. in e-commerce and healthcare applications.

*Dangerous and threatening episodes:* For example, being chased by a tiger, gory images (mutilated body) and erotic content all increase arousal and invoke emotions ranging from fear to anger, whereas pleasant images (e.g. flowers, sunset) tend to decrease it, i.e. have calming effects and produce pleasurable emotional responses.

*Characters:* Characters can appear threatening or benevolent depending on their appearance or dress, e.g. disfigured people appear threatening and evoke emotions ranging from fear to disgust. Characters familiar from popular culture may be selected for the desired emotional reactions.

*Dialogue:* Spoken dialogue is probably the most powerful tool for creating emotional responses, from threats to empathy. Emotional effects are additive, so choice of character with a threatening appearance, complemented by a menacing voice tone and an aggressive dialogue, reinforces the emotions of anxiety and fear.

Although the above ideas can improve the attractiveness of interfaces, they are no guarantee that these effects will be achieved. Design is often a trade-off between ease of use and stimulating and aesthetic design; for instance, the use of progressive disclosure to promote flow may well be perceived by others as being difficult to learn. Visual effects often show considerable individual differences and learning effects, so a well-intentioned design might not be successful. The advice, as with most design, is to test ideas and preliminary designs with users to check interpretations, critique ideas and evaluate their acceptability.

# 6  Design Examples

This section illustrates use of some of the above principles in websites which were evaluated to demonstrate that the design features actually do enhance user experience. The user experiences for three website designs from the same art gallery domain were experimentally compared [25] to evaluate interactive features including interactive guides, animations and 3D effects (see Fig. 6). The application domain of all three websites was the same (art galleries), although they varied in their interactive features, as shown in Table 1.

Egocentric navigation places the user's viewpoint within the interactive world, in contrast to exocentric navigation where the user presence (e.g. an avatar in SecondLife) is within the user's field of view. Animated pop-ups extend the basic mouseover effect [56] with a scripted animation in response to the mouse trigger. Hypermedia navigation follows the basic paradigm of web-based interaction [4].

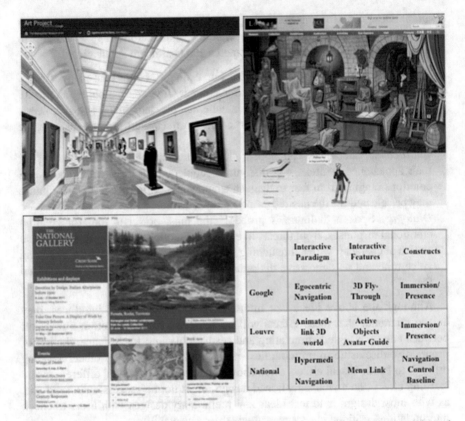

**Fig. 6** The websites used in the study: the Google Art Project (*top left*), the Louvre (*top right*) and the National Gallery (*bottom left*)

**Table 1** Interactivity in the three websites

|  | Interactive Paradigm | Interactive Features | Constructs |
|---|---|---|---|
| **Google** | Egocentric navigation | 3D fly-through | Immersion/presence |
| **Louvre** | Animated-pop-up effects | Graphical objects Avatar guide | Immersion/presence |
| **National Gallery** | Hypermedia navigation | Menu link | Navigation control baseline |

The Google Art Project[1] was chosen for its 3D "street view" technology, in which users can navigate by an interactive fly-through and interact with 2D images within

[1] http://www.googleartproject.com/en-gb/.

a 3D gallery space. Interactive features of the Louvre[2] website included an avatar guide (a cartoon character) and animated objects. Users could navigate using the animated links from the interactive objects and the avatar (which had limited interactivity, as users could not ask questions). There was an option to turn off the animated guide, leaving users to freely navigate the site through a more traditional menu-based website layout. The third site, the National Gallery[3] provided a control condition with simple menus and traditional hypermedia navigation within a standard grid style layout.

Google Art followed UE design principles by using the interactive metaphor of a 3D world through which the user could navigate by fly-through controls, thus enhancing engagement by immersion and presence. Fly-through navigation also enables users to control the pace of their flow experience. The Louvre design also used a semi-3D interactive world through which the user could navigate with similar controls. It implemented the UE design heuristics for characters (use of the avatar), design for arousal (oddity in interactive objects and pop-ups), dynamic media using video and speech, as well as design for salience. The National Gallery site, in contrast, contained few design features to promote user engagement apart from an interactive map of the gallery which had pop-up descriptions and illustrations of the content in gallery rooms. This implemented arousal heuristics for dynamic media and oddity.

## 6.1 Evaluation of User Experience

UE was assessed in a within-group, repeated measures design where the exposure to websites was counterbalanced, but the order of presentation (home page only, task 1, task 2) was not. Participants completed an affect-rating questionnaire at each task step and a full set of questionnaires (usability, aesthetics, service quality, affect, overall preference) after the home page and task 2. As might be expected, the users' rating of both the Louvre and Google Art was more favourable than for the National Gallery on a variety of measures including emotion, arousal, aesthetics and hedonics [28]. User engagement showed a dramatic task effect, increasing after home page viewing to interactive tasks, for all sites. Overall there was little to choose between the Louvre and Google Art on overall preference and satisfaction, although differences in user experience were revealed in user interviews. The fly-through interaction in Google was appreciated by most users; however, a minority found it confusing and difficult to control. Google was also criticized for response time problems when rapid movement and zooming in to view pictures produced judder in the display. Response time problems in updating the graphical 3D world disrupted

[2]http://www.louvre.fr/en (Site design has since changed with avatar guide and animated links removed).
[3]http://www.nationalgallery.org.uk/.

**Fig. 7** Enhanced (*left*) and standard (*right*) interactive versions of the same museum website

the flow experience and presence. The Louvre design was appreciated by most users, but there was a minority who did not like the avatar which was difficult to turn off. These users found the presence of the avatar and its speech annoying. In contrast, the graphical 3D world, interactive objects and pop-up explanations received only positive comments. These reactions demonstrate that while application of design heuristics does produce good UE for the majority, some design features may not be appreciated by a minority of users.

We have found that interactive metaphors in 3D graphical worlds generally produce good UE; for instance, in another museum website illustrated in Fig. 7, the graphical world with a telescope metaphor for zoom in and timeline navigation produced more favourable user ratings than a traditional menu-link interface with the same content. In contrast, avatars can be a double-edged sword; while generally they are engaging, minor design flaws, such as suboptimal appearance of the characters [36], inability to control interaction with the avatar [25] and unnatural speech [1] can destroy the effect of presence and flow.

## 7  Conclusions

While there is no simple "silver bullet" for UE design, I hope this chapter has given some pointers towards the concepts and criteria which need to be considered. User experience will vary widely between domains. When goal-oriented use is the priority, good usability and delivering utility that matches users' needs will be paramount; however, when more discretionary use and entertainment are important, user experience will be enhanced by 3D interactive worlds and the other design features covered in this chapter. As user interaction becomes more sophisticated, in a future with 3D graphics, speech and holographic representations of people, even more mundane applications will need to be designed with flow, presence and immersion in mind. The nature of interaction may therefore become a more important selling point for the interactive systems of the future when users expect more excitement at the interface. The reason for this trend is not surprising. As any technology advances, the means of interacting with it invariably becomes more complex. In spite of the inexorable advance of technology, people still prefer interacting with others in the real world; however, we are increasingly accepting technically mediated surrogates for human interaction. Google glasses (augmented reality), Google Street View, SecondLife and Social Media (e.g. YouTube and Facebook) are accepted technologies. The design concepts present in these technologies will set the standard for interactive user experience in the future.

# References

1. Al-Qaed, F., Sutcliffe, A.G.: Adaptive decision support system (ADSS) for B2C e-commerce. In: Proceedings 8th International Conference on Electronic Commerce, pp. 492–503. ACM Press, New York (2006)
2. Beck, K.: Extreme Programming Explained: Embracing Change. Addison-Wesley, New York (1999)
3. Benford, S., Giannachi, G., Koleva, B., Rodden, T.: From interaction to trajectories: designing coherent journeys through user experiences. In: Proceedings: CHI 2009: 27th International Conference on Human Factors in Computing Systems, pp. 709–718. ACM Press, New York (2009)
4. Benyon, D., Turner, P., Turner, S.: Designing Interactive Systems: People, Activities, Contexts Technologies. Pearson Education, Harlow (2005)
5. Berlyne, D.E.: Conflict, Arousal, and Curiosity. McGraw-Hill, New York (1960)
6. Blythe, M.A., Overbeeke, K., Monk, A.F., Wright, P.C.: Funology: From Usability to Enjoyment. Kluwer, Boston (2004)
7. Bolchini, D., Garzotto, F., Sorce, F.: Does branding need web usability? A value-oriented empirical study. Interact 2, 652–665 (2009)
8. Buxton, B.: Sketching User Experiences: Getting the Design Right and the Right Design. Elsevier, Amsterdam (2007)
9. Callele, D., Neufeld, E., Schneider, K.: Emotional requirements in video games. In: Proceedings: 14th IEEE International Requirements Engineering Conference RE06, pp. 299–302. IEEE Computer Society Press, Los Alamitos (2006)
10. Carroll, J.M.: The Nurnberg Funnel: Designing Minimalist Instruction for Practical Computer Skill. MIT Press, Cambridge (1990)
11. Carroll, J.M.: Making Use: Scenario-Based Design of Human-Computer Interactions. MIT Press, Cambridge (2000)
12. Clark, H.H.: Using Language. Cambridge University Press, Cambridge (1996)
13. Cockton, G., Kujala, S., Nurkka, P., Höttä, T.: Supporting Worth Mapping with Sentence Completion. Lecture Notes in Computer Science, vol. 5727. Springer, Berlin (2009)
14. Cooper, A., Reimann, R., Cronin, D.: About Face 3: The Essentials of Interaction Design. Wiley, Indianapolis (2007)
15. Csikszentmihalyi, M.: Flow: The Classic Work on How to Achieve Happiness, Revised edn. Rider, London (2002)
16. Cyr, D., Head, M., Ivanov, A.: Perceived interactivity leading to e-loyalty: development of a model for cognitive-affective user responses. Int. J. Hum. Comput. Stud. 67(10), 850–869 (2009)
17. De Angeli, A., Brahnam, S.: I hate you! Disinhibition with virtual partners. Interact. Comput. 20, 302–310 (2008)
18. De Angeli, A., Sutcliffe, A., Hartmann, J.: Interaction, usability and aesthetics: what influences users' preferences? In Proceedings: Conference on Designing Interactive Systems, DIS-06, pp. 271–280. ACM Press, New York (2006)

19. De Bruijn, O., De Angeli, A., Sutcliffe, A.G.: Customer experience requirements for e-commerce web-sites. Int. J. Web Eng. Technol. **3**(4), 441–464 (2007)
20. Diefenbach, S., Hassenzahl, M.: The "beauty dilemma": beauty is valued but discounted in product choice. In: Proceedings of the CHI 2009 Conference on Human Factors in Computer Systems, pp. 1419–1426. ACM Press, New York (2009)
21. Djajadiningrat, J.P., Gaver, W.W., Frens, J.W.: Interaction relabelling and extreme characters: methods for exploring aesthetic interactions. In: Boyarski, D., Kellogg, W.A. (eds.) Proceedings of DIS2000 Designing Interactive Systems: Processes, Practices Methods and Techniques, pp. 66–71. ACM Press, New York (2000)
22. Dourish, P.: Where the Action Is: The Foundations of Embodied Interaction. MIT Press, Cambridge (2004)
23. Fogg, B.J.: Persuasive Technology: Using Computers to Change What We Think and Do. Morgan Kaufmann, San Francisco (2003)
24. Hart, J.: Evaluating user engagement and interaction for design. Ph.D. thesis, University of Manchester (2014)
25. Hart, J., Sutcliffe, A.G.: Love it or hate it! The UX of interactivity and user types. In: Proceedings of CHI 2013. ACM Press/Digital Library, New York (2013)
26. Hartmann, J., Sutcliffe, A.G., De Angeli, A.: Investigating attractiveness in web user interfaces. In: Proceedings of CHI 2007. ACM Press, New York (2007)
27. Hartmann, J., Sutcliffe, A.G., De Angeli, A.: Towards a theory of user judgment of aesthetics and user interface quality. ACM Trans. Comput. Hum. Interact. **15**(4), 15 (2008)
28. Hassenzahl, M.: The interplay of beauty, goodness and usability in interactive products. Hum. Comput. Interact. **19**, 319–349 (2004)
29. Hassenzahl, M., Monk, A.: The inference of perceived usability from beauty. Hum. Comput. Interact. **25**(3), 235–260 (2010)
30. Hassenzahl, M., Tractinsky, N.: User experience: a research agenda. Behav. Inf. Technol. **25**, 91–97 (2006)
31. Hassenzahl, M., Schöbel, M., Trautmann, T.: How motivational orientation influences the evaluation and choice of hedonic and pragmatic interactive products: the role of regulatory focus. Interact. Comput. **20**, 473–479 (2008)
32. Hassenzahl, M., Diefenbach, S., Göritz, A.S.: Needs, affect, and interactive products: facets of user experience. Interact. Comput. **22**(5), 353–362 (2010)
33. Hoffman, D.L., Novak, T.P.: Marketing in hypermedia computer mediated environments: conceptual foundations. J. Market. **60**, 50–68 (1996)
34. Jennett, C., Cox, A.L., et al.: Measuring and defining the experience of immersion in games. Int. J. Hum. Comput. Stud. **66**(9), 641–661 (2008)
35. Karapanos, E., Zimmerman, J., Forlizzi, J., Martens, J.B.: User experience over time: an initial framework. In: Proceedings of the CHI 2009 Conference on Human Factors in Computer Systems, pp. 729–738. ACM, New York (2009)
36. Khan, R.F., Sutcliffe, A.G.: Attractive agents are more persuasive. Int. J. Hum. Comput. Interact. **30**(2), 142–150 (2014)
37. Kristof, R., Satran, A.: Interactivity by Design: Creating and Communicating with New Media. Adobe Press, Mountain View (1995)
38. Kujala, S., Roto, V., et al.: UX curve: a method for evaluating long-term user experience. Interact. Comput. **23**, 473–483 (2011)
39. Lavie, T., Tractinsky, N.: Assessing dimensions of perceived visual aesthetics of websites. Int. J. Hum. Comput. Stud. **60**, 269–298 (2004)
40. Lee, S., Koubek, R.: Understanding user preference based on usability and aesthetics before and after actual use. Interact. Comput. **22**(6), 530–543 (2010)
41. Lidwell, W., Holden K., Butler, J.: Universal Principles of Design. Rockport, Gloucester (2003)
42. Lindgaard, G., Dudek, C., et al.: An exploration of relations between visual appeal, trustworthiness and perceived usability of homepages. ACM Trans. Comput. Hum. Interact. **18**(1), 1–30 (2011)

43. Magni, M.M., Taylor, S., Venkatesh, V.: To play or not to play? A cross temporal investigation using hedonic and instrumental perspectives to explain user intentions to explore a technology. Int. J. Hum. Comput. Stud. **68**, 572–588 (2010)
44. McCarthy, J., Wright, P.: Technology as Experience. MIT Press, Cambridge (2005)
45. McMahan, R.P., Kopper, R., Bowman, D.A.: Principles for designing effective 3D interaction techniques. In: Hale, K.S., Stanney, K.M. (eds.) Handbook of Virtual Environments: Design, Implementation and Applications. CRC Press, Boca Raton (2014)
46. Mendoza, V., Novick, D.G.: Usability over time. In: Proceedings of International Conference on Design of Communication: Documenting and Designing for Pervasive Information, pp. 151–158. ACM Press, New York (2005)
47. Mullet, K., Sano, D.: Designing Visual Interfaces: Communication Oriented Techniques. SunSoft Press, Englewood Cliffs (1995)
48. O'Brien, H.: The influence of hedonic and utilitarian motivations on user engagement: the case of online shopping experiences. Interact. Comput. **22**(5), 344–352 (2010)
49. O'Brien, H., Lebow, M.: A mixed methods approach to measuring user experience in online news interactions. J. Am. Soc. Inf. Sci. Technol. **64**(8), 1543–1556 (2013)
50. O'Brien, H., Toms, E.: What is user engagement ? A conceptual framework for defining user engagement with technology. J. Am. Soc. Inf. Sci. Technol. **59**(8), 938–955 (2008)
51. Payne, J.W., Bettman, J.R., Johnson, E.J.: The Adaptive Decision Maker. Cambridge University Press, Cambridge (1993)
52. Porat, T., Tractinsky, N.: It's a pleasure buying here: the effects of web-store design on consumers' emotions and attitudes. Hum. Comput. Interact. **27**(3), 235–276 (2012)
53. Reeves, B., Nass, C.: The media equation: how people treat computers, television and new media like real people and places. CLSI/Cambridge University Press, Stanford/Cambridge (1996)
54. Romero, P., Cavillo-Gamez, E.: An embodied view of flow. Interact. Comput. **26**(6), 513–527 (2013)
55. Short, J., Williams, E., Christie, B.: The Social Psychology of Telecommunications. Wiley, Chichester (1976)
56. Sundar, S.S., Bellur, S., Oh, J., Xu, Q., Jia, H.: User experience of on-screen interaction techniques: an experimental investigation of clicking, sliding, zooming, hovering, dragging and flipping. Hum. Comput. Interact. **29**, 109–152 (2014)
57. Sutcliffe, A.G.: Assessing the reliability of heuristic evaluation for website attractiveness and usability. In: Proceedings HICSS-35: Hawaii International Conference on System Sciences, pp. 1838–1847. IEEE Computer Society Press, Los Alamitos (2002)
58. Sutcliffe, A.G.: Multimedia and Virtual Reality: Designing Multisensory User Interfaces. Lawrence Erlbaum Associates, Mahwah (2003)
59. Sutcliffe, A.G.: Designing for user engagement: aesthetic and attractive user interfaces. In: Carroll, J.M. (ed.) Synthesis Lectures on Human Centered Informatics. Morgan Claypool, San Rafael (2009)
60. Sutcliffe, A.G., Carroll, J.M.: Generalizing claims and reuse of HCI knowledge. In: Johnson, H., Nigay, L., Roast, C. (eds.) People and Computers XIII; Proceedings of BCS-HCI '98, pp. 159–176. Springer, Berlin (1998)
61. Sutcliffe, A.G., De Angeli, A.: Assessing interaction styles in web user interfaces. In: Costabile, M.F., Paterno, F. (eds.) Proceedings of Interact 2005, pp. 405–417 (2005)
62. Teo, H.H., Oh, L.B., Liu, C., Wei, K.K.: An empirical study of the effects of interactivity on web user attitude. Int. J. Hum. Comput. Stud. **58**(3), 281–305 (2003)
63. Tractinsky, N., Shoval-Katz, A., Ikar, D.: What is beautiful is usable? Interact. Comput. **13**(2), 127–145 (2000)
64. Travis, D.: Effective Colour Displays: Theory and Practice. Academic Press, Boston (1991)
65. Trevino, L.K. Lengel, R.H., Daft, R.L.: Media symbolism, media richness, and media choice in organizations: a symbolic interactionist perspective. Commun. Res. **5**, 553–574 (1987)
66. Tuch, A.N., Roth, S.P., et al.: Is beautiful really usable? Towards understanding the relation between usability, aesthetics and affect in HCI. Comput. Hum. Behav. **28**, 1596–1607 (2012)

67. Weibel, D., Wissmath, B.: Immersion in computer games: the role of spatial presence and flow. Int. J. Comput. Games Technol. **2011**, Article ID 282345 (2011)
68. Wirth, W., Hartmann, T., Bocking, S., et al.:  A process model of the formation of spatial presence experiences. Media Psychol. **9**, 493–525 (2007)
69. Witmer, B.G., Singer, M.J.: Measuring presence in virtual environments: a presence questionnaire. Presence **7**, 225–240 (1999)
70. Wu, J., Lu, X.: Effects of extrinsic and intrinsic motivators on using utilitarian, hedonic, and dual-purposed information systems: a meta-analysis. J. Assoc. Inf. Syst. **13**(3), 153–191 (2013)

# User Engagement with Digital Health Technologies

Patty Kostkova

## 1 Introduction

Recently, there has been a digital revolution in healthcare [30]. Over the last two decades, billions of dollars' worth of investments have been directed into ICT (information and communications technologies) solutions for healthcare. "Knowledge is the enemy of disease, the application of what we know will have a bigger impact than any drug or technology likely to be introduced in the next decade", famously predicted Sir Muir Gray, Director of the United Kingdom (UK) National Health System (NHS) National Knowledge Service and NHS Chief Knowledge Officer over 10 years ago [25] when he established the National Electronic Library for Health in the UK [26].

New evidence-based digital libraries and web portals designed to keep busy clinicians up to date with the latest evidence were created in the UK and USA [34]. Digital libraries have formed a subset of online health portals [8, 10, 44] and have been increasingly providing key information about clinical care, up-to-date policies and guidelines and essential underlying evidence-based knowledge [60]. Further, serious (educational) games are new arrivals that have established themselves firmly in the spectrum of health online resources contributing to health knowledge, awareness and subsequently health outcomes. One of the key challenges is how to methodologically assess their educational impact without decreasing user enjoyment and engagement. Online virtual communities of practice (VCoP) in the health domain have enabled collaborative work over geographical distances and barriers; however, keeping them sustainable remains a challenge.

How have digital health technologies actually been assessed? The typical methods for assessing them (and the core method of engagement) have been to investigate

P. Kostkova (✉)
Department of Computer Science, University College London, London, UK
e-mail: p.kostkova@ucl.ac.uk

© Springer International Publishing Switzerland 2016
H. O'Brien, P. Cairns (eds.), *Why Engagement Matters*,
DOI 10.1007/978-3-319-27446-1_6

their effectiveness in providing information through searching and browsing. User preferences for information access and navigation behaviour on medical portals have been widely researched to improve usability and access to information [44]. While it is known that user perceived behaviour differs from actual online behaviour [47, 61] combined methods are required to gain a realistic picture.

However, how do we define, assess and ultimately improve engagement with these resources? With more research being undertaken, the focus of health resources evaluation has started to shift towards impact evaluation [9] and assessment of knowledge, attitude and behaviour change; this development has been mirrored in traditional library domains [49].

Overall, in this chapter, we focus on health online resources delivering evidence and improving knowledge, their impact in clinical settings at the point of care, the role of serious games for health and, finally, engagement of individuals and communities. We define user engagement from the perspective of these four themes:

1. Knowledge and attitude change
2. Impact at the point of care
3. Integrative digital storytelling
4. Professional communities of practice

In each section, we discuss one of these four core themes using the particular definition of engagement (above) and methodological framework for digital health technology; these are applied to a real case study from health domain. The structure of this chapter is illustrated in Table 1. For the purposes of this chapter, we do not investigate the evaluation of behaviour change.

**Table 1** Four themes for user engagement, digital health technologies and case studies

| Theme | Digital health technology | Case study project |
|---|---|---|
| Knowledge and attitude change | Internet portals | Bugs and Drugs |
| Impact at the point of care | Digital libraries | National Resource for Infection Control |
| Integrative digital storytelling | Serious games | Edugames4All |
| Professional communities of practice | Virtual Communities of Practice and collaborative Web 2.0 technology | FEMwiki |

# 2 Knowledge and Attitude Change

## 2.1 Knowledge and Attitude

Disseminating "explicit knowledge" (i.e. knowledge that can be written down) [59] could be considered one of the fundamental aims of Internet health portals aiming to equip users with the knowledge necessary to carry out their work, whether that be appropriate clinical guidelines, relevant articles for an assignment or evidence to support decision-making.

There is general consensus on the definition of attitude, that it involves placing value or judgment on something or someone. Fishbein and Ajzen suggest that "Attitude refers to a person's favourable or unfavourable evaluation of an object, event or person" [22] or "the degree to which performance of the behaviour is positively or negatively valued" [2]. In the medical context, attitudes are important as the value or judgment a healthcare professional places on the information held within the portal may affect the impact this information has on their work [22]. This is of equal importance for patients and citizens who are looking after their own health and well-being.

There have been studies looking at users' ability to search and find specific information on the Internet [17], but there has not been enough consideration of whether the users of health information websites have actually remembered this information and whether it has had any impact on their knowledge or attitudes.

Assessing knowledge and attitude independently provides a valuable proxy of user engagement; however, for wider impact, understanding the relationship between knowledge and attitude change is important. Through administrating two identical sets of questions assessing knowledge and attitude before and after using an online health portal, we could:

- Test for changes in knowledge
- Test for changes in attitudes
- Evaluate the relationship between changes in knowledge and changes in attitude

## 2.2 Relationship Between Knowledge and Attitude Change

It is all very well to improve people's knowledge, but if this has no impact on their attitude and subsequent behaviour, then in this case, it would be a futile exercise. Therefore, the knowledge and attitude change evaluation was designed in a complementary way to show the correlation between these variables.

This approach has been piloted with a small digital library in the healthcare domain (Bugs and Drugs) where library users were asked a series of questions before using the library and then asked the same questions after using the library, showing positive changes in knowledge and attitude [42, 43].

## 2.3   Case Study: Bugs and Drugs

Bugs and Drugs (www.antibioticresistance.org.uk) is a website aimed at the general
public about antimicrobial resistance [46]. It was funded by the UK Department
of Health and provides an interface for the general public. Bugs and Drugs was
developed under the umbrella of the health digital library (DL) called National
electronic Library for Communicable Disease (NeLCD) [67, 69], which later
became the National electronic Library of Infection (NeLI) in the UK (www.
neli.org.uk) [35–37, 44]. NeLI further enhanced access to evidence by semantic
navigation to infection resources [15, 16, 28]. Bugs and Drugs provided a small
collection of information to help reduce the unnecessary prescribing of antibiotics,
i.e. changing attitudes and eventual behaviour.

### 2.3.1   Changes in Knowledge and Attitude

To evaluate changes in knowledge about antibiotics and antibiotic resistance, the
user was asked to decide whether seven statements about antibiotics were true
or false. Some of the "answers" or correct versions of the statements were more
obvious in the site than others, e.g. one question ("People become resistant to
antibiotics": True or False?) was the subject of the current tip of the month present
on every page of the site.

To evaluate changes in attitude, the user was asked to rank their agreement with
six statements on a Likert scale of 1 (strongly disagree) to 5 (strongly agree). Four
of these statements were about the user's attitude to information on the site, e.g.
"Antibiotics help to reduce the duration of pain in AOM (acute otitis media—a
common childhood ear infection)". How the user evaluates that information will
be seen in their attitude to the statement after using the site, i.e. to what extent
they agree or disagree with it. Other Likert scale statements were about the user's
attitudes to prescribing antibiotics for AOM, "Doctors should prescribe antibiotics
for AOM" and "I would expect an antibiotic for me/my child if I/they had AOM".
Answers to these statements will indicate clearly the user's attitude with respect to
the use of antibiotics in AOM in general and in their own situation.

### 2.3.2   Relationship Between Knowledge Change and Attitude Change

The knowledge questions on antibiotics were reflected in the attitude questions
on AOM and a question on user learning self-assessment to indicate further
correlations. To evaluate our AR test bed, these results are essential as the ultimate
aim of the antimicrobial resistance website is to contribute to reducing inappropriate
prescription of antibiotics. If people know that antibiotics are not an effective
treatment for certain infections as a result of using the site but would still expect
one from their doctor for those infections, then the site has only half done its job.

### 2.3.3    Results

The antimicrobial resistance site was tested in the Science Museum, London, as part of their "live science" programme. Over a period of 7 days during UK February school holidays, 227 people took part in the study. Of these, 177 completed both questionnaires. A paired t-test was performed to test the statistical significance of changes between pairs of questionnaires. The detailed results for each question are illustrated in Table 2.

There was a significant change in the mean score for the true/false statements (1 for correct answer, 0 for incorrect or "don't know") of users before (mean = 4.33) and after using the site (mean = 4.90 $p < 0.001$). With respect to individual statements, there were significant changes in the answers to four of the seven statements. The largest change was from 9.6 % of users getting the answer right to statement 1b ("People can become resistant to antibiotics") before using the site to 45.76 % getting this answer correct after using the site ($p < 0.001$). This reflects the visual impact of the answer to this question in the site, as it was the focus of the tip of the month on the home page.

With respect to changes in attitudes, the most significant change (mean from 3.44 to 2.74, $p < 0.001$) was for the statement about the duration of antibiotic course in the ear infection indicating that after using the site, people were tending to neither disagree nor agree with the statement, rather than agree. For the two statements examining attitudes to prescribing, there were significant decreases in the mean scores (i.e. levels of agreement) for both "I would expect an antibiotic for me or my child if I/they had AOM" and "Doctors should usually prescribe antibiotics for AOM", indicating that maybe this "new" information the users had learned could have an impact on their potential behaviour.

Comparing the actual changes in knowledge and attitude for individual users, Fig. 1 shows the relationship between users' change in knowledge score and their

**Table 2** Agreement before and after using the site with changes in mean scores, p values from a paired t-test and associated confidence intervals (CI) for statements testing attitude to information on the site

|  | % (n) agree before | % (n) agree after | Change in mean | p | 95% CI |
|---|---|---|---|---|---|
| Antibiotics are effective in acute otitis media | 64% (113) | 38% (67) | -0.52 | 0.0003 | -0.79 to -0.25 |
| 10-day courses are more effective than 3-day courses of antibiotics in AOM | 42% (74) | 21% (38) | -0.70 | 0.000007 | -0.99 to -0.42 |
| Antibiotics help reduce the duration of pain in AOM | 46% (82) | 32% (57) | -0.23 | 0.09271 | -0.49 to 0.03 |
| You are more likely to have a complication from AOM if you do not have antibiotics | 44% (78) | 23% (41) | -0.49 | 0.00041 | -0.76 to -0.23 |

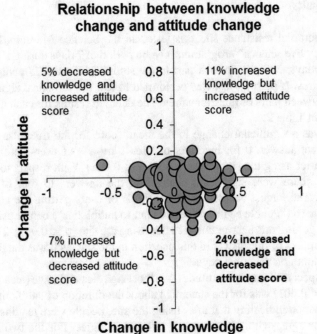

**Relationship between knowledge change and attitude change**

**Fig. 1** Relationship between change in knowledge and change in attitude to prescribing of antibiotics in AOM for individual users. The size of the bubbles indicates the number of users at that point

change in attitude towards prescribing. 24.24 % of users increased their knowledge score and decreased their attitude score (i.e. they were less likely to expect antibiotics for AOM). 10.10 % of users did not change their knowledge score but decreased their attitude score. Changes in knowledge do not always equal changes in attitude, particularly when knowledge is applied to a personal situation such as the prescribing of antibiotics for AOM, so using these figures we can suggest that 34.34 % of users increased their knowledge about antibiotics and resistance and allowed that knowledge to change their attitude to the prescribing of antibiotics in AOM.

The mean, mode and median scores for "I have learnt something new after using this site" indicated that users did generally feel they had learned from the site. This is supported by the fact that for 45.19 % of users, increases in knowledge scores matched the perception that they had learned from the site. In contrast, 17.31 % of users thought they had learned but actually decreased their knowledge score.

# 3 Impact at Point of Care

## 3.1 Definition of Impact in the Context of Digital Library

In addition to knowledge and attitude change, health digital libraries aimed at professionals need to deliver more impact at the point of care. "Impact concerns long-term and sustainable changes introduced by a given intervention in the lives of beneficiaries. Impact can be related either to the specific objectives of an intervention or to unanticipated changes caused by an intervention; such unanticipated changes may also occur in the lives of people not belonging to the beneficiary group. Impact can be either positive or negative, the latter being equally important to be aware of" [7].

Users were asked if the library has ever had an impact on their professional knowledge or whether they applied the knowledge or attitude in their work [41]. Various research findings in psychology suggest that knowledge and attitude can be indicators of behaviour [1, 3], and therefore, this research used them as proxy measures for digital library impact [22]. To assess behaviour, we drew from Dervin's model that is defined as "a model of methodology, rather than a model of a set of activities or a situation" [70]. Dervin's sense-making model [14] is considered to be a model of the "how to" of information seeking. The holistic approach we propose in the next section investigates the knowledge provided by the DL in the decision-making context of the individual user and directly at the point of care.

## 3.2 The Impact-ED Model

In order to address the impact of digital libraries at the point of care, we developed the Impact-ED evaluation framework measuring impact on four dimensions of digital libraries—content, community, services and technology, as defined in [45]. Data collected by qualitative and quantitative methods were triangulated to analyse pre- and post-visit questionnaires to assess the clinical query or aim of the visit and subsequent satisfaction with each visit to the site, mapped against weblog analysis for each session, and data from semi-structured interviews.

The Impact-ED (Impact Evaluation for Digital Libraries) model on which the methods for evaluation were developed is shown in Fig. 2. It was developed to meet a set of impact evaluation criteria developed in a systematic review of digital library evaluations [41], and the full details can be found in [32, 41, 45]. The model is based around previously published digital library dimensions [24] and enables development of an impact score if evaluations are consistently based around one model [31].

The Impact-ED provides a set of criteria around which questionnaires and interviews are designed to collect appropriate data. The four dimensions are assessed to answer key questions about the DL impact from the point of community,

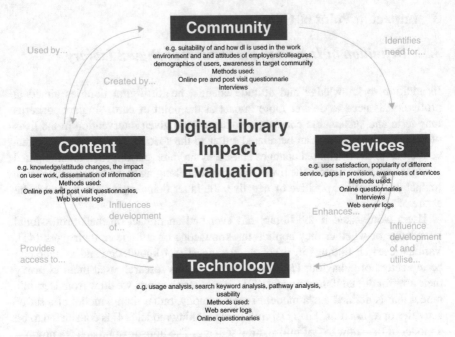

**Fig. 2** Impact-ED impact evaluation framework

services, technology and content (see [32] for full details). The methods used
in the model to collect data included online questionnaires (investigating use
of the DL/web portal within the work environment); online pre- and post-visit
(sense-making) questionnaires (investigating real-time, real-world use and how
knowledge and attitudes change); online tasks (investigating how users complete
tasks to find information within the library and how this changes knowledge and
attitudes); weblog analysis (showing what users actually did within the DL); and
semi-structured interviews (complimenting these other methods by providing more
in-depth qualitative data that expands on issues identified in the questionnaires and
weblogs).

In Fig. 2, it is illustrated how the DL evaluation methods are used together in a
study flow diagram (Fig. 3).

### 3.2.1 The Impact Score

The framework defines a method for triangulating the data sets collected from
the questionnaires, weblogs and interviews. Weblogs were statistically analysed to
calculate length and time of visits, while statistical tests, such as Fisher's exact test,
independent t-test and analysis of variance (ANOVA), were used to evaluate the
pre- and post-questionnaire data. Qualitative analysis was applied to semi-structured
interview results to determine the outcome for each criterion from all three data sets.

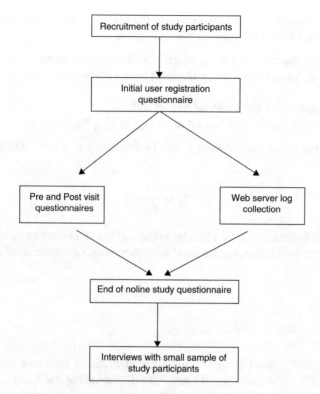

**Fig. 3** Framework for digital library impact evaluation methods

The *impact score* is defined as follows: data obtained from the pre- and post-visit questionnaires coded to show where there was a strengthening of knowledge or change in knowledge or gain in knowledge as a result of a visit to the library. For each visit where this occurred, the library scored 1. A running total is kept until all visits have been scored, and this is then divided by the total number of visits analysed. The formula is shown below:

$$\text{Impact score } I = K/V_t$$

where $V_t$ = total number of visits analysed and $K$ = knowledge score (where $K$ = sum of number of visits where either a change/strengthening or gain in knowledge is recorded).

In order to gain a comparative figure, we look at the reasons for "no impact" by recording reasons given by users. Where the digital library had no impact on user knowledge, it is possible to establish a known maximum achievable score based on the areas in which the library design is in control, i.e. if a reason for no impact is that the user could not find any information related to their query, then the impact score could have been improved by either adding information where it was lacking or by improving the navigation or organisation of the library so the available information is more easily found. The calculation is as follows:

Reason for no impact 1 ($R_1$) = e.g. No relevant information found
Reason for no impact 2 ($R_2'$) = e.g. Couldn't access document
$R_3$ etc.
$V_{R_x}$ = total number of visits with no impact coded $R_x$
Known maximum achievable impact score $I_{max} = (\sum_x V_{R_x})/V_t + I$

Therefore, the actual impact score $I_A$ can be calculated as a ratio with the $I_{max}$ as follows:

$$I_A = \frac{I}{I_{max}}$$

Using the definition, the $I_A$ can also be calculated for all outputs or services rather than just an overall figure, e.g. personal education, training/education of other staff, etc.


## 3.3 Case Study: NRIC

Since May 2015, the UK-based online portal National Resource for Infection Control (NRIC: www.nric.org.uk) has been disseminating the latest evidence in infection prevention and control for professionals in healthcare settings and social care in the UK as well as internationally [39, 72], stressing the need to share evidence-based resources with professionals at the point of care [71, 73] in particular around major outbreaks [74]. But what difference is NRIC making to those who use it?

In order to use the Impact-ED model on NRIC, the framework needs to be mapped onto the specific situation of this digital library. Based on the generic model, Fig. 2, an NRIC specific mapping in accordance with the four dimensions was undertaken and can be found in Fig. 4.

The four dimensions of the Impact-ED model were applied to NRIC. The NRIC community has been involved in identifying the need for services and, in some cases, involved in creating and reviewing content for the library. The Internet technology, based on IBM Lotus Domino web server with a Dublin Core (DC) metadata tagged documents, was designed in order to provide the services required and to ensure consistent access to content throughout the library. The content is freely accessible to the community although a minority of external documents have restricted access. The aim of Impact-ED is to see the infection control content evaluated to allow improvement of the technology to increase the impact of the content on the user community.

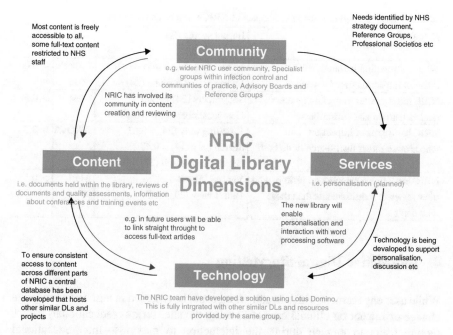

**Fig. 4** Mapping the NRIC library onto the Impact-ED model

### 3.3.1 Results

The very positive outcome of this study demonstrated that NRIC had an impact on user knowledge in 52.8 % of visits (n = 38). The main reasons for no impact were that not enough information was found (n = 16) and the user couldn't access the document (n = 4). NRIC has a positive impact in many areas of user work including policy development, training and education, implementing changes in practice and business case or proposal preparation.

Calculating impact scores for these different groups resulted in the hypotheses shown in Table 3. Statistical tests were performed to validate the data. The Kolmogorov-Smirnov test determined that the data was normally distributed.

Table 3 shows that if people find related information in NRIC, then this does have an impact on their knowledge. However, there was no statistical significance for any of the other hypotheses despite the differences in impact scores. This is possibly due to the small sample numbers involved and a larger evaluation may provide more significant results.

**Table 3** Statistical significance of the impact of NRIC services and features

| Hypothesis | Impact scores ($I_A$) (no. of visits) | Test | p |
|---|---|---|---|
| When information is found in NRIC it has an impact on user knowledge | Information found (47) = 0.74<br>Information not found (24) = 0.13 | Fisher's exact | < 0.001 |
| NRIC has a greater impact on its newsletter readers than on non-subscribers | Subscribers (24) = 0.55<br>Non-subscribers (10) = 0.48 | t-test | > 0.5 |
| NRIC has a greater impact on visitors who browse rather than search or do both | Browsing only (24) = 0.63<br>Search only (17) = 0.47<br>Browse and search (27) = 0.52 | ANOVA | > 0.5 |
| NRIC has a greater impact on visitors who view reviewer's assessments than those who don't | Viewed (5) = 0.6<br>Didn't view (29) = 0.52 | t-test | > 0.5 |

# 4 Interactive Digital Storytelling

While user engagement with a health portal could be assessed in terms of knowledge change or impact on clinical care after using the site, serious (educational) games require users to engage during the interaction to maximise their educational opportunity. This is of particular importance for serious health games [19] that use storytelling as the paradigm [56].

Interactive digital storytelling (IDS) games [29], using story and narrative as the educational intervention in games, are particularly popular game mechanics increasing user engagement through interaction with the story while delivering both entertainment and health educational content [54]. Serious health games are typically aimed at teaching a particular set of learning objectives (LOs) assessed using pre- and post-tests to provide information regarding the efficiency of the game, as well as feedback for the player about his/her knowledge, further enhancing the educational value of the game and contributing to player's knowledge. It has been shown that feedback is vital for learning, as it is necessary to encourage "deep" learning and engage students with the subject [27].

However, assessments using tests and questionnaires are known to be disengaging for students and bring additional inconsistencies and bias to the tested knowledge. Thus, seamlessly integrating tested LO into the story narrative prior to and after playing the game provides an engaging instrument for knowledge assessment without losing players' attention, immersion and engagement.

## 4.1 IDS Seamless Evaluation (SE) Framework

This section will first introduce the structure of an IDS framework and present the extensions to the framework required for evaluation to be seamlessly integrated

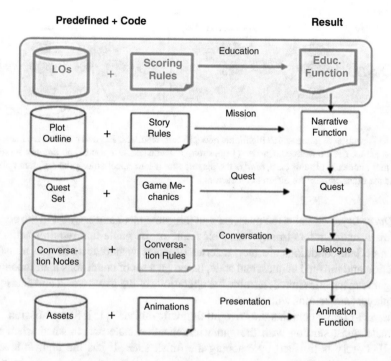

**Fig. 5** User-centered seamless evaluation framework

into the game. The IDS game framework (see Fig. 5) is based on four conceptual layers for authoring that we enhanced by incorporating the Education Layer. The five layers are: Presentation Layer, Conversation Layer, Quest Layer, Mission Layer and Education Layer. A detailed description of the first four layers can be found in [63]. Here, we briefly introduce the layers, by focusing on the methodological enhancement necessary for an integration of the seamless evaluation and on the Education Layer, the enhancement necessary for the Conversation Layer.

For reasons of clarity, a brief definition of the four layers is discussed to set the scene—full details can be found in [51, 52].

*Presentation Layer* contains the assets/animations needed to deliver the IDS. It consists of animation for characters, rooms, items, etc., in the game and the motion models that are used to describe how the virtual characters move or behave. Together they form the game animation function.

*Conversation Layer* is the main means of interaction and content presentation [15]. This layer consists of conversation nodes and conversation rules. A conversation node (CN) is a line of text/or a sentence recited by a player character. The conversation rules show which player is saying what and in which context they are saying it. For example, a rule could be a virtual character that greets the player at the beginning of the game. Another rule states that the virtual character greets the player only if the player does it first.

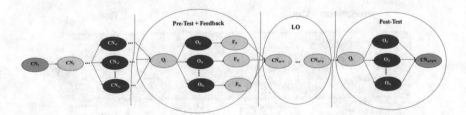

**Fig. 6** A section of game which highlights how pre-test, feedback, LO and post-test are integrated in the game. *CN* conversation node, *Q* question, *F* feedback, *O* option. The *colours* represent different characters; in this case, *blue* is the player, who has to select among the different options, while the other *colours* are different characters

*Quest Layer* contains the quest set and the game mechanics. Quest in the context of this research refers to any "story element" of the game that requires activation when certain conditions are met, a series of states visited according to transition function and finished at quest end state, based on a set of conditions met. It contains the game mechanics that determine the operations of the game world and deals with the player interactions with the game.

*Mission Layer* contains the "overall dramatic outline" [15]. Story Mission is an ultimate quest starting with the game initialisation state and finished when then the IDS story is finished by reaching the finish state. It has the highest level of abstraction as the IDS.

*Education Layer* is the new layer added to the framework. It consists of LOs and scoring rules. The LOs contain a high-level description of the LO delivered through the game. For example, an LO could be: "One should only use antibiotics with a doctor's permission". The scoring rules consists of rules describing how the LO evaluation contributes to the player's score. For example, how many points the player gets for answering correctly one of the questions in the game (Fig. 6).

## 4.2   Case Study: Edugames4all

Seamless evaluation integrated into a role-playing game utilises problem-based learning (PBL) [18]: the GHD (Global Handwashing Day) Game [56] builds on the European e-Bug project that teaches children about hygiene [12, 20, 21, 38]. The game is an educational IDS game that relies heavily on the narrative. It aims to reinforce the importance of hygiene, focusing on handwashing, and enforces the learning through a game tutorial [53].

### 4.2.1 Game Narrative

The player is placed in the e-Bug agency and she/he is introduced to her/his boss, Big C. Also here, the player meets Alyx who is the player's partner and helps him/her during the investigation. After the introductions are made, Big C introduces the problem that Hugh Gaego, a famous actor, is supposedly poisoned, and the player has to decipher the mystery: whether it was a case of an alleged poisoning or not and who the guilty party is, if any, for poisoning Hugh. The state space of the game allows the player to explore different parts of the game, by making it non-linear and allowing different options during the investigation. Not all the paths lead to an answer, and they are not all mandatory for solving the mystery. Although totally integrated into the game flow, the questions assess the educational content presented (Fig. 7). The questions are spread throughout the game but asked before the player is exposed to game mechanics through which she/he can learn about the objectives being asked. The questions are asked in an abstract manner, in order to see whether the player understands the scientific concept and if what she/he learns is generalised. However, the LOs are delivered both in an abstract manner and through the game mechanics. If the player gets an answer wrong, the correct answer is given to the player, in order to correct misconceptions and allow the player to improve his/her knowledge and engagement during the game play.

Following the SE evaluation framework, the post-questions that assess the knowledge after the LO was delivered were asked towards the end of the game when the investigation was over, and the player returned to the headquarters for debriefing Big C—who asked the player the same set of questions as when the questions were asked for the first time (Fig. 8).

**Fig. 7** Example of an evaluation question integrated in the game

**Fig. 8** Example of a question at the end of the game, during the debriefing

### 4.2.2 Results

The key to understanding the impact of the seamless evaluation is the first assessment; however, the seamless evaluation can only demonstrate useful results if the positive education impact is not affected. The participants played the game either in a controlled environment (in a school with a teacher present with 50 min to finish the game) or online at their convenience. The schools at which the evaluation took place were located in London and Glasgow, UK.

The seamless evaluation was assessed through a mixed method, combining a survey (performed at the end of the game playing session) with observations during the playing sessions. The effectiveness of the game in conveying the LOs was assessed through the experimental studies in which participants had to play the game from beginning to end. For measuring the statistical significance of the effectiveness of the game in conveying the educational content, we used a paired t-test.

One hundred and forty-five participants were considered for the evaluation, selected based on whether they finished the game or not. The main reason for this decision is the fact that the evaluation is integrated in the game and the post-evaluation is towards the end of the game; therefore, for a player who did not finish the game, the results of the evaluation were not available. The end survey was completed by 21 participants (incomplete surveys were not considered).

Ninety-five percent of the players realised that they had to choose one of the options presented. The players who realised that they have to select one of the presented options were asked to rate how these affected their game experience on

**Table 4** The results for how people perceived that the seamless evaluation affected their experience

| # | Option | % |
|---|--------|---|
| 1 | They obstructed my game experience | 6 |
| 2 | It wasn't too bad, they didn't discourage me but I would prefer not to have them | 12 |
| 3 | They did not affect me in any way | 24 |
| 4 | It was good having them, they had made the game more interesting | 44 |
| 5 | They enriched my game experience, they engage me more into the game | 12 |

a five-point Likert scale, presented in Table 4. As can be seen, half of the players consider the questions to be a good addition to the game: 12 % stated that they enriched their game experience, while 44 % said that they made the game more interesting. Among the rest, 24 % were not affected in any way by the integrated questions, and the rest were affected in a negative manner. This can lead to the conclusion that, for most of the players, the integrated evaluation does not only facilitate the assessment but can also improve the game experience and enhance engagement.

To summarise, the results of the seamless evaluation assessment indicate players' strong preference of this method. Moreover, most players considered the questions as an enhancement to the game. The effectiveness of the game at conveying the educational content was performed using a paired t-test on the number of correct answers the players had on the pre- and post-questionnaire. The results show that the difference between the players pre- and post-questionnaire questions is statistically significant ($p = 0.01, \sigma = 2.20$).

## 5 Professional Communities of Practice

We have focused so far on engagement of a single user with health websites, portals, digital libraries and serious games through knowledge and attitude changes, impact assessment at point of care and seamless evaluation of IDS games. However, humans are community beings—communities have always been the key to our communication, interaction and social and professional lives. Traditional communities of practice (CoP) have been the cornerstone of professional life [68]; however, with the recent rise in online social networks (OSN) dedicated to professional communities, professional VCoPs have enabled interactions over geographical and cultural boundaries [57]. These are of pivotal importance in the medical domain [48]. Recent research investigated community interaction at health events [64], but the underlying roles and dynamics of VCoPs are of key importance for engagement. They also underpin the relationship between roles in traditional CoP and VCoPs in online activities. Unlike many studies evaluating large networks a posteriori with no insight into the user base, through a collaboration with real CoPs, we could develop a roles framework for engagement and experiment with a real community, enabling us to better understand actions on both sides of the digital divide.

Do leading experts in a real community naturally become moderators of online discussions, or does the influence change the pattern of interaction? What factors play a role in keeping an ongoing and long-term interest in VCoP engagement? These are some of the aims of our research conducted with users of the FEMwiki portal and the CoPs of epidemiologists.

## 5.1 Communities of Practice and Their Virtual Counterparts (VCoP)

Unlike ad hoc online social networks, professional CoP has a long history in the organisation of traditional societies, as defined by Wenger [68]:

> Communities of practice are groups of people who share a concern or a passion for something they do and learn how to do it better as they interact regularly.

According to Wenger, CoPs are characterised by the domain, the community and the practice. Professional communities in the medical domain have a history spanning centuries (such as the Royal Societies); however, new digital social networks and collaborative activities have transformed traditional human ties to virtual interaction [62]. The evolution of online communities has been studied for a long time, from a user or community perspective [4–6]; however, our focus is engagement through the synergy and dynamics between VCoP and CoP roles.

In the virtual world, online discussions (e.g. "ask the expert" forums) in fact "crowdsource" scientific contributions, but sustainable active engagement remains sparse. There are a number of ways to define the roles of CoPs—these include champion, moderator, practice leader, sponsor, member and facilitator [57]. In VCoP context, Dale [11] differentiates these roles according to their increasing level of engagement, anonymous reader and anonymous commentator, and after registration, commentator with attribution, "ask a question" with attribution, blog writer, mentor and expert. In the health domain, we define the roles this way in the framework below, in Table 5, drawing from our initial work establishing roles on a wiki portal [33, 40].

Please note that if it is not stated "anonymous" in Table 5, then "registered" users were assumed.

Definitions for the wiki section (non-self-explanatory terms) are as follows:

- Original author: recognising the author of the resource prior to being turned into online project
- Author: creator of a new wiki page
- Contributor(s): any user who made a contribution to an existing wiki page
- Editor: responsible for quality control and has the right to authorise the page as "approved", enabling a specific dual versioning for each page of user-generated edits while maintaining editorial control over the quality of the resource (one editor per page)

**Table 5** Taxonomy of roles in VCoP

| Role | VCoP | Wiki project | Discussion forum project |
|------|------|--------------|--------------------------|
| Level 1 | No friend | Anonymous reader | Anonymous reader |
| Level 2 | Follower | Reader | Reader |
| Level 3 | Mutual followers | Contributor | Initiator of a thread |
| Level 4 | Friends | Author/ Original Author | neither (replies 2nd or later) |
| Level 5 | Editor | 1st reply | |
| Level 6 | | Both 1st poster and 1st replier, (these are naturally the most active members of the community) | |

## 5.2   Case Study: FEMwiki

In the next section, we will apply our framework on the Field Epidemiology Manual Wiki (FEMwiki, www.femwiki.com) online community (VCoP). FEM Wiki is an online wiki training resource consisting of growing online wiki training resource consisting of wiki pages defining key terms and procedures in field epidemiologists and active discussion forum.

FEMwiki was developed to support the European training programme "European Programme for Intervention Epidemiology Training" (EPIET, ecdc.europa.eu/en/epiet/). Investigating the real CoP, EPIET, together with its online FEM Wiki counterpart, we could better understand the roles, their dynamics and the relationships and implications for engagement. In the final set of results, we provide a comparison between FEMwiki and another medical community, Medicines Support Unit for Optometrists (MSU).

### 5.2.1   Discussion Forum: Dynamics of the Roles

We analysed the longitudinal data from user forum discussion. Figure 9 is an illustrative snapshot giving an idea of an evolution of the network taken by a moving week-long window in the period 2010–2012.

As seen in Fig. 9, the majority of nodes are red (only active nodes are depicted), indicating 1st replies, while blue nodes (indicating both activities, 1st posts and 1st replies) are on a similar level. Green nodes, 1st posters (typically, those asking questions in discussions), are in the minority on this snapshot. However, as we used a week-wide sliding window analysis approach, this was the only way to generate a longitudinal changing data.

Figure 10 is illustrating the growth in users contributing to the forum discussion with respect to the roles: the increasing number of 1st poster indicates a widening community, while the main success in terms of engagement is increase of 1st responders and "both". Although a step in the right direction, analysing the user base indicates these are still centered around the European Centre for Disease Prevention and Control (ECDC) and EPIET CoP. The dynamics in forum discussions is strongly

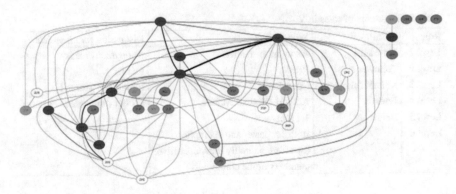

**Fig. 9** Forum dynamics with illustrative snapshot of activities

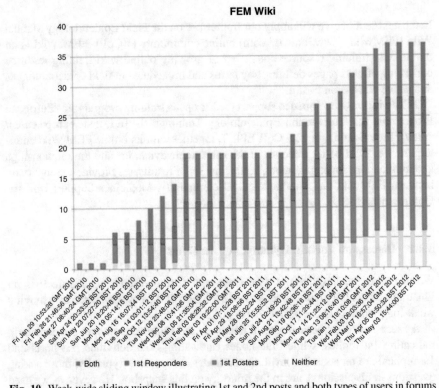

**Fig. 10** Week-wide sliding window illustrating 1st and 2nd posts and both types of users in forums

reflecting the CoP roles; however, the growing number of users who started posting as well as sending 1st posts in the forum has tripled since the launch of the project (15 members up from 5). This indicates engagement of new users asking questions (including those from outside of Europe). However, for sustainability of the portal, the pool of "blue" (8) and "red" (5) users willing to respond needs to be adequately expanded or a dedicated moderator engaged.

## 5.2.2  Relationship Between Discussion Forum and Wiki

We also investigated the relationship between the forum and wiki activity—this includes any contributions regardless of roles. As discussed above, 483 wiki pages have been subject to over 3000 edits made by a total of 33 different registered users. On the forums for discussing pages, there are 95 forum discussions since January 2010, with over 200 posts. Thirty-seven distinct users have made comments.

However, the overlap between these groups (wiki contributors/authors and forum posts) is 20 users out of 33 and 37. Figure 11 shows the monthly number of page edits and forum posts on FEMwiki.

Naturally, users in the intersection of activities are those senior members of the EPIET community and core staff from the European Centre for Disease Prevention and Control (ECDC)—an agency that is responsible for running EPIET and FEM Wiki.

## 5.2.3  FEM Wiki Semantic Navigation Model

FEMwiki framework is structured using a domain taxonomy editable by users in the same way as the actual content. The taxonomy browser on the front page

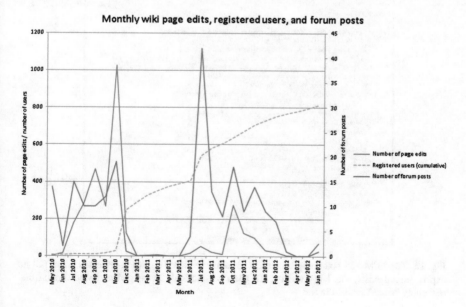

**Fig. 11**  Signups, forum discussion

of the wiki allows users to immediately see and navigate the organisation of the repository. User-friendliness of ontology editors is another challenge. In the FEM Wiki framework, we utilised the wiki user interface users have been using for collaborative editing of the medical content for an entirely different purpose: the wiki page also serves as a user-friendly taxonomy editor, thus, offering a seamless experience to users and increasing engagement with the VCoP.

In order to elicit more edits from users, the entire field epidemiology taxonomy is displayed on the navigation page (rather than just pages with existing content). A colour coding is used to draw user attending to empty pages ("stubs") and to distinguish between various types of content; see Fig. 12. The taxonomy editor supports colour-coding for the dual versioning of pages: (A) Yellow is the link to the latest version of the page. (B) Green is the link to the expert-reviewed (and approved) page—clicking on the text "approved version" will lead to the reviewed version. Further, (C) question mark is for pages that do not have an expert-reviewed version (indicated by the question mark icon)—the link will lead to the latest version. (D) Green only indicates pages where the latest version is also the expert-reviewed version—the link leads to this common version. Any edits to the page will cause a new latest version to be created. Finally, (E) red illustrates (and visually draws attention to) pages tagged as "stubs" where content has not been developed yet. By simply looking at the colour-coded taxonomy browser, users can see which pages have expert-reviewed versions and can either choose to see that version or a later unapproved version if one exists (Fig. 12). The user can also see "stub" pages

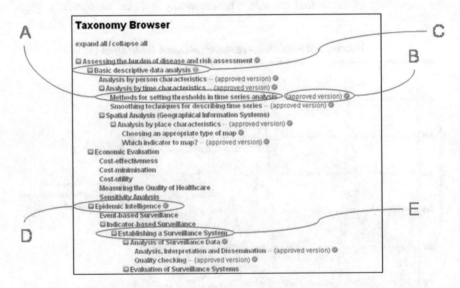

**Fig. 12** The FEMwiki taxonomy browser: (A) latest version; (B) expert-reviewed page; (C) no expert version exists, only latest version; (D) latest version is also the expert-reviewed version; and (E) empty "stubs" marked in *red*

marked in red—this feature is specifically designed to highlight parts of the wiki content that need to be filled in and to encourage users to start this process.

The user-friendly semantic taxonomy with the same interface to modify the parent-child tree structure as the pages themselves further engages users in contribution and resulted in 12 new nodes in taxonomy (not possible to add without editable taxonomy) and 15 filled stubs which otherwise would not be created. Four percent of registered users contribute new content, and those who contribute to editing pages are also active in discussion forums.

### 5.2.4 Comparison of Two Health Communities: FEMwiki and MSU

In the final section, we examine two independent CoPs and a theory of engagement developed around medical scientific Internet portals: FEMwiki (www. femwiki.com), dealing with field epidemiology, and Medicines Support Unit for Optometrists (MSU, www.med-support.org.uk), supporting therapeutic prescribing by optometrists. The user bases are geographically dispersed (mainly throughout the UK for MSU and throughout Europe for FEMwiki). Both sites provide centrally authored information to specialists and have means for user discussion. Each was created to order, but FEMwiki is more highly structured than MSU. In FEM Wiki, users can directly edit the content, but to guarantee quality, changes must be approved before the changes are made official. In MSU, changes can be suggested informally via the forum [23].

We collected the messages that were posted on the discussion forums of the communities and extracted networks of users. Each node corresponds to a user, with arcs linking the nodes of users who were involved in the same discussion (see Fig. 13).

While it is clear from Fig. 13 that each community has a moderator or a set of very engaged users, Figure 14 shows more details—the number of connections for each node in the networks—and Table 6 summarises some key statistics. Each network has a number of users who are involved in many discussions; these seem to be mainly senior project leaders or administrators. There is an almost linear decline to users who were only involved in one or two discussions (possibly they only had a specific question that was answered to their satisfaction). Users with many connections are involved in many discussions and therefore may have more knowledge and experience to share.

Further, ongoing research is required to expand our understanding of engagement strategies in relation to actions taken to engage the actual CoP members.

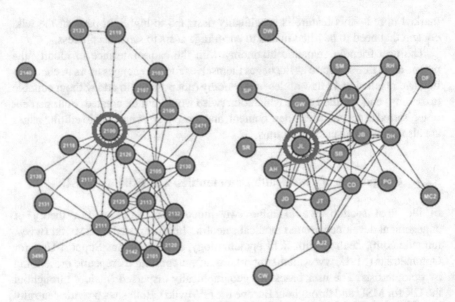

**Fig. 13** The user networks extracted from FEM Wiki (*left*) and MSU (*right*). The nodes with most connections are *highlighted*

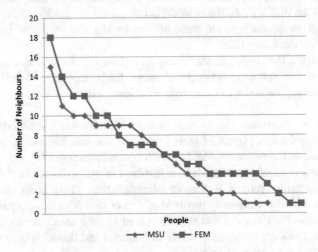

**Fig. 14** The numbers of neighbours for each node in Fig. 13

# 6 Conclusions

In this chapter, we discussed the role of user engagement with health technologies. We specifically focused on health Internet portals, digital libraries, serious games and collaborative online spaces for development of VCoP underpinned by real CoPs.

**Table 6** Summary statistics
for the two communities

| | FEMwiki | MSU |
|---|---|---|
| Nodes | 23 | 20 |
| Edges | 73 | 62 |
| Average Degree | 6.35 | 6.20 |
| Diameter | 3 | 4 |
| Average Path Length | 1.80 | 1.82 |
| Graph Density | 0.289 | 0.326 |

In particular, we focused on the role of user engagement with health technologies aimed at knowledge and attitude change, the impact in clinical settings at the point of care, seamless assessment of serious IDS games and, finally, roles enabling engagement of professional CoP.

Firstly, with regard to knowledge and attitude change, we defined a correlation method highlighting the relationship between these two measures and illustrated this approach using the case study: the "Bugs and Drugs" project.

Secondly, Impact-ED is a framework defining the impact of a health digital library at the point of care along four DH dimensions: community, services, technology and content. We illustrated the Impact-ED and calculated the impact score on assessment of the National Resource for Infection Control.

Thirdly, IDS games are increasingly important platforms delivering health educational messages while entertaining users. The seamless evaluation (SE) framework enhancing the IDS layers was developed to enable assessment of users' knowledge against learning objectives (LOs) while keeping players entertained. SE was implemented on edugames4all games and GHD and demonstrated users' preferences for this method.

Finally, engagement measures for VCoP were defined in terms of user roles in the VCoP and their relationships to the real CoP. Engagement dynamics in the online wiki, discussion forums and collaborative editing of the navigation taxonomy was analysed through the FEMwiki project.

However, there are still a number of challenges and barriers: frequent changes of technology platforms and subsequent usability issues might jeopardise user engagement with health portals [58]. New methods are required to analyse cross-platform engagement with growing segments of users using mobile phones and tablets as their primary devices, who are typically very interactive and on the go, thus creating porting challenges [55]. Designing for children's engagement is particularly challenging [50], as are the multilingual aspects and localisation of health technologies [66]. Rapidly expanding use of wearable and tracking devices creates a new need for understanding user engagement with technology for monitoring health and well-being with the primary goal to achieve behaviour change. Finally, increasingly virtual professional CoPs resembling social networks rather than mirroring more traditionally structured CoPs bring new opportunities and challenges for community engagement.

In this chapter, we outlined four major themes for user engagement with health technologies, presented four methodological frameworks and illustrated their use with case studies representing real-world medical communities and resources.

To summarise, user engagement with health technologies is essential for their success, but more fine-grained definition of their purpose, ranging from education to online community interaction to the impact at the point of care, is essential for choosing the appropriate methodological framework. Technological challenges, usability issues and technology access barriers within workplaces or learning environments (hospitals, schools) were identified as key obstacles that hinder user engagement. This is further enhanced by the fast speed of technological evolution and the need for co-authoring to reduce developmental costs [65]. However, when it comes to the ongoing investment in maintenance and improving existing health resources, the notoriously underfunded healthcare and educational sectors are often lagging behind. Finally, promotion of health technologies and resources, essential for users to actually be aware and find the portal or game, brings another set of challenges requiring right strategies and sufficient resources [13].

# References

1. Ajzen, I.: The theory of planned behaviour. Organ. Behav. Hum. Decis. Process. **50**, 179–211 (1991)
2. Ajzen, I.: The theory of planned behavior diagram. Icek Ajzen's home page. Available at: http://people.umass.edu/aizen/tpb.diag.html, November 2006
3. Ajzen, I., Manstead, A.S.R.: Changing health-related behaviors: an approach based on the theory of planned behaviour. In: van den Bos, K., et al. (eds.) The Scope of Social Psychology: Theory and Applications, pp. 43–63. Psychology Press, New York (2007)
4. Arguello, J., Butler, B.S., Joyce, E., Kraut, R., Ling, K.S., Rosé, C., Wang, X.: Talk to me: foundations for successful individual-group interactions in online communities. In: Proceedings of the SIGCHI Conference on Human Factors in Computing Systems, pp. 959–968. ACM Press, New York (2006)
5. Backstrom, L., Huttenlocher, D., Kleinberg, J., Lan, X.: Group formation in large social networks: membership, growth, and evolution. In: Proceedings of the 12th ACM SIGKDD International Conference on Knowledge Discovery and Data Mining, pp. 44–54. ACM Press, New York (2006)
6. Backstrom, L., Kleinberg, J., Lee, L., Danescu-Niculescu-Mizil, C.: Characterizing and curating conversation threads: expansion, focus, volume, re-entry. In: Proceedings of the 6th ACM International Conference on Web Search and Data Mining, pp. 13–22. ACM Press, New York (2013)
7. Blankenberg, F.: Methods of Impact Assessment Research Programme: Resource Pack and Discussion Paper for the Case Studies Phase. Oxfam UK and Novib, The Hague (1995)
8. Borgman, C.: Designing digital libraries for usability. In: Bishop, A.P., van House, N.A., Buttenfield, B.P. (eds.) Digital Library Use: Social Practice and Evaluation, pp. 85–118. MIT Press, Cambridge, MA (2003)
9. Chowdhury, G.G., Chowdhury, S.: Introduction to Digital Libraries. Facet Publishing, London (2003)
10. Chowdhury, S., Landoni, M., Gibb, F.: Usability and impact of digital libraries: a review. Online Inf. Rev. **30**(6), 656–680 (2006)

11. Dale, S.: Communities of Practice: turning conversation into collaboration. Semantics UK, 2009
12. de Quincey, E., Kostkova, P., Jawaheer, G., Farrell, D., McNulty, C., Weinberg, J.: Evaluating the online activity of users of the e-Bug web site. J. Antimicrob. Chemother. **66**(Suppl. 5), v45–v49 (2011)
13. de Quincey, E., Kostkova, P., Jawaheer, G: Promoting e-Health Resources: Lessons Learned. LNICST, vol. 69, pp. 103–110. Springer, Berlin (2011)
14. Dervin, B.: Audience as listener and learner, teacher and confidante: the sense-making approach. In: Dervin, B., Foreman-Wernet, L., Lauterbach, E. (eds.) Sense-Making Methodology Reader: Selected Writings of Brenda Dervin, pp. 215–232. Hampton Press, Cresskill (2003)
15. Diallo, G., Khelif, K., Corby, O., Kostkova, P., Madle, G.: Semantic browsing of a domain related resources: the corese-neli framework. In: Proceedings of the 2008 IEEE/WIC/ACM International WI'08 Conference, December 2008, vol. 3, pp. 50–54
16. Diallo, G., Kostkova, P., Jawaheer, G., Jupp, S., Stevens, R.: Process of building a vocabulary for the infection domain. In: 21st IEEE International Symposium on Computer-Based Medical Systems, pp. 308–313 (2008)
17. Eysenbach, G., Kohler, C.: How do consumers search for and appraise health information on the world wide web? Qualitative study using focus groups, usability tests and in-depth interviews. Br. Med. J. **324**(7337), 573–577 (2002)
18. Farrell, D., Kostkova, P., Lecky, D., McNulty, C.: Teaching children hygiene using problem based learning: the story telling approach to games based learning. In: Proceedings of the 2nd Workshop on Story-Telling and Educational Games (STEG) (2009)
19. Farrell, D., Kostkova, P., Lazareck, L., Weerasinghe, D.: Cerc story-game engine: an open source technology to power story based investigation games. In: Proceedings of the Med-e-Tel, pp. 181–185 (2010)
20. Farrell, D., Kostkova, P., Weinberg, J., Lazareck, L., Weerasinghe, D., Lecky, D., McNulty, C.: Computer games to teach hygiene: an evaluation of the e-bug junior game. J. Antimicrob. Chemother. **66**(Suppl. 5), v39–v44 (2011)
21. Farrell, D., Kostkova, P., Lazareck, L., Weerasinghe, D., Weinberg, J., et al.: Developing web games to teach microbiology. J. Antimicrob. Chemother. **66**(Suppl 5), v33–v38 (2011)
22. Fishbein, M., Ajzen, I.: Belief, Attitude, Intention, and Behavior: An Introduction to Theory and Research. Addison-Wesley, Reading, MA (1975)
23. Fowler, D., Szomszor, M., Hammond, S., Lawrenson, J., Kostkova, P.: Engagement in online medical communities of practice in healthcare: analysis of messages and social networks. In: Kostkova, P., Szomszor, M., Fowler, D. (eds.) eHealth 2011. Lecture Notes in Computer Science, vol. 91, pp. 154–157. Springer, Berlin (2012)
24. Fox, E., Marchionini, G.: Progress towards digital libraries: augmentation through integration. Inf. Process. Manag. **35**, 219–225 (1999)
25. Gray, M.: On knowledge and disease. www.gurteen.com/gurteen/gurteen.nsf/id/knowledge-and-disease (2004)
26. Gray, M.J.A., de Lustignan, S.: National electronic library for health (NeLH). Br. Med. J. **319**, 1476–1479 (1999)
27. Higgins, R., Skelton, A., Hartley, P.: The conscientious consumer: reconsidering the role of assessment feedback in student learning. Stud. High. Educ. **27**(1), 53–54 (2009)
28. Jupp, S., Stevens, R., Bechhofer, S., Yesilada, Y., Kostkova, P.: Knowledge representation for web navigation. In: International Workshop on Semantic Web Applications and Tools for the Life Sciences (SWAT4LS 2008), November 2008
29. Koenitz, H., Ferri, G., Haahr, M., Sezen, D., Sezen, T.: Interactive Digital Narrative: History, Theory and Practice. Routledge, New York (2015)
30. Kostkova, P.: Grand Challenges in Digital Health. Front. Public Health **3**, 134 (2015)
31. Kostkova, P., Madle, G.: User-centred evaluation model for medical digital libraries. In: Riaño, D. (ed.) K4HelP 2008. Lecture Notes in Artificial Intelligence, vol. 5626, pp. 92–103. Springer, Berlin (2009)

32. Kostkova, P., Madle, G.: What impact do healthcare digital libraries have? An evaluation of national resource of infection control at the point of care using the Impact-ED framework. Int. J. Digit. Libr. **13**(2), 77–90 (2013)
33. Kostkova, P., Szomszor, M.: The FEM Wiki project: a conversion of a training resource for field epidemiologists into a collaborative Web 2. In: Szomszor, M., Kostkova, P. (eds.) Social-Informatics and Telecommunications Engineering. LNICST, vol. 69, pp. 119–126. Springer, Berlin (2011)
34. Kostkova, P., Mani-Saada, J., Weinberg, J.R.: Do you read the literature properly, and if you do how can others benefit from it. In: Proceedings of PHLS Conference (2002)
35. Kostkova, P., Mani-Saada, J., Weinberg, J., Madle, G.: User customisation of agent profiles in the national electronic library for communicable disease. In: Proceedings of HDL (2003)
36. Kostkova, P., et al.: Agent-based up-to-date data management in national electronic library for communicable disease. In: Nealon, J., Moreno, T. (eds.) Applications of Intelligent Agents in Health Care. Whitestein Series in Software Agent Technologies, pp. 105–124 (2003)
37. Kostkova, P., Diallo, G., Jawaheer, G.: User profiling for semantic browsing in medical digital libraries. In: Proceedings of the 5th European Semantic Web Conference (ESWC'08). Lecture Notes in Computer Science, vol. 5021, pp. 827–831. Springer, Berlin (2008)
38. Kostkova, P., Weinberg, J., Lecky, D., McNulty, C., Farrell, D., de Quincey, E.: ebug – teaching children hygiene principles using educational games. Stud. Health Technol. Inform. **160**, 600–604 (2010)
39. Kostkova, P., Fowler, D., Weinberg, J., Wiseman, S.: Major infection events over 5 years – how is media coverage influencing online information needs of healthcare professionals and the public? J. Med. Internet Res. **15**(7), e107 (2013)
40. Kostkova, P., Bosman, A., Prikazsky, V.: Femwiki: crowdsourcing semantic taxonomy and wiki input todomain experts while keeping editorial control: mission possible! In: Proceedings of Digital Health 2015, DH '15. ACM Press, New York (2015)
41. Madle, G.: Impact-ED: a new model of digital library evaluation. Ph.D. thesis, City University, London (2009)
42. Madle, G., Kostkova, P., Mani-Saada, J., Weinberg, J.R.: Evaluating the changes in knowledge and attitudes of digital library users. In: Research and Advanced Technology for Digital Libraries, pp. 29–40. Springer, Berlin (2003)
43. Madle, G., Kostkova, P., Mani-Saada, J., Weinberg, J., Williams, P.: Changing public attitudes to antibiotic prescribing: can the internet help? Inform. Prim. Care **12**(1), 19–26 (2004)
44. Madle, G., Kostkova, P., Mani-Saada, J., Roy, A.: Lessons learned from evaluation of the use of the national electronic library of infection. Health Informatics J. **12**(2), 137–151 (2006)
45. Madle, G., Kostkova, P., Roudsari, A.: Impacted – a new model of digital library impact evaluation. In: Proceedings of the ECDL 2008. Lecture Notes in Computer Science, vol. 5173, pp. 100–105. Springer, Berlin (2008)
46. Madle, G., Kostkova, P., Weinberg, J.: Bugs and drugs on the web: changes in knowledge of users of a web-based education resource on antibiotic prescribing. J. Antimicrob. Chemother. **63**(1), 221–223 (2009)
47. Madle, G., Menna, S., Kostkova, P., Berger, A., Cognat, S.: User information seeking behaviour: perceptions and reality. An evaluation of the WHO labresources internet portal. Inform. Health Soc. Care **34**(1), 30–38 (2009)
48. Mani-Saada, J., Madle, G., Williams, P., Kostkova, P.: Initial experience with developing communities of practice around the national electronic library for communicable disease. In: Proceedings of 1st Healthcare Digital Libraries Workshop (HDL 03) at ECDL (2003)
49. McNicol, S.: The eVALUEd toolkit: a framework for the qualitative evaluation of electronic information services. Vine **34**(4), 172–175 (2004)
50. Molnar, A., Kostkova, P.: If you build it would they play? Challenges and solutions in adopting games for children. In: Proceedings of ACM SIGCHI Conference on Human Factors in Computing Systems "Let's Talk About Failures: Why Was the Game for Children Not a Success?" (2013)

51. Molnar, A., Kostkova, P.: On effective integration of educational content in serious games: text vs game mechanics. In: IEEE International Conference on Advanced Learning Technologies, pp. 299–303 (2013)
52. Molnar, A., Kostkova, P.: Seamless evaluation integration into IDS educational games. In: International Conference on the Foundations of Digital Games, pp. 322–329 (2013)
53. Molnar, A., Kostkova, P.: Gaming to master the game-game usability and game mechanics. In: IEEE 3rd International Conference on Serious Games and Applications for Health (SeGAH), pp. 1–7. IEEE (2014)
54. Molnar, A., Kostkova, P.: Learning through interactive digital narratives. In: Koenitz, H., Ferri, G., Haahr, M., Sezen, D., Sezen, T.I. (eds.) Interactive Digital Narrative: History, Theory and Practice, pp. 200–210. Routledge, New York (2015)
55. Molnar, A., Kostkova, P.: Mind the gap – from desktop to app. In: Proceedings of Digital Health 2015, DH '15, pp. 15–16. ACM Press, New York (2015). doi:10.1145/2750511.2750537
56. Molnar, A., Farrell, D., Kostkova, P.: Who poisoned hugh? – the star framework: integrating learning objectives with storytelling. In: Oyarzun, D., Peinado, F., Young, R.M., Elizalde, A., Méndez, G. (eds.) Interactive Storytelling. Lecture Notes in Computer Science, vol. 7648, pp. 60–71. Springer, Berlin (2012)
57. Nickols, F.: Communities of Practice Roles & Responsibilities. Distance Consulting (2003)
58. Oliver, H., Diallo, G., de Quincey, E., Kostkova, P., Jawaheer, G., Alexopoulou, D., Habermann, B., Stevens, R., Jupp, S., Khelif, K., Schroeder, M., Madle, G.: A user-centered evaluation framework for the Sealife semantic web browsers. BMC Bioinf. 10(Suppl 10), S14 (2009). doi:10.1186/1471-2105-10-S10-S1
59. Rowley, J.: The wisdom hierarchy: representations of the DIKW hierarchy. J. Inf. Sci. 33(2), 163–180 (2007)
60. Roy, A., Kostkova, P., Carson, E., Catchpole, M.: Web-based provision of information on infectious diseases: a systems study. J. Health Inform. 12(4), 274–292 (2006)
61. Roy, A., Kostkova, P., Catchpole, M., Carson, E.: Do users do what they think they do? A comparative study of user perceived and actual information searching behaviour in the national electronic library of infection. In: Kostkova, P. (ed.) eHealth 2009. LNICST, vol. 27, pp. 96–103. Springer, Berlin (2010)
62. Smith, M.A., Kollock, P.: Communities in Cyberspace. Routledge, New York (1999)
63. Sxilas, N., Duman, J., Richle, U., Boggini, T.: Using highly interactive drama to help young people cope with traumatic situations. In: Interactive Storytelling. Lecture Notes in Computer Science, vol. 6432, pp. 279–282. Springer, Berlin (2010)
64. Szomszor, M., Kostkova, P., Cattuto, C., Barrat, A., Alani, H., Van den Broeck, W.: Providing enhanced social interaction services for industry exhibitors at large medical conferences. In: Developments in E-Systems Engineering (DeSE), pp. 42–45. IEEE (2011)
65. Torrente, J., O'Brien, B., Alesky, W., Fernandez-Manjon, B., Serrano-Laguna, Á., Fisk, C., Kostkova, P.: Introducing mokap: a novel approach to creating serious games. In: Proceedings of Digital Health 2015, DH '15. ACM Press, New York (2015)
66. Weerasinghe, D., Lazareck, L., Kostkova, P., Farrell, D: Evaluating of popularity of multilingual educational web games – do all children speak English? In: Szomszor, M., Kostkova, P. (eds.) ehealth 2010. LNICST, vol. 69, pp. 44–53. Springer, Berlin (2011)
67. Weinberg, J.R., Mani-Saada, J., Smith, K.: The national electronic library for communicable disease (NeLCD). In: FIS Conference, UK (2000)
68. Wenger, E.: Communities of Practice: Learning, Meaning and Identity. Cambridge University Press, Cambridge (1998)
69. Williams, P., Madle, G., Weinberg, J., Kostkova, P., Mani-Saada, J.: Information for the public about disease: usability issues in the development of the national electronic library for communicable diseases. Aslib Proc. New Inf. Perspect. 56(2), 99–103 (2004)
70. Wilson, T.D.: Models in information behaviour research. J. Doc. 55(3), 249–270 (1999)
71. Wiseman, S., Kostkova, P.: Where did infection prevention & control (IP & C) guidance and policy go? In: IPC 2013 Conference, London (2013)

72. Wiseman, S., Kostkova, P., D'Souza, S., Mani-Saada, J., Madle, G.: Evidence-based infection control – a national resource. Br. J. Infect. Control. **17**(3), 13–14 (2006)
73. Wiseman, S., Jawaheer, G., Kostkova, P.: Evidence and global access: the importance of sharing resources. In: Proceedings of ESCAIDE 2010 (2010)
74. Wiseman, S., Kostkova, P., de Quincey, E., Jawaheer, G.: Providing guidance during the swine flu outbreak in 2009: an evaluation study of the national resource for infection control (NRIC). In: Proceedings of the 14th International Conference on Infectious Diseases (ICID), vol. 14, p. e105 (2010)

# Engagement in Information Search

**Ashlee Edwards and Diane Kelly**

## 1 Introduction

Engagement is a multifaceted concept, and approaches to studying it vary across disciplines. In the education field, engagement is often understood to be the extent to which a student interacts with classroom material; research in this area often focuses on how teachers can present this material in more interesting and inviting ways [29]. In organizational psychology, the focus has been on how to create a workplace where employees stay invigorated and enthusiastic [40]. In cognitive psychology, engagement is studied from the perspective of understanding goal orientation, perceived ability, and motivation [31]. The common thread in all this work is the focus on creating positive subjective experiences for people so they stay motivated while performing activities. Engagement in the context of information search systems research has been anchored by similar goals: discovering what makes an interface (and search) engaging, creating search interfaces that promote engagement, and, to a lesser extent, understanding how to measure engagement. An underlying assumption of this work is that engagement creates a more positive search experience.

In this chapter, we focus on engagement in the context of interactive information search systems research, which "blends research from information retrieval (IR), information behavior, and human-computer interaction (HCI) to form a unique research specialty that is focused on enabling people to explore, resolve, and manage their information problems via interactions with information systems. Interactive information retrieval (IIR) research comprises studies of people's information search behaviors, their use of interfaces and search features, and their interactions with systems" [23, p. 745]. The main goal of an interactive information search

A. Edwards • D. Kelly (✉)
University of North Carolina at Chapel Hill, Chapel Hill, NC, USA
e-mail: aedwards@unc.edu; dianek@email.unc.edu

© Springer International Publishing Switzerland 2016                                    157
H. O'Brien, P. Cairns (eds.), *Why Engagement Matters*,
DOI 10.1007/978-3-319-27446-1_7

system is to help people resolve their information needs by providing a mechanism for them to interact with a set of information objects (e.g., web pages, scholarly research articles, newspaper articles). Typically, such interaction is initiated with a query and continues until the searcher has resolved his or her information need. This might take place during a single search episode or across multiple search episodes. This basic mode of search is perhaps best illustrated by reference to Google, where a searcher submits a keyword query describing his or her information need and receives a set of search results. The searcher can then use these results as a way to access content. Most of the studies reviewed in this chapter focus on retrieval of textual information objects, although a few studies focusing on other types of objects are included when appropriate. Most of the studies also focus on retrieval in the context of Internet-based systems and general-purpose search services that are freely available on the web, as opposed to proprietary database systems, search services associated with a single website or digital library, or enterprise search systems. Some systems are studied in their natural states (e.g., studies of Google or Yahoo!), while others are experimental systems where the researchers either modified a commercial system or created a completely new system.

We first review conceptualizations and definitions of engagement. Next, we discuss the contexts in which researchers have examined engagement, which provide insight about the multifaceted nature of engagement and how many different aspects of the search system and search experience can impact engagement. Specifically, we review work that considers engagement in the context of search user interfaces, search tasks, content and architecture, and individual differences. Following this, we describe several large-scale search log studies of engagement. Next, we discuss several studies that have attempted to compare, contrast, and integrate different measures of engagement. Finally, we conclude by considering the future of engagement in information search research.

## 2  Defining and Measuring User Engagement in Search

Researchers have primarily examined engagement by focusing on signals that can be extracted from search logs such as clicks and dwell time. A search log is "a file of the communications (i.e., transactions) between a system and the users of that system" [21, p. 408]. Communications that are typically studied include queries people issue, clicks people make on hyperlinks, and the amount of time between subsequent communications (e.g., dwell time). These communications are typically referred to as search interaction data or search behavior data. The use of search log signals is the most common way researchers have measured engagement.

Generally, the underlying assumption is greater frequency of certain behaviors, such as clicks and dwell times, indicates more engaged users. In other words, users who are more engaged will communicate more with the search system and communicate with it for a longer period of time. This approach to defining engagement can be observed in both large-scale studies of search logs and small-scale laboratory studies. Our examination of the literature also shows that the term *engagement* is increasingly being used to describe observed patterns and sets of search behaviors, even if it is not initially posited as a construct that drives research inquiry (cf. [15, 26]). Regardless of how it is defined, measured, or discussed, user engagement has become a key concern of information search systems researchers.

Search log signals can be useful since they provide information about a person's activities; however, using behavioral signals alone to define engagement is problematic because many of these same signals have been used to indicate other things about a person's search experience. For example, increases in behavioral signals have been used to indicate frustration, confusion about the task, uncertainty about where to find information, information relevance, and user satisfaction. Since these behavior-based measures do not capture the cognitive or affective parts of search engagement, important information about search context is missed. In addition, these signals alone do not wholly capture engagement as it has been conceptually defined in some of this research. For example, although Lehmann et al. [27] define engagement as the "quality of the user experience associated with a desire to use the web application" (p. 1), they only use behavioral signals to measure engagement, which do not adequately capture the quality of the experience or a person's desire to use an application. Solid measurement of latent constructs such as engagement relies on clear conceptual definitions of what is being measured as well as a clear mapping between conceptual and operational definitions (i.e., measures).

While much of the work has focused on using behavioral signals to measure engagement, O'Brien and colleagues [32–35] have used psychometric theory to create self-report measures to capture engagement. O'Brien and Toms [33] define engagement as a "category of user experience characterized by attributes of challenge, positive affect, endurability, aesthetic and sensory appeal, attention, feedback, variety/novelty, interactivity, and perceived user control" (p. 7). Building on this conceptual definition, O'Brien and Toms [34] created and evaluated a 31-item scale to measure engagement, called the user engagement scale (UES). Six attributes of engagement were identified using factor analysis: *perceived usability, aesthetics, focused attention, felt involvement, novelty,* and *endurability*, which capture the cognitive, affective, and usability-related attributes of user experience.

The UES is one of the first instruments to measure engagement in the context of information search. Importantly, it has undergone extensive validity and reliability testing [33, 34]. It is also one of the first measures of engagement designed to help researchers who are working more closely with users; while many of the behavioral-based measures are useful in the context of large-scale search log analysis, they do not characterize the entire user experience. Researchers often gather data directly from participants using questionnaires or interviews, and it is critical to have valid and reliable measures that allow researchers to obtain this type of feedback.

When considering how engagement has been studied in research with self-report measures such as those administered via questionnaires, it is important to distinguish between measures such as the UES, which have undergone extensive testing, and sets of questions researchers ask that have not been tested. Researchers without training in the behavioral sciences often group all self-report measures together and dismiss them because they are subjective. However, when constructed correctly, such measures can provide a valid and reliable signal. While many of the studies reviewed in this chapter elicit self-report data from research participants, in most cases, these items were created on an ad hoc basis, and there is no guarantee they adequately capture engagement. Such ad hoc collections of items also make it difficult to compare results across studies to generate a more thorough understanding of how and when engagement happens during information search and how it manifests itself in search behaviors.

Although the UES was initially evaluated in the context of e-commerce, it is increasingly being used to evaluate more general information search experiences [1, 4, 30]. Initial studies of its generalizability to the information search domain have been conducted [35] along with studies to understand its relationship to log data and other types of data such as physiological signals, eye tracking, and cursor movements [2, 32]. This work is discussed throughout this chapter. Ultimately, a variety of definitions and combinations of measures likely offer researchers the most robust understanding of search engagement and, depending on the type of study being conducted, different definitions and sets of measures might be more or less appropriate and feasible.

## 3 Search User Interfaces

The search user interface aids users "in the expression of their information needs, in the formulation of their queries, in the understanding of their search results, and in keeping track of the progress of their information-seeking efforts" [17, p. 1]. While researchers in information search have been interested in designing usable interfaces for quite some time, they have only recently moved beyond a focus on functional requirements and adopted the position that search interfaces should also be engaging and that search experiences should be pleasurable [6]. The work reviewed in this section has either used the UES to evaluate search interfaces or used terms like engagement when describing the goals and outcome of the work.

One of the first studies to use the UES to understand user experience in the context of search interfaces evaluated the display of vertical search results [4]. The study's authors examined differences between an interface that blended vertical results into web search engine results pages (SERPs) and an interface that displayed vertical results separately on individual SERPs that could be accessed via tabs. Arguello et al. [4] did not use the complete UES in their study and also made several modifications to the items they did use. This limited their ability to make strong claims about the validity of the modified set of items, which had been established in previous work [34]. However, previous testing of the UES was done in an e-commerce setting, and the authors argued that the changes were needed to make the scales more suitable for the evaluation of search interactions. Most of the changes consisted of replacing words like "shopping" with "searching." In addition, the researchers dropped the aesthetics subscale as the basic elements of the interface remained constant throughout. Finally, the researchers indicated they deleted one item from each of the attention and endurability subscales after pilot participants reacted unexpectedly to them. Ultimately, [4] used the UES subscales focused attention, felt involvement, perceived usability, and endurability and added a subscale about search effectiveness. Reliability analysis of responses to these modified subscales demonstrated that these items had good reliability.

Arguello et al. [4] did not find any significant differences between responses to these items according to interface. They went on to compare participants' interface preferences with their post-task questionnaire ratings on these subscales and found that people who preferred one interface rated it higher along all aspects, specifically for attributes such as endurability and perceived usability. Participants who preferred one of the interfaces said they found it more visually appealing and felt the information was better organized and easier to understand, reinforcing the importance of usability. These findings are interesting because they show that engagement is related to a person's preferences, and without knowing this preference, aggregate engagement scores for two or more interfaces might appear similar even when they produce different user experiences.

Moshfeghi et al. [30] evaluated whether adding a timeline and a named-entity component to a news search system would improve engagement and whether engagement could be predicted based on interaction data. They created a search interface where a participant clicked on search results that were presented on a timeline in order to access content. In addition to the timeline, they added a list of entities for a given search result. For example, for a given entry such as (US) republican debates, the named entity list contained items such as "Newt Gingrich," "Herman Cain," and "Rick Perry."

Participants were recruited from Mechanical Turk and given explicit instructions about the assignment and how much time they would have to complete it (120 min). Engagement was measured using the UES. Similar to [4], Moshfeghi et al. [30] modified the UES by changing the wording of the items for a news context, and each question was structured to ensure forced choice instead of a range of values. They found that participants who used the enhanced interface rated felt involvement, endurability, novelty, and aesthetics (subscales of the UES) higher, which demonstrates the importance of moving beyond a purely functional assessment to more completely understand the user's search experience.

Bateman et al. [5] created an interface where participants interacted with their previous search data and were able to compare themselves to three archetypes: the typical participants, search experts, and topical experts. Search experts were defined as frequent users of search operators, and topical experts were defined as having visited ten search results within the category. One version of the interface allowed participants to compare themselves to these archetypes, and the other did not. Engagement was derived from interactions found in participants' log data, specifically attributes such as time spent examining search results, likelihood of returning to the dashboard, and an affective learning dimension. The researchers (without mentioning engagement directly) also referenced engagement when they discussed participants' interest in learning and insights when using the interface.

Participants were most interested in and felt they gained more insight about themselves from the data about characteristics of search engine use and data on special search engine features and advanced query operators they viewed. Participants rated the comparison interface much higher than one that did not allow comparison and were also more likely to report that the comparison interface would alter their search behavior later. Unlike the studies described above, this study focused on people's interactions with personalized content.

The structure and layout of a website and search interface is referred to as a representational context. Representational context includes the designer's decisions about how to represent actions that can be performed (e.g., search box, search button), the placement of elements and icons on a page, and even the icons themselves. Subsequently, representational *stability* refers to the extent to which this representational context is maintained over the course of the entire search experience. Representational stability can be examined both within a single system and also across systems that are used to perform a similar function. For example, most major search systems employ interfaces that use a single box for query entry and a rank ordering of search results. Duin and Archee [13] posited that representational context must remain stable in order for the participant to become engaged.

Webster and Ahuja's research [46] supports the relationship between engagement and representational stability by developing a model of disorientation and engagement in web systems. This model states that navigation systems affect perceived disorientation, which affects engagement, which affects both performance and future use. Engagement was operationalized as when a system "holds [a subject's] attention and they are attracted to it for their intrinsic rewards" [20, p. 58] and was measured with a seven-item questionnaire that contained items such as "the site kept me totally absorbed in the browsing" or "the site held my attention." To evaluate their model, Webster and Ahuja [46] tested a simple navigation system against a global navigation system and an enhanced navigation system. The simple navigation system contained only hyperlinks, and these hyperlinks disappeared while the participant scrolled. The global navigation system contained a site map, a search form, and nested navigation bars (i.e., a parent topic contained child topics), but the navigational features also disappeared while scrolling. The enhanced global navigation system had the same features as the global one but kept the features visible while scrolling. Their findings supported the model in that participants in both the global and enhanced global navigation conditions reported less disorientation, and participants in the enhanced global navigation system had the best performance. This group's high performance was also positively related to engagement, showing that navigational aspects of a search interface can affect engagement. Perceptions of navigation and orientation are shown to help maintain representational integrity, providing a link between engagement and usability.

Feild et al. [15] also wanted to support orientation and engagement during the transition from the SERP to the content page by adding clickable snippets on the SERP. These snippets contained text from the document that matched the participant's query, and clicking on these snippets took participants directly to where that text was located in the document. Feild et al. [15] measured engagement with the system by calculating differences in views on the landing page, path length, gaze fixations, time until fixation on the answer passage, and scroll distance. They found that participants had lower time until fixation on the passage with the answer, lower fixations, and lower scroll distance when using the system with the clickable snippets with gradual transition. This indicates that for most of Feild et al.'s metrics, participants were engaged with and performed better using systems with clickable snippets. These results demonstrate that interventions can improve engagement and search performance, but they challenge prior notions that familiarity and comfort (i.e., a stable representational context) with a system are a necessary but not sufficient condition for engagement. More work is needed to understand what kinds of interventions improve engagement while not overwhelming the user.

This notion of stability is also supported by work on the effect of different user interface interaction modalities on engagement [42]. Interaction modality refers to mouse-based interaction patterns, specifically zoom, drag, slide, mouseover, cover flow, and click to download. Sundar et al. investigated these modalities on six artificial websites. Layout, page content, and color were kept constant between interaction modalities. These modalities allowed participants to access "hotspots" or links to information embedded in the website. Sundar et al. [42] defined engagement as a combination of participant attitudes, actions, skill, and behavior toward the content. They hypothesized that different types of interaction modalities would lead to different levels of perceptual bandwidth or the "range of sensory and preliminary attentional resources available to individuals" (p. 1478), referring to the resources a person has for understanding and perceiving interactivity in an interface; Sundar et al. defined this conceptually as "users memory for interface content" (p. 1478). Reeves and Nass [38] stated that perceptual bandwidth is increased by perceptual interfaces, which offer people "more and different sensory channels" (p. 65) than traditional interfaces. This suggests that perceptual interfaces or increases in perceptual bandwidth can change interest in the content of an interface.

Perceptual bandwidth was measured in terms of recall and recognition, perceived interactivity, actions, behavioral intention toward content and the website, and attitudes toward content. Sundar et al. [42] found significant differences between modalities; specifically, the slide modality showed higher recall than the zoom in/out modality. Participants who used the cover flow and mouseover actions performed more actions overall than the other modality types. Some participants preferred modality types that gave them more control over their content, while others preferred modality types that allowed them to perform more actions. Sundar et al. remind us that interaction modalities can make content more absorbing and generate positive feelings, which are closely related to the interest and cognitive absorption that occurs during engagement. The distinct preference for modality among participants indicates that users want to maintain representational stability, though representational stability may be subject to variation across individuals.

Sundar et al. [42] collected attitude data and found that certain actions such as the mouseover led to more positive attitudes than cover flow, which led to more negative attitudes. This also shows that some interaction types are generally more preferable than others. Some users, referred to as "power users" (who were identified based on a questionnaire containing items about liking, skill, and dependence on technology) preferred modality types that gave them more control over their content, while other users who were not "power users" preferred modality types that allowed them to perform more actions, demonstrating the importance of individual differences. Other research has suggested that control is important in engagement [46], and this work showed that control might be more critical to engaging some users than others.

Teevan et al.'s findings [43] challenge the notion of representational stability as necessary for engagement. In this study, Teevan et al. studied one important structural element of search systems: latency. Latency refers to the interval between an action and the response. High latency can be thought of as disruptive to representational stability because it disrupts a person's ability to maintain representational context. The purpose of this study was to examine how participants interacted with a search system that prioritized high-quality results over speed. Specifically, Teevan et al. looked at querying behavior with navigational queries (those that "targeted specific web pages" (p. 2)) and informational query types (those that are "intended to find information about a topic" (p. 2)). The researchers also examined two post-query behaviors: abandonment rate and time to first click. Engagement was examined and was defined as engagement with the search results in the form of more search interaction behaviors. Teevan et al. found that click frequency decreased as page load times increased, which the authors claimed signaled a loss of interest. However, the results showed no increase in search abandonment (which is also posited as evidence of disengagement) as load times increased. They explain this by stating there is a point beyond which load times can increase without causing higher search abandonment rates. It is also possible that the clicking was more deliberate, as participants anticipated the page load times and wanted to be sure they clicked on the most fruitful result. Participants were asked how long they would be willing to wait if they knew search engines would give them the best response, versus an acceptable response, and most said they were willing to wait much longer for the best response. This indicated that participants may be able to tolerate shifts in their representational context and adapt to them if they receive some benefit.

Arapakis et al. [1] investigated the impact of response latency on the click behavior of participants and the point at which response latency becomes noticeable in two studies. The first study looked at participants' sensitivity to latency and used two manipulations: response latency and site speed. Response latency refers to the time between a user's action and the perception of the response. Site speed was operationalized as either slow (a search site with a slow response) or fast (a search site with a fast response). They found that participants were more likely to notice the response latency if it climbed above 1000 ms. In the second study, they measured the effect of response latency on user engagement using the *focused attention* subscale of the UES (modified for a search context), satisfaction, and click behavior. They found a small effect for focused attention in participants in the fast condition, which suggests that these participants felt more deeply involved in the search task. They also found that though there were no significant differences in frustration, participants' positive search engine bias (the belief that the search system was helpful) was correlated with focused attention and perceived usability in both speed conditions. This suggests that search engine bias affects the way that participants interpret system response. Lastly, they found that participants were more likely to click on a result from a SERP that had been returned with low latency. This paper showed that conditions we may see as unfavorable to engagement (such as low latency) could encourage positive behaviors such as more examination of search results.

Work on engagement and search interfaces has shown that the interface can be crucial in fostering and maintaining engagement throughout the search session and that altering the traditional search interface to include elements that allow users to reflect on their own behaviors, and compare them to others, can potentially improve user engagement. This body of research also shows that representational stability, while important to engagement, may be one facet where individual differences are important. The literature reviewed here shows that users can tolerate shifts in their representational contexts and that users can express preferences for different kinds of interaction.

## 4  Search Tasks

When people decide to use an information search system, they often do so because they have an information need. In much of the search system research, a user's information need is encapsulated in a search task. This is especially true in laboratory studies where researchers assign search tasks to users so they have some (controlled and prescribed) reason to use a search system. Search tasks have been defined as "goal-directed activities carried out using search systems" [44, p. 1134] and as "a task that users need to accomplish through effective interaction with information systems" [28, p. 1823]. The impact of different types of search tasks on information search behavior and the user experience has been of great interest to information search researchers during the last 10 years [44]. While in the past researchers have measured task properties, such as difficulty and complexity [47], recently researchers have begun to evaluate the relationship between search tasks, search task properties (e.g., difficulty), and engagement.

O'Brien and Toms [35] evaluated the generalizability of the UES to exploratory search tasks by asking people to complete three complex, situated tasks that required them to make a decision. Using results from 381 participants, they found that the UES factor loadings differed from those observed in the initial evaluation of the UES, which was evaluated in the context of an e-commerce setting [34]. While the perceived usability, aesthetics, and focused attention factors remained distinct, the novelty, felt involvement, and endurability were indistinguishable. They also found a negative correlation between focused attention and perceived usability, which differed from the original study [33]. O'Brien and Toms explain this by stating that the laboratory setting may have impacted the relationship between flow and usability and that in naturalistic settings, flow and usability may be more closely correlated. The assigned tasks may have inhibited the participant's ability to achieve a flow state. Focused attention scores were also lower than scores for other factors, which O'Brien and Toms [33] speculate was a result of participants' focus on task completion rather than on the content of the task.

Jiang et al. [22] illustrated the importance of task when they measured how different kinds of tasks affected search behavior, relevance judgments, and interest. While Jiang et al. did not conceptually define engagement, they used the term interest when characterizing participants' search behaviors. Participants were given tasks defined by a goal (specific or amorphous) and the required information behavior (either factual or intellectual). These two dimensions created four sets of tasks: known item (factual and well defined), known subject (factual and amorphous), interpretive (intellectual and well defined), and exploratory (intellectual and amorphous). Jiang et al. measured interest in the search results by unique clicks per query, unique fixations per query, and SERP views per query. All of these behavioral measures dropped significantly over the course of the search session, and Jiang et al. present this as evidence that a person's interest in the search task decreased during the course of the search session. When considered alongside O'Brien and Toms' findings [35], this finding is likely related to the search context, that is, a laboratory study with assigned search tasks and a task time limit. While these findings might have limited applicability to real-world search, especially when task time is unlimited, they suggest what researchers might expect when assigning search tasks with a fixed search time to research participants; that is, participants might begin to disengage as they approach the task time limit. This is also consistent with conceptual model of engagement in [33], which depicted points of disengagement arising from external forces and constraints.

It is also useful to consider the work of Borlund et al. [8] and others [9, 37] who have investigated differences in user experience and interest between assigned search tasks and genuine search tasks, or search tasks created by users, as this work demonstrates how the content of the task can potentially impact engagement. This is consistent with earlier conceptualizations of flow, where interest in one's task was found to be central to experiences of flow [12] and Borlund's recommendations [7] that simulated work tasks be those to which participants relate and find topically interesting. Borlund et al. [8] found that 76 % of participants attributed time spent searching on their genuine task to it being interesting versus 38 % for a simulated task. They also found that participants spent more time searching during genuine tasks and generally found them more difficult. This finding is interesting since it suggests that difficulty is, in part, related to interest in the task, and in an unexpected way. It might be the case that when a person is more interested in a task, they have more emotional investment, which translates into greater perceptions of task difficulty. Poddar and Ruthven [37] found that participants had greater positive emotions and made more use of various search strategies when completing their own search tasks versus assigned search tasks, so the source of the task can impact user experience and effort expended.

While the studies described above focused on understanding how search task properties impact engagement, at least one study has examined the relationship between search task type and engagement in the context of creating reusable tasks for laboratory search studies [24]. Kelly et al. [24] created and evaluated a set of search tasks that were proposed to vary in terms of cognitive complexity. The researchers examined participants' behaviors as they completed tasks of different levels of cognitive complexity as well as their ratings of these tasks along a number of dimensions, including difficulty and engagement. The hope was that more cognitively complex tasks would be rated as more engaging because of the increasing amounts of cognition they required. Results showed that the two most cognitively complex tasks were rated as significantly more engaging than the least cognitively complex task. Participants also exhibited significantly more effort (e.g., queries, clicks) completing more cognitively complex tasks, which is aligned with work that posits increased search behavior is related to increased engagement. The difficulty, of course, is untangling temporal order to show cause and effect; that is, do more engaging tasks cause a person to exhibit more search effort, or does more search effort cause a person to become more engaged?

Interestingly, in Kelly et al.'s study [24], when participants were asked to rank tasks according to level of engagement, the signal was not as clear (except for the least cognitively complex tasks which were mostly rated as the least engaging). This result suggests that the content of the task likely played a role in engagement and, more specifically, the user's interest in the content. This implies that researchers who are constructing assigned search tasks for laboratory use should not only consider the structure of the tasks but also the topic of the tasks if they wish to study searchers who are engaged. Of course, discovering what interests an individual participant before a study becomes a challenge as well as maintaining some parity among the potentially large number of topical areas that are likely to interest participants. Thus, an important future research direction is to understand how search tasks can be developed to foster or inhibit engagement in experimental settings.

## 5 Content and Architecture

In the previous section, we discussed how the content of a search task potentially impacts a person's experiences of engagement. Research has also shown that the content of the information sources with which a user interacts plays an important role in engagement. Arapakis et al. [3] used the *focused attention* subscale of the UES in conjunction with other measures to observe what attributes of news articles and comments were important to participants. They examined several attributes: genre, sentimentality of the article (the richness of the emotional tone of the article), polarity (positivity or negativity), and time of publication. Articles were then selected from three categories: crime, entertainment, and science. Participants indicated their interest before and after the task. Arapakis et al. found that participants who read articles they labeled as interesting exhibited higher levels of focused attention. They also found that interest in the article and enjoyment experienced from reading it were higher when the topic of the article had a strong sentiment and negative connotations.

Linking content focus and attention, Rokhlenko et al. [39] looked at how interest in peripheral content, such as advertisements, varied based on interest in the primary content on the page. Participants (Mechanical Turk workers) were asked to read news articles until they felt they had discovered the purpose of an article and then were instructed to answer questions based on the text. Results showed most participants missed the ads entirely; only a quarter of participants paid any attention to the ad image surrogates. Rokhlenko et al. [39] found that participants who spent a lot of time reading the content on a web page had higher recall for the advertisement images than participants who read less. If interest can serve as an indicator of engagement, then this study showed that engagement with content could lead to higher recall for peripheral images. This study also helps confirm that when participants are engaged, they tend to display deeper information processing behaviors such as reading and absorbing more content. If engaged participants are able to recall many different types of information, then it is possible that engagement could lend itself to expanding attentional resources.

Song et al. [41] examined whether degraded search relevance had an effect on engagement. The researchers defined engagement both in terms of frequency of search engine reuse and behavioral signals. Participants in this study were given a search algorithm that provided low-quality search results or received the normal search engine algorithm. Song et al. analyzed the session data of search logs from 2.2 million users. Query attributes such as queries issued per session, length, success, click-through rate, type, and session length as well as frequency of search engine usage were used to measure engagement. Song et al. found that though engagement decreased overall, there was some indication that participants might have been engaged. Participants in the treatment group issued more queries overall, issued more navigational queries, reformulated their queries more, and clicked on more results. They surmise that this search behavior could reflect increased effort, a consequence of struggling to complete the search with poor search results. This means that, for the engagement metrics defined in this study, engagement was initially negatively correlated with relevance. Song et al. then tried to predict engagement using search behaviors and found that the number of clicks was the highest correlated feature with engagement. This study established a link between behavioral signals and engagement as induced by effort. In particular, effort invokes the factors of felt involvement and focused attention, which, as this study showed, can be induced by negative influences rather than positive ones.

Perhaps the most revealing studies are those that combine changes in both content and navigational structure. Chen et al. [10] examined the effect of disorientation on engagement with a website given the breadth, familiarity, and media richness of the site. Two websites were created with different structures: the "broad" structure contained two levels, while the "deep" structure contained four levels. Familiar sites contained stationery products, while unfamiliar sites contained industrial products. Media richness was also manipulated; "media rich" sites contained images and videos, while "lean media" sites contained only text. Chen et al. [10] found that participants preferred websites that had a deeper structure and were more engaged with a site that had unfamiliar structure and lean media richness in addition to deeper structure. Higher disorientation was linked to less engagement and lower intentions to use the website in future. This study shows that engagement does not always occur when a participant is completely comfortable and familiar with a web interface. Rather, a combination of novelty and familiarity can foster engagement.

Colbert and Boodoo [11] examined the effect of web content noncompliance on engagement. Some attributes of noncompliance were minor, such as grammatical errors, but also included direct barriers to information-seeking such as a lack of same-page links and obscure heading levels. Participants were subject to an advertising campaign on both sites, and there were 11 advertisements, with between 7 and 43 keywords and phrases per advertisement. Four attributes of engagement were defined in this study: time spent on site, pages per visit, ratio of revisits to first visit, and bounce rate, or whether the participant spends time on a single page only versus multiple pages. They found the compliant website more engaging across all metrics and in particular for return visits. Colbert and Boodoo believed that web standard compliance in the form of fewer well-placed words increases engagement. This study suggests that engagement can occur at the micro-level; if the structure and content of a site does not facilitate information-seeking, then a person will not be engaged and may leave the site prematurely. It is encouraging as it suggests that by following web standards, website designers can increase the engagement of their sites. These studies demonstrate that the content of a search system is just as important as the representational context in keeping users engaged with a website, suggesting that engagement is highly sensitive to both major and minor changes in a search interface.

# 6 Individual Differences

So far, we have discussed how interface features, search tasks, and information content and design relate to engagement. Individual differences have also been shown to have an effect on engagement. Heinstrom [18] looked at the relationship among individual differences, information-seeking behaviors, and engagement in the context of a naturalistic study. The individual differences investigated included personality traits, learning approach preferences, and disciplinary differences. Master's students writing theses were chosen to participate, and three questionnaires were used: the NEO Five-Factor Inventory, the Approaches and Study Skills Inventory for Students, and a questionnaire about information-seeking behaviors. Three information-seeking patterns were discovered: fast surfing, broad scanning, and deep diving. Fast surfing was a search pattern characterized by minimal effort in both information-seeking behaviors and content analysis, while broad scanning was an exploratory search pattern characterized by wide searches and many information searches. Deep diving, however, was characterized by expending considerable effort on the search as well as looking for high-quality documents. The behavior most closely related to engagement was deep diving. Heinstrom [18] noted that they seemed "focused and structured" (p. 1446) in their searches and searched to gain a thorough understanding of the topic rather than just scanning for information. There was also an interaction among information-seeking pattern, engagement, and content: broad scanners were more engaged with documents that gave them new information, while fast surfers were more interested in documents that were easy to read and were less academically challenging. Topical engagement was more likely to occur in relaxed settings presumably because of the absence of time pressure.

This work supports the notion that engagement is highly context and topic dependent. Since the students in this study were completing master's theses, there was an inherent interest in the topic and task that likely lent natural motivation to searches. These results also suggest that differences in personality and information-seeking styles will impact what experiences a person finds engaging. This finding is similar to the one described in [4], where participants' engagement ratings were tied to their interface preferences.

## 7  Large-Scale Analysis of Commercial Search Logs

Lehmann and colleagues have conducted a number of studies that provide a good illustration of how engagement has been studied in the context of large-scale search logs [25–27]. In one of their first studies, Lehmann et al. [25] proposed and evaluated three interaction-based models of engagement: a general model, a time-based model, and a user-based model. Using search log data from millions of people, three measures of engagement were defined and examined in the context of each model: popularity, activity, and loyalty. *Popularity* was defined as the number of users that visit a site (including number of clicks). *Loyalty* was defined as the frequency with which a person returns to a site and how often they dwell on the site. *Activity* was defined as total dwell time on the site and number of page views per visit. Lehmann et al.'s general model of engagement [25] focused primarily on popularity and clicks on a site, the time-based model was more focused on loyalty, and the user-based model was more focused on an individual user's behavioral patterns.

Lehmann et al. [26] continued this work by proposing the concept of *networked user engagement*, which refers to engagement within a network of websites. This work focused on user clicks among different websites and posited users with high network engagement would make clicks among the websites within the network. They found that users performed more goal-oriented behaviors on a weekday (Wednesday), while they performed more browsing activities on the weekend. They also found that some users who were more active with regard to search behavior (referred to as VIP users) navigated more frequently between sites and had higher rates of return to previously visited sites than users who were less active. This conceptualization differed from the previous one in that it focused on activity within a collection of websites as opposed to activity at an individual website.

Lehmann et al. [27] furthered their work on engagement by focusing on user engagement with many tasks simultaneously and analyzed online multitasking and engagement using two behavioral signals: dwell time and page views. Transforming these signals into metrics like attention shift, attention range, cumulative actions, visits, and sessions, Lehmann et al. grouped different kinds of sites based on levels of engagement and proposed a model in which dwell time and page views were conceptualized as tree-streams, or paths through which participants click at the session level. Shopping and mail sites were found to have high activity per visit and also short times between visits, indicating that participants progressively became more focused on their tasks. Search sites, front pages, and auction sites had lower dwell time overall but higher dwell time per session and had high cumulative activity numbers, indicating that participants spent more time completing more activities. The most engaging set of sites had high ranges of attention shift and attention range, indicating that when participants did return to the site, they spent more time than before.

Dupret and Lalmas [14] investigated the usefulness of absence time, or the time between two user visits, as a metric of user engagement. This was based on the assumption that users who are engaged will return to a site sooner, meaning that their absence times will be shorter. Most unique to this work was that the researchers used survival analysis. Survival analysis is based on a "death and resuscitation" model, whereby users "survive" past a given time, and "hazard rate," which refers to the probability a user will die at a given time; thus, a higher hazard rate implies a lower survival rate. In this example, a high hazard rate is associated with a lower absence time (meaning a user is returning more frequently). They found that faster time to click was associated with higher hazard rate, suggesting that if users click quickly, they are likely more engaged. They suggest that click three, which contributed weakly to the hazard rate of five clicks, may be associated with greater user engagement because it suggests more perusal of search results and thus more cognitive investment. Lastly, they found more views than distinct queries are associated with longer absence times.

Finally, Ortiz-Cordova and Jansen [36] investigated whether behavioral signals could be used to identify "high-revenue" participants, or those who were more engaged with site content and advertisements. They defined engagement in terms of new visits, number of pages visited during the duration of the session, time spent on a site, click-through rate, ads clicked, ad impressions, and rate of return to the site. The researchers classified participants into three clusters, low, medium, and highly engaged, and identified different kinds of revenue streams generated by each cluster. Participants in the highly engaged cluster spent the most time on the site, visited the most content, and clicked on the most ads, while those in the low engagement cluster typically visited few pages and clicked on little content. Generally, revenue streams were higher if participants clicked on the ads and had a higher number of page visits.

## 8 Multiple Measures of Engagement

We started this chapter by discussing how engagement has been defined and measured in information search research. We turn our attention back to this topic by examining studies that have attempted to combine different measures including behavioral measures, self-report measures, and eye-tracking and physiological data. While many of the studies discussed above used both objective and subjective measures of engagement, researchers have only recently started investigating how these measures are related to one another, along with other types of measures. O'Brien and Lebow [32] used the UES in conjunction with the Cognitive Absorption and System Usability Scales to examine which attributes were important during information-seeking experiences within an online news context. They combined these self-report measures with physiological signals in order to get a better understanding of engagement. Participants completed one task, with a time limit of 20 min, followed by the psychometric scales and an interview. O'Brien and Lebow [32] found that participants who rated their level of interest in an article higher were also more engaged. They also found that participants who were less engaged spent more time browsing and visited more web pages but had increased physiological signals. Participants who reported the highest levels of engagement spent the least amount of time browsing, visited the least amount of web pages, and spent the least time reading but had lower physiological signals. This study also found low, negative correlations between physiological signals and the psychometric scales used.

Arapakis et al. [2] investigated the usefulness of mouse gestures and gaze behavior as possible indicators of engagement with search results. Participants were given one interesting and one uninteresting news-related task (and a corresponding corpus) and had their cursor movements and eye fixations recorded. In addition to this, affect was measured via the PANAS and focused attention subscale of the UES, modified to reflect a news context. Arapakis et al. found a correlation between gaze behavior and engagement, specifically that participants had more fixations when reading an interesting article, looked more at the content of the article, and had longer visits. When the article was not interesting to participants, they fixated on other content on the page. Arapakis et al. also found that negative emotions had a greater influence on mouse movements than positive ones, suggesting that lack of engagement may be more detectable through cursor movement than engagement.

In our review, we found two studies by Grafsgaard and colleagues that have used part of the UES to evaluate intelligent tutoring systems, along with facial expression analysis and skin conductance [16, 45]. Grafsgaard et al. [16] were interested in investigating the usefulness of facial expression analysis in understanding the affective states of engagement and frustration. Sixty-five participants interacted with a programming tutor through a web interface. Their facial expressions and skin conductance were recorded, though the researchers did not report the skin conductance results in their paper. Students were given the endurability subscale of the UES, modified for a learning context, as well as questions about temporal demand, performance, and frustration from the NASA-TLX. They found that endurability was predicted by rises in participants' inner eyebrows, while temporal demand was predicted by rises in participants' outer eyebrows. Performance was predicted by mouth dimpling, and frustration was predicted by brow lowering. The major contribution of this paper was its linkages of facial expressions to measures of engagement and frustration.

In a follow-up study, Vail et al. [45] reviewed the utility of one of the Big Five personality traits (extraversion and its opposite introversion) in conjunction with facial and postural gestures as predictors of engagement and frustration. Seventy-seven participants had their personality traits measured and facial and postural gestures recorded during a web-based tutoring session. Engagement was measured via the focused attention, felt involvement, and endurability subscales of the UES, modified for a learning context. They found that feedback from the tutor was a feature of the predictive model for extraverts and that engagement and learning gains were positively and negatively affected by feedback from the tutor. Frustration was more often correlated with changes in posture and seat movement for extraverts. For introverts, engagement was correlated with forward postural movements, while frustration was correlated with backward postural movements, indicating that introverts express their feelings behaviorally rather than with dialogue. This study reinforces the idea that individual differences, and specifically personality differences, can play a role in how a person experiences and expresses engagement.

# 9   Conclusions

It has been observed that engagement is integral to system success [19], and the work reviewed in this chapter supports this idea. System success is a complex mix of attributes such as system response time, content and results quality, the user interface, and subjective experience. While in the past research in the area of information search has emphasized the functional aspects of search systems such as performance and usability, there has been growing interest in creating engaging search experiences for searchers and understanding more about searchers' emotional experiences during search. This chapter reviewed some of the research within the information search research specialty that has focused on engagement and related constructs like interest.

This review illustrated the challenges of studying engagement. The extent to which someone is engaged depends on a variety of factors including the structure and ease of use of the system, performance of the system, content within it, complexity and difficulty of search tasks, how searchers perceive all of these variables, and whatever individual differences they bring to the search situation. Our role as researchers is to meet the needs of searchers by understanding how these aspects contribute to experiences of engagement and subsequently applying this understanding to the design of search tools that foster engaging experiences. In recent years, information search research has been dominated by studies of searchers' interactions with SERPs; an interesting consequence of focusing on engagement is that now a wider view including both interactions with SERPs and the information objects themselves is required.

One way we can address some of the challenges of studying engagement is to examine both the behavior of the searcher and their subjective experiences. While it is easy to discount self-report data as flawed and unreliable, searchers are really the only ones who can tell us if they are engaged. It is also easy to discount behavioral-based measures because they can be ambiguous and only represent the potential manifestation of engagement. However, this physical manifestation is an important part of engagement and provides a useful and unobtrusive way to operationalize engagement. In many environments and contexts, especially at scale, it is not possible to ask people about their experiences, so refining the use of these signals as standalone measures is important. The examination of physiological signals, facial expressions, and eye-tracking data, along with behavioral and self-report measures, are likely productive ways to start refining theoretical models of engagement and methods for measuring engagement in different contexts.

# References

1. Arapakis, I., Bai, X., Cambazoglu, B.B.: Impact of response latency on user behavior in web search. In: Proceedings of the 37th International ACM SIGIR Conference on Research & Development in Information Retrieval, pp. 103–112 (2014)
2. Arapakis, I., Lalmas, M., Valkanas, G.: Understanding within-content engagement through pattern analysis of mouse gestures. In: Proceedings of the 23rd ACM International Conference on Conference on Information and Knowledge Management, pp. 1439–1448 (2014)
3. Arapakis, I., Lalmas, M., Cambazoglu, B.B., Marcos, M.C., Jose, J.M.: User engagement in online news: under the scope of sentiment, interest, affect, and gaze. J. Assoc. Inf. Sci. Technol. **65**, 1988–2005 (2014)
4. Arguello, J., Wu, W.C., Kelly, D., Edwards, A.: Task complexity, vertical display and user interaction in aggregated search. In: Proceedings of the 35th International ACM SIGIR Conference on Research and Development in Information Retrieval, pp. 435–444 (2012)
5. Bateman, S., Teevan, J., White, R.W.: The search dashboard: how reflection and comparison impact search behavior. In: Proceedings of the SIGCHI Conference on Human Factors in Computing Systems, pp. 1785–1794. ACM Press, New York (2012)
6. Belkin, N.J.: Some(what) grand challenges for information retrieval. SIGIR Forum **42**, 47–54 (2008)
7. Borlund, P.: The IIR evaluation model: a framework for evaluation of interactive information retrieval systems. Inf. Res. **8**(3), 1–5 (2003)
8. Borlund, P., Dreier, S., Byström, K.: What does time spent on searching indicate? In: Proceedings of the 4th Information Interaction in Context Symposium, pp. 184–193 (2012)
9. Capra, R., Sams, B., Seligson, P.: Self-generated versus imposed tasks in collaborative search. In: Collaborative Information Seeking: Bridging the Gap Between Theory and Practice (CIS). Workshop at the Meeting of the American Society for Information Science and Technology (2011)
10. Chen, J.V., Lin, C., Yen, D.C., Linn, K.P.: The interaction effects of familiarity, breadth and media usage on web browsing experience. Comput. Hum. Behav. **27**, 2141–2152 (2011)

11. Colbert, M., Boodoo, A.: Does' letting go of the words' increase engagement: a traffic study. In: ACM CHI 2011 Extended Abstracts on Human Factors in Computing Systems, pp. 655–667. ACM Press, New York (2011)
12. Csikszentmihalyi, M.: Flow: The Psychology of Optimal Experience. Harper-Perennial, New York (1991)
13. Duin, A.H., Archee, R.: Distance learning via the world wide web: information, engagement, and community. In: Selber, S. (ed.) Computers and Technical Communication: Pedagogical and Programmatic Perspectives, pp. 149–169. Erlbaum, Hillsdale, NJ (1997)
14. Dupret, G., Lalmas, M.: Absence time and user engagement: evaluating ranking functions. In: Proceedings of the 6th ACM International Conference on Web Search and Data Mining, pp. 173–182. ACM Press, New York (2013)
15. Feild, H., White, R.W., Fu, X.: Supporting orientation during search result examination. In: Proceedings of the SIGCHI Conference on Human Factors in Computing Systems, pp. 2999–3008. ACM Press, New York (2013)
16. Grafsgaard, J.F., Wiggins, J.B., Boyer, K.E., Wiebe, E.N., Lester, J.C.: Automatically recognizing facial expression: predicting engagement and frustration. In: Proceedings of the 6th International Conference on Educational Data Mining, pp. 43–50 (2013)
17. Hearst, M.: Search User Interfaces. Cambridge University Press, Cambridge (2009)
18. Heinström, J.: Broad exploration or precise specificity: two basic information seeking patterns among students. J. Am. Soc. Inf. Sci. Technol. **57**, 1440–1450 (2006)
19. Hwang, M.I., Thorn, R.G.: The effect of user engagement on system success: a meta-analytical integration of research findings. Inf. Manag. **35**(4), 229–336 (1999)
20. Jacques, R., Precce, J, Carey, J.T.: Engagement as a design concept for hypermedia. Can. J. Educ. Commun. **24**, 49–59 (1995)
21. Jansen, B.J.: Search log analysis: what it is, what's been done, how to do it. Libr. Inf. Sci. Res. **28**, 407–432 (2006)
22. Jiang, J., He, D., Allan, J.: Searching, browsing, and clicking in a search session: changes in user behavior by task and over time. In: Proceedings of the 37th International ACM SIGIR Conference on Research & Development in Information Retrieval, pp. 607–616. ACM Press, New York (2014)
23. Kelly, D., Sugimoto, C.R.: A systematic review of interactive information retrieval evaluation studies, 1967–2006. J. Am. Soc. Inf. Sci. Technol. **64**(4), 745–770 (2013)
24. Kelly, D., Arguello, J., Edwards, A., Wu, W.C.: Development and evaluation of search tasks for IIR experiments using a cognitive complexity framework. In: Proceedings of SIGIR International Conference on the Theory of Information Retrieval, pp. 7–10 (2015)
25. Lehmann, J., Lalmas, M., Yom-Tov, E., Dupret, G.: Models of user engagement. In: User Modeling, Adaptation, and Personalization, pp. 164–175 (2012)
26. Lehmann, J., Lalmas, M., Baeza-Yates, R., Yom-Tov, E.: Networked user engagement. In: Proceedings of the 1st Workshop on User Engagement Optimization, pp. 7–10 (2013)
27. Lehmann, J., Lalmas, M., Dupret, G., Baeza-Yates, R.: Online multitasking and user engagement. In: Proceedings of the 22nd ACM International Conference on Information and Knowledge Management, pp. 519–528 (2013)
28. Li, Y., Belkin, N.J.: A faceted approach to conceptualizing tasks in information seeking. Inf. Process. Manag. **44**, 1822–1837 (2008)
29. Linnenbrink, E.A., Pintrich, P.R.: The role of self-efficacy beliefs in student engagement and learning in the classroom. Read. Writ. Q. **19**(2), 119–137 (2003)
30. Moshfeghi, Y., Matthews, M., Blanco, R., Jose, J.M.: Influence of timeline and named-entity components on user engagement. In: Advances in Information Retrieval, pp. 305–317 (2013)
31. Nes, L.S., Segerstrom, S.C., Sephton, S.E.: Engagement and arousal: optimism's effects during a brief stressor. Personal. Soc. Psychol. Bull. **31**(1), 111–120 (2005)
32. O'Brien, H., Lebow, M.: Mixed-methods approach to measuring user experience in online news interactions. J. Am. Soc. Inf. Sci. Technol. **64**, 1543–1556 (2013)
33. O'Brien, H., Toms, E.G.: What is user engagement? A conceptual framework for defining user engagement with technology. J. Am. Soc. Inf. Sci. Technol. **59**, 938–955 (2008)

34. O'Brien, H., Toms, E.G.: The development and evaluation of a survey to measure user engagement. J. Am. Soc. Inf. Sci. Technol. **61**, 50–69 (2010)
35. O'Brien, H., Toms, E.G.: Examining the generalizability of the user engagement scale (UES) in exploratory search. Inf. Process. Manag. **49**, 1092–1107 (2013)
36. Ortiz-Cordova, A., Jansen, B.J.: Classifying web search queries to identify high revenue generating customers. J. Am. Soc. Inf. Sci. Technol. **63**, 1426–1441 (2012)
37. Poddar, A., Ruthven, I.: The emotional impact of search tasks. In: Proceedings of the 3rd Symposium on Information Interaction in Context, pp. 35–44 (2010)
38. Reeves, B., Nass, C.: The Media Equation: How People Treat Computers, Television, and New Media Like Real People and Places. Cambridge University Press, New York, NY (1996)
39. Rokhlenko, O., Golbandi, N., Lempel, R., Leibovich, L.: Engagement-based user attention distribution on web article pages. In: Proceedings of the 24th ACM Conference on Hypertext and Social Media, pp. 196–201 (2013)
40. Schaufeli, W.B., Salanova, M.: Enhancing work engagement through the management of human resources. In: Naswall, K., Hellgren, J., Sverke, M. (eds.) The Individual in the Changing Working Life, pp. 380–402. Cambridge University Press, Cambridge (2008)
41. Song, Y., Shi, X., Fu, X.: Evaluating and predicting user engagement change with degraded search relevance. In: Proceedings of the 22nd International Conference on World Wide Web, pp. 1213–1224 (2013)
42. Sundar, S.S., Xu, Q., Bellur, S., Oh, J., Jia, H.: Beyond pointing and clicking: how do newer interaction modalities affect user engagement? In: CHI'11 Extended Abstracts on Human Factors in Computing Systems. ACM Press, New York (2011)
43. Teevan, J., Collins-Thompson, K., White, R.W., Dumais, S.T., Kim, Y.: Slow search: information retrieval without time constraints. In: Proceedings of the Symposium on Human-Computer Interaction and Information Retrieval, pp. 1–10 (2013)
44. Toms, E.: Task-based information searching and retrieval. In: Ruthven, I., Kelly, D. (eds.) Task-Based Information Searching and Retrieval, pp. 43–59 (2011)
45. Vail, A.K., Grafsgaard, J.F., Wiggins, J.B., Lester, J.C., Boyer, K.E.: Predicting learning and engagement in tutorial dialogue: a personality-based model. In: Proceedings of the 16th International Conference on Multimodal Interaction, pp. 255–262 (2014)
46. Webster, J., Ahuja, J.S.: Enhancing the design of web navigation systems: the influence of user disorientation on engagement and performance. MIS Q. **30**, 661–678 (2006)
47. Wildemuth, B.W., Freund, L., Toms, E.G.: Untangling search task complexity and difficulty in the context of interactive information retrieval studies. J. Doc. **70**, 1118–1140 (2014)

# User Engagement with Interactive Media: A Communication Perspective

**Jeeyun Oh and S. Shyam Sundar**

## 1 Introduction

Recently, Google launched "Engagement Ads" with the goal of optimizing "user engagement." According to Google, this new model of advertising metric will replace the old pay-per-click model—by which advertisers are charged every time users click an ad regardless of whether they have actually watched or read it. Instead, engagement ads expand a display ad once the user has hovered over it for 2 s. This 2-s hover is considered evidence that the ad has grabbed the users' attention and they are ready to be further engaged with the content.

The idea of a *cost-per-engagement* model is not new. Advertising researchers and industry professionals have long wondered how to effectively measure user engagement with digital media content, going beyond simple clicking or hovering. Digital media offer unprecedented opportunities for both users and content providers—users can control what they want to see, while content providers can create more interactive, engaging content and precisely track users' behaviors. With the rise of new media, we have an abundance of media technology that could aid the communication process between users and message sources. Users can personalize their media settings, choose what they want to see, be involved in social networks, and control the pace and format of information they want to receive.

Interactivity is perhaps the most distinguishable feature of modern media technology that could summarize all these capabilities. Interactivity allows users to take a number of actions that control information flow instead of passively

J. Oh (✉)
Robert Morris University, Moon Township, PA, USA
e-mail: oh@rmu.edu

S.S. Sundar
The Pennsylvania State University, University Park, PA, USA
e-mail: sss12@psu.edu

© Springer International Publishing Switzerland 2016
H. O'Brien, P. Cairns (eds.), *Why Engagement Matters*,
DOI 10.1007/978-3-319-27446-1_8

receiving it, providing various interaction techniques—e.g., users can swipe, zoom, and mouse over content on a website and click through several layers of hyperlinks to open hidden content. As the term itself implies, interactivity rests on the notion of active users who can control both media content and interface. Interactivity has been defined in several different ways—two-way, reciprocal communication and synchronicity [40, 50], personalization capability of the system [35, 78], the degree of user control [42, 58], and technological affordances that allow users to determine the medium, source, and message of communication [62]. In this chapter, we adopt the last mentioned definition of interactive media, with a focus on the three central elements of communication.

For communication researchers, interactive media call for a completely new way of studying user engagement. Researchers now want to take into account users' capabilities to change the content and form of mediated messages. The key question is, when interactive media allow users to intervene in the process of message delivery, are users more engaged with the media content? Or, do interactive media merely distract users from the content, with interface features that consume users' cognitive capacity? Over the last few decades, communication researchers have made significant progress in answering these questions. Scholars have debated whether the interactive components of the website can engage users or simply distract them [8, 13, 60–62]. Up to this point, previous studies in the field have focused on examining whether interactive media pose an opportunity or a challenge in terms of engaging users with the content that is transformed by new technology. For instance, scholars have examined the effects of interactive product websites on consumers' attitudes and behaviors [36, 38, 54] and the effects of online news websites on users' cognitive processing [23, 61, 65, 76].

In our view, the more significant question for future research is how we could design "truly interactive" media—interfaces that engage users with the content and thus further enhance the communication between the source and the receiver. Like user engagement with traditional media, user engagement with new media also aims to encourage users to pay attention to the message rather than any peripheral features surrounding the message and be affected by the message cognitively and emotionally. Building upon previous studies in the field of communication, we summarize various definitions of user engagement with media and move on to discuss the interface and content characteristics that could enhance user engagement with interactive media. Next, we discuss why engagement matters by pointing out persuasive outcomes that we could expect when we adopt and design interactive media. Data from an empirical study will then be used to demonstrate that user engagement, when defined according to both behavioral and psychological dimensions, can significantly mediate the effects of interactive media on attitudinal and behavioral outcomes in an anti-smoking website. The chapter will conclude that user engagement is a crucial mediator in the process of persuasion involving interactive media.

## 2 Defining User Engagement with Interactive Media

Although the term *user engagement* has been widely used in the field of communication, rigorous definitions of user engagement are scarce. Our literature review reveals that there are at least three common factors to define the concept of user engagement with media: (a) strong cognitive and emotional focus on media content; (b) attraction, curiosity, and interest toward the medium or interface; and (c) voluntary participation influenced by media content.

One of the most common ways of defining user engagement with media is the degree to which users become cognitively and affectively focused on media content. TV viewers are engaged when they are emotionally involved in a program and watch the whole program sequence with attention [18]. Consumers are engaged when they feel inspired by an ad [12] or become cognitively committed and emotionally attached to the ad or brand website [29, 43, 74]. Similarly, engagement with narrative has been defined as a story's success in "directing a reader's thought toward the story and its themes" [59, p. 437]. Narrative engagement is often called as "transportation," which refers to the feeling of being "lost" in a story whereby all mental systems and capacities become focused on events occurring in the narrative [10, 26]. Recently, Busselle and Bilandzic [11] developed a scale of *narrative engagement* that reflects the strength of the cognitive and emotional focus on the story: narrative understanding (ease in comprehending narrative), attentional focus (absence of distraction), emotional engagement (feeling for and with character), and narrative presence (sensation of leaving the actual world and entering the story).

Apart from user engagement driven by media content, researchers have also found that user engagement can be driven by the interface or task itself. User engagement with a multimedia system has been defined as a user's intrinsically motivated attraction to the system [15, 34] and "a state of playfulness which includes attention focus, curiosity, and intrinsic interest" with the presentation of multimedia [75, p. 65]. Extending the previous definitions, Sundar [62] points out at least three factors that engage users with an interactive website—customization, multimodality, and contingency. Customization refers to the ability to control users' own communication setting based on their preference. For instance, portal websites provide tools by which users can personalize the look and feel of the home page or synchronize the website with users' mobile devices or other applications. Multimodality refers to the degree to which the interface allows multiple input modes of communication, such as speech, touch, gaze, gesture, or a variety of mouse-based interaction. Finally, contingency refers to the degree to which a given message is contingent upon reception of the previous message and the ones preceding that. For instance, the tagging feature on Facebook allows users to exchange messages in a contingent manner by encouraging a response to the previous posting, eventually resulting in a threaded interaction of interdependent messages.

With the rise of social media, user engagement can be equated to social media engagement, which is described in more detail in McCay-Peet and Quan-Haase's chapter in this book. Social media engagement commonly refers to consumers' voluntary information-sharing behaviors [19, 22, 24, 48]. In other words, user engagement in social networking and marketing is characterized as engagement of one user that drives the engagement of other users. Engaged users are known to generate electronic word of mouth (eWOM)—any positive or negative statements about a product or a company that spread to other users via the Internet [30] and thereby generating "viral" messages [27]. A number of measures have been suggested to capture this voluntary sharing behavior, including the number of comments and reviews on a company blog, the amount of consumer-generated media (CGM), and the frequency of forwarding the content to someone else [49]. Recently, the social media industry has used user engagement metrics based on cost-per-follower on Twitter [14] and cost-per-Like on Facebook [33].

There are relatively few studies that propose a definition of user engagement with all of the three factors summarized above—(a) strong cognitive and emotional focus on media content; (b) attraction, curiosity, and interest toward medium or interface; and (c) voluntary participation influenced by media content. Exceptions include a scale proposed by O'Brien and Toms [45] and a model of user engagement by Oh et al. [46]. O'Brien and Toms [45] proposed a comprehensive scale of user engagement in an e-commerce environment. They found that novelty and aesthetics of the website lead to focused attention to the website and involvement with a shopping task, which results in perceived usability of the system and willingness to use the system again and recommend it to others in the future. In their scale, *novelty* and *aesthetics* reflect users' attraction to the media system or interface, *focused attention* and *felt involvement* capture cognitive and emotional focus on media content, and the *endurability* of system use represents evaluations of success and voluntary participation to recommend the website to others.

Oh et al. [46] explicated the concept of user engagement as a construct that has four dimensions: physical interactions, cognitive experience, absorption, and outreach through one's social network. User engagement is a point on the user involvement continuum, which is marked by *physical interactions* with media and *cognitive experience* that lead to user *absorption* with content, finally cumulating as behavioral outcomes in the form of *outreach*.

In this framework, users are attracted by visual features, sounds, motion, touch, and the novelty of interface and physically interact with the interface features by watching, clicking, swiping, hovering, etc. This *physical interaction* can serve to expand their cognitive experience, "the extent to which the user processes preliminary information from the interface as well as the media content, which is marked by an activation of the users' sensory mechanisms." Next, the stage called *absorption* summarizes previous definitions related to strong cognitive and emotional focus on media content. *Absorption* refers to the stage where the individual is consciously involved in an interaction, and more specifically with the content of the interaction, with almost complete attention in the activity. Finally, behavioral participation is called outreach in this model—collective, voluntary behavior of users that shares their thoughts regarding a specific media content.

Table 1 summarizes the theoretical and operational definitions of user engagement based on the three common defining factors of user engagement: (a) cognitive

**Table 1** Theoretical and operational definitions of user engagement based on three defining factors: Cog = cognitive and emotional focus on media content; Att = attraction, curiosity, and interest in medium or interface; and Vol = voluntary participation

| Theoretical definition | Operational definition | Cog | Att | Vol | Object of engagement |
|---|---|---|---|---|---|
| A psychological state where the message recipient is cognitively and affectively invested in a narrative [56] | The degree to which viewers (a) make sense of the thread of the story and characters, (b) pay attention to the program, (c) feel that they are inside the world created by the story, and (d) are affected emotionally by the story [11] | x | | | Narrative |
| To be focused with a TV program cognitively and emotionally [18] | Watching a single video continuously [20]; watching a television show with other people and interacting with other platforms like the Internet or cell phones while watching a program [3, 18] | x | | x | TV show |
| A positive, interactive psychological state where users' attention was willingly given and held [34] | The degree to which (a) the user perceives that his or her attention is focused on the interaction, (b) the user's curiosity is aroused during the interaction, and (c) the user finds the interaction intrinsically interesting [15] | x | x | | Presentation |
| Cognitive and affective commitment to the brand as personified by the website or other computer-mediated entities [43] | The degree to which users are (a) personally engaged with the brand website by seeking stimulation, inspiration, self-esteem and enjoyment and (b) socially engaged with the website by participating with others and socializing on the website [12] | x | | x | Website |
| Voluntary behaviors of forwarding the brand message toward their friends, family members, and work colleagues [19] | The degree to which users are involved in opinion seeking, opinion giving and opinion passing on social media [16] | | | x | Website |

(continued)

**Table 1** (continued)

| | | | | | |
|---|---|---|---|---|---|
| Emotional, cognitive and behavioral connection that exists, at any point in time and possibly over time, between a user and a resource [4] | The degree to which users have have focused attention to the website, perceive the website easy-to-use, aesthetically appealing, and evoking curiosity, feel involved during the task, and become willing to use the application in future or recommend it to others [45] | x | x | x | Website |
| A form of user experience which includes both (a) a psychological state where the user appraises the quality of media and becomes absorbed in media content and (b) a behavioral experience with which the user physically interacts with the interface and also socially distributes the content [46] | The degree to which users (a) physically interact with the interface, (b) cognitively process the preliminary information about the quality of the interface, (c) feel absorbed in the mediated content, and (d) are willing to distribute the content to other users [46] | x | x | x | Website |

and emotional focus on media content; (b) attraction, curiosity, and interest in medium or interface; and (c) voluntary participation. This chapter defines user engagement based on all three components—user engagement is a psychological state where the user appraises the quality of media and becomes cognitively and emotionally absorbed in media content, followed by a behavioral experience with which the user physically interacts with the interface and also socially distributes the content.

# 3   What Determines User Engagement with Interactive Media

Whereas interactive and visually appealing interface features have been highlighted with the rapid development of media technology, there is no agreement among previous studies on what exactly determines user engagement with interactive media. Some scholars argue that interactive media lead to shallow processing and superficial interaction with media content [13] and often prevent users from being immersed in a narrative [73]. By contrast, other studies have found that interactive media can promote further processing of media content when users are highly involved with the topic, by demanding more user actions and thereby resulting in systematic processing of content [41]. On the other hand, the mere presence of interactivity can serve as a positive peripheral cue such that users with low involvement positively evaluate the credibility of website without further elaboration [63]. In fact, user engagement with interactive media is a complex phenomenon that involves several precursors and moderators.

## 3.1   Medium/Interface Characteristics

Scholars have suggested that visually attractive and easy-to-use interfaces can engage users with a website: interfaces that adopt real-world features such as 3D animation, gravity, or inertia lead to better task efficiency and greater learning outcomes [1, 37, 71]. The perceived attractiveness of the interface has been found to increase the system's perceived usability and even trustworthiness [39, 45]. The perceived usability of the system is said to enhance users' behavioral intention to use the website in the future and recommend it to other users [45] and system adoption [72].

The interactivity effects model proposed by Sundar [62] suggests that three forms of interactivity (i.e., modality interactivity, source interactivity, and message interactivity) are key precursors of user engagement. The three types of interactivity affect individuals' cognition, attitudes, and behavior by adjusting the level of user engagement with media content. Recently, a series of experimental studies performed by Sundar and his colleagues found ample empirical evidence to support this model.

First, when interactivity provides a variety of ways for accessing content (*modality interactivity*) such as zooming, 3D carousel, and slideshow, it can affect users' preliminary assessment of the interface and lead to different levels of user engagement with content. Sundar et al. [68] examined the effects of six on-screen interaction techniques (click to download, drag, mouse over, slide, zoom, and 3D carousel) on users' assessment of the interface and their engagement with an informational website, as well as the effects of four combinations of the six interaction techniques (slide+click, slide+mouse over, drag+mouse over, and drag+zoom) on user engagement. Results from two experiments suggested that different interaction techniques indeed create significant differences in terms of the amount of interaction with the main content, users' memory and attitudes, and user engagement defined as cognitive absorption. They showed that users' preliminary interface assessment was a key precursor of the positive effects of modality interactivity on user engagement. Interface assessment includes three factors: the perceived naturalness in the ways users could control changes on the website (natural mapping), how intuitive the interaction with the website was (intuitiveness), and how easily they could use the website (ease of use). In other words, an interaction technique enhanced user engagement (i.e., losing tracking of time and being immersed in the activity) only when users perceived the interface as natural, intuitive, and easy to use.

Secondly, user engagement can be enhanced and maintained over time by source interactivity—the type of interactivity that provides users an opportunity to customize and create content [67]. *Source interactivity* has been defined as the degree to which the interface lets the user serve as the source of communication, e.g., customize one's portal or create one's own content [62]. Sundar et al. [67] created 12 different versions of a portal website and examined the effects of three different source interactivity tools—a functional customization tool that enables users to choose gadgets and feeds, a cosmetic customization tool that enables them to change background themes, and a blog tool that allows them to create a post and share it with confederates who were thought to be other users. After using the portal website for 2 weeks, users reported being more engaged with the website if they had a chance to create personal content on their blog, especially when the blog had a cosmetic customization tool or moderate amount of functional customization for gadgets and feeds.

*Message interactivity*, defined as the degree to which a website allows the exchange of messages between the user and the system (human-computer interaction) or between users (computer-mediated communication), has been found to imbue the sense of back-and-forth interaction, i.e., perceived contingency. This user perception can heighten user engagement with the content, which leads to other cognitive, attitudinal, and behavioral outcomes. Bellur and Sundar [5] investigated the effect of an interactive question and answer (Q&A) tool on college students' engagement with health information. The level of message interactivity was varied as the level of threadedness (looping mechanism) employed in the Q&A dialogue. In this study, user engagement was operationalized as three factors:

(a) fun and enjoyment, (b) immersion, and (c) the amount of control. The study found that the high message interactivity condition—where the system displayed the entire interaction history—led to greater perceptions of contingency (i.e., increased sense of dialogue and back and forth) and subsequently resulted in greater user engagement with the website than did the control condition.

Interaction history and synchronous chat were found to increase participants' user engagement with a movie search site [69]. The two message interactivity tools increased users' perceived contingency that subsequently led to greater user engagement, such as losing track of time and feeling immersed while browsing the website, especially when participants believed that they were chatting with a human agent, not an artificial one. The heightened user engagement was, in turn, associated with positive attitudes and behavioral intentions toward the website. Users evaluated the website with a human agent as more appealing, attractive, useful, and of high quality and were more willing to recommend the website to others and know more about the website in the future, even though the content of dialogue between participants and the chat agent remained the same across conditions.

In sum, medium/interface features that can induce user engagement include three species of website interactivity—modality interactivity that enhances the interface's naturalness, intuitiveness, and ease of use, source interactivity that allows users to create content and customize the interface, and message interactivity that boosts the sense of contingency of the interaction between the user and the website or among users.

## 3.2 Individual Difference: Power Usage

Previous studies also found that individual differences moderate users' attitudes toward websites. Although not many findings directly suggest that these individual differences have an effect on user engagement, related outcomes such as user attitudes toward the website are known to be affected by individual characteristics. Often, the three types of website interactivity (i.e., modality, source, and message interactivity) interact with a certain set of user characteristics and affect user engagement. In particular, power usage, the degree to which a user is competent to deal with new media technologies, has been found to moderate the effects of interactive media on user engagement.

Compared with novice users, power users are those who are highly experienced in new technology, have more competence, and fully exploit the potential of the technology [6, 53, 64]. Previous studies found that the effects of modality interactivity and source interactivity on user engagement and attitudes are moderated by power usage. Sundar et al. [68] showed that power users evaluated the same content as more credible and likeable when the interface provided simpler interaction techniques, such as mouseover or click, whereas non-power users preferred to explore newer techniques, such as 3D carousel or slider. This finding suggests that power users would rather focus on the underlying site content with simpler techniques than spend time figuring out complicated tools.

As for source interactivity, power users are known to appreciate a customizable website. Sundar and Marathe [64] found that power users and non-power users react differently to a customizable news-aggregator website. Power users showed more positive attitudes toward the content and website when they customized the website, whereas non-power users showed more positive attitudes when the site personalized the content for them.

## 4 Why User Engagement Matters: Persuasive Potential of User Engagement with Interactive Media

How to engage users has been a key question for both media scholars and industries, but the effects of user engagement are yet to be fully discovered. When users feel engaged, what exactly happens to them cognitively? What are the cognitive and behavioral outcomes of user engagement? Several theoretical approaches have been suggested for examining the ways in which interactive media engage users, e.g., a curvilinear model of interactivity [8], the mediated moderation model of interactivity [9], a dual-process model of interactivity effects [41], and the model of interactivity effects on user engagement [62]. Although the outcome of user engagement can vary depending on how it is defined and when and where users are involved, these models all point out that engaged users would experience significant changes in their cognitive and emotional processing and attitudes and behaviors regarding media content. In the following sections, our literature review and empirical example will show that two types of user engagement are powerful mediators for persuasive outcomes—imagery engagement and cognitive engagement.

### 4.1 Imagery Engagement

One of the concepts closely related to user engagement is presence [21, 70]. Presence has been defined as a sense of "being there" in a mediated environment [7, 32]. An immediate outcome of feeling presence is cognitive and emotional focus on media content, i.e., user engagement. The mechanism by which presence leads to greater user engagement is based on a basic feature of human perception—we have not evolved enough to distinguish the mediated content from real-world objects [51]. When interactive media allow users to observe and control a virtual object in a manner that is similar to the way they perform the behavior in the real world, they can easily create real-life imagery in their minds.

This real-life imagery is a key factor to further engage users with media. The degree to which users construct vivid mental imagery of objects in a computer-

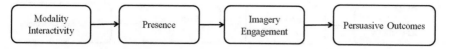

**Fig. 1** Effect of imagery engagement

mediated environment can be called *imagery engagement*. In cognitive psychology, it has been known that visually imagined things are more powerful to govern people's actual behaviors than are the things from purely logical reasoning [55]. When it comes to media, visual imagery constructed in users' minds as a result of reading or watching a narrative is an indicator of the degree to which users are engaged in the story [26]. When technology engages users with a real-world-like stimulus and elicits imagery engagement, it can persuade users—it enhances credibility of messages [57]; forms more confident, enduring, and resistant attitudes [25]; induces stronger beliefs and more positive attitudes about claims made on the website [17, 36]; and even leads to greater behavioral intention to actually perform the simulated behavior [54].

Thus, when users can interact with objects and products through modality interactivity that simulates real-world phenomena, the interaction can create feeling of presence in users' minds. Subsequently, the feeling of presence may shape more vivid mental imagery in users' minds, which can lead to more persuasiveness. Figure 1 describes this hypothesized effect of imagery engagement.

## 4.2 Cognitive Engagement

Engaged users are also said to devote all available perceptual resources to process the stimulus at hand, which generates *cognitive engagement*. Cognitive engagement can be defined as the degree to which users feel attraction, curiosity, and fun during interaction. Especially, modality interactivity is said to increase the degree to which we can mentally represent the mediated information [52, 62]. Anti-drug or anti-smoking campaign websites often employ modality interactivity that heightens user experience. For instance, when individuals move a mouse from left to right along a slider that shows a drastic change in a drug-addicted brain, users are adjusting their motor response to drag their mouse, at the same time perceptually coding the visual changes according to their mouse movement, and finally, cognitively processing the graphical information that shows areas of activity in the addict's brain.

During this process, individuals' perceptual bandwidth [52] will be expanded compared with the situation where they passively receive stimuli from media, especially when the interface enables users to have natural, easy-to-use, and intuitive interaction with the system [68]. O'Brien and Toms [44] also point out that usability of the website is a prerequisite for user engagement. Thus, as long as modality interactivity creates a more natural, intuitive, and easy-to-use interface, the increased

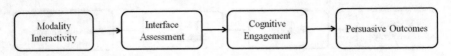

**Fig. 2** Effect of cognitive engagement

perceptual bandwidth through interactivity will be fully used to mobilize their perceptual, motor, and cognitive abilities, which in turn creates further engagement with the website. However, if interaction with the system is error-prone or not intuitive enough, it would be more difficult for users to be completely immersed in the browsing experience.

When users' perception and cognition are fully activated, they appreciate the interaction further, feeling more fun and control. Xu and Sundar [79] created a high-interactivity condition where a website allowed users to spin, zoom, and mouse over the product image and a low-interactivity condition where the users were only allowed to scroll through different product images. As a result of interacting with the product image in the high-interactivity condition, users reported having more fun and feeling in control, which led to more positive attitudes and greater behavioral intention than in the low-interactivity condition. Thus, cognitively engaged users not only explore the content fully but also enjoy the task more and have more positive attitudes toward the whole website afterwards. Figure 2 summarizes the effect of cognitive engagement discussed so far. Interface assessment includes intuitiveness, naturalness, and ease of use.

In sum, user engagement matters because it enhances the persuasive potential of interactive media by inducing imagery engagement and cognitive engagement. The following empirical study suggests that these two types of user engagement indeed mediate the relationship between interactive media and persuasive outcomes on an anti-smoking website.

## 5   An Empirical Example

User engagement has been measured in previous studies, but there were relatively few studies that comprehensively measured both behavioral and psychological aspects of user engagement. To rectify previous methodological shortcomings, this study measured physical interaction with the website as well as self-reported user engagement, and examined if the mediators can indeed enhance the persuasive effects of an anti-smoking website by using a bootstrapping method [28]. A 2 (Modality interactivity: Control vs. Slider) X 3 (Message interactivity: Low vs. Medium vs. High) full-factorial, between-subjects lab experiment was conducted to collect data. Only the procedure and outcomes directly related to the effect of modality interactivity will be discussed in this chapter. Full details of the study can be obtained from Oh and Sundar [47].

## 5.1 Participants and Procedure

Participants were recruited from undergraduate classes at Penn State, in exchange for extra credit ($N = 167$). The final sample included 97 females (58.1%) and 70 males (41.9%), with an average age of 19.6. First, a 5-min, self-administered online questionnaire that included smoking status measures along with a consent form was sent to participants. The second part of the study was administered in a media laboratory. Participants were given a browsing task on an anti-smoking website. The questionnaire software randomly assigned each participant to one of the six conditions. Instructions asked participants to fully browse the website and spend as much time as they needed. They were told that the site contained three different topics and asked to explore all three topics and learn as much as they could. On average, participants spent 317.08 s browsing the entire website ($SD = 149.07$, $Min = 30.37$ s, $Max = 682.98$ s). After they finished browsing the site, they were asked to fill out another online questionnaire. The entire study session lasted approximately 40 min.

## 5.2 Stimulus

Six prototype websites (2 (Modality interactivity: Control vs. Slider) X 3 (Message interactivity: Low vs. Medium vs. High)) were constructed for this study. The six prototypes differed only in their interactive features. With the exception of the interactivity features employed, all six versions of the prototype shared the same content and the same page layout. The prototype website was titled "Tobacco-Free State College." The prototype website had three different topical health outcomes linked to smoking: "How smoking affects your looks," "How smoking affects your brain," and "How smoking affects your respiratory system." The name of the website, "Tobacco-Free State College," was located at the top left corner of the web page. Right next to the logo of "Tobacco-Free State College," the site provided a simple mission statement, "To protect the people in State College from the dangers of tobacco."

Modality interactivity was operationalized as the presence (Slider condition) or absence (Control condition) of sliders. In the Control condition, each of the three topics contained two to three static images related to the topic (i.e., looks, brain, and respiratory system affected by smoking) (Fig. 3). In the Slider condition, a drag-and-slide bar was located under the same-sized images. Images of a female's face, brain activity, and lungs changed as participants moved the slider horizontally across the bar. Instead of showing images discretely like in the Control condition, the images were morphed into one so that they showed gradual change upon slider movement across the horizontal axis (Fig. 4).

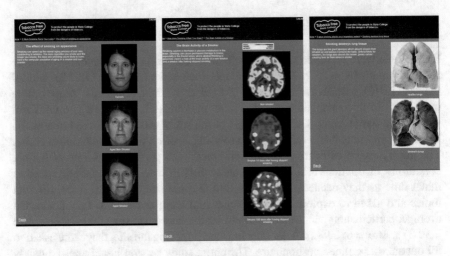

**Fig. 3** Control condition

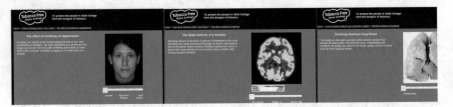

**Fig. 4** Slider condition

## 5.3 Measurement

### 5.3.1 User Engagement

*Imagery engagement* was measured by three items adapted from Schlosser [54]. Three questions asked participants to what extent they could construct vivid mental imagery of negative outcomes of smoking while browsing the website ranging from 1 (not at all) to 9 (a lot), such as "How much did the website's features help you imagine the effects of smoking?", "How easily could you picture the effects of smoking in your mind?", and "How easily did the website let you visualize the effects of smoking?" ($M = 7.44$, $SD = 1.26$, Cronbach's $\alpha = 0.88$). *Cognitive engagement* was measured by six items obtained from Agarwal and Karahanna [2]: "I had fun interacting with the site," "The site's features provided me a lot of enjoyment," "I was bored (reverse-coded)," "I felt as if my curiosity was excited," "I felt as if my imagination was aroused," and "I felt that my interest was evoked" ($M = 5.43$, $SD = 1.53$, $\alpha = 0.88$). Finally, this study measured physical interaction with the interface. *The number of clicks on the slider* was measured by the frequency of dragging and releasing the slider bar. Thus, it was measured for only those in the

Slider condition (N = 78). On average, participants clicked the slider 4.46 times (*SD* = 2.54, *Min* = 0, *Max* = 13).

### 5.3.2 Persuasive Outcomes

For *attitudes toward anti-smoking messages*, participants indicated how well six adjectives from Sundar [61] (believable, informative, insightful, objective, interesting, and clear) describe the persuasive messages on a 9-point scale ($M = 7.22$, $SD = 1.22$, $\alpha = 0.82$). Attitudes toward the website comprised nine items selected from Sundar [61] and Sundar et al. [66]. Participants were asked to indicate how well nine adjectives (appealing, useful, positive, good, favorable, attractive, pleasant, likeable, and interesting) described the website on a 9-point Likert scale ($M = 6.54$, $SD = 1.58$, $\alpha = 0.93$). Participants' behavioral intention was measured by three items adapted from Hu and Sundar [31]. Participants responded to six statements on a 9-point Likert scale, indicating the likelihood that they would perform the following behaviors: "recommend this website to others," "forward this website to my acquaintances," "visit this website again in the future," "visit other websites similar to the one that I just browsed," and "save this web page for future browsing" ($M = 3.53$, $SD = 2.31$, $\alpha = 0.96$).

### 5.3.3 Mediators

As described in Figs. 1 and 2, presence and interface assessment were proposed as precursors to user engagement. Presence was measured using three items obtained from Witmer and Singer [77] on a 9-point Likert-type scale: "How well could you move or manipulate objects while browsing? (ranging from 1 = not very well to 9 = very well)," "How much did the visual aspects of the website involve you? (ranging from 1 = not at all to 9 = a lot)," and "How completely were all of your senses engaged while browsing? (ranging from 1 = not completely to 9 = completely)" ($M = 6.52$, $SD = 1.76$, Cronbach's $\alpha = 0.76$). Interface assessment comprised three statements:64 "My interaction with the website was intuitive," "The ways that I used to control the changes on the website seemed natural," and "The website was easy to use" ($M = 7.06$, $SD = 1.30$, Cronbach's $\alpha = 0.63$).

## 5.4  Results

### 5.4.1 Imagery Engagement

The indirect effects of modality interactivity on attitudes toward the anti-smoking messages through presence and imagery engagement were examined. We used a bootstrapping procedure with 5000 bootstrap samples and bias-corrected confidence intervals [28]. The analysis revealed a significant indirect effect through both mediators ($B = 0.11$, $SE = 04$, 95 % CI from 0.04 to 0.23). Modality interactivity (i.e., the slider) increased the feeling of presence during the browsing task such that participants felt as if they were able to manipulate a real-world object. The enhanced feeling of presence enabled participants to more easily visualize the effects of smoking. Subsequently, this heightened imagery engagement led to more positive attitudes toward the anti-smoking messages that were delivered by the website such that the messages were believable, informative, insightful, objective, etc. Thus, imagery engagement mediated the relationship between modality interactivity and participants' attitudes toward the persuasive messages (Fig. 5).

### 5.4.2 Cognitive Engagement

The mediating effects of interface assessment and cognitive engagement were also significant for attitudes toward anti-smoking messages ($B = 0.04$, $SE = 0.02$, 95 % CI from 0.01 to 0.10). Participants in the Slider condition evaluated the website as more natural, easier, and more intuitive. This heightened interface assessment predicted greater cognitive engagement in the browsing task such that the website provided more fun and excited curiosity while browsing than did the Control condition. Finally, increased cognitive engagement was associated with greater agreement that the anti-smoking messages on the site were believable, informative, insightful, objective, etc. In sum, cognitive engagement mediated the relationship between modality interactivity and participants' attitudes toward the persuasive messages (Fig. 5).

### 5.4.3 Physical Interaction

Finally, the number of clicks on the slider was also positively associated with imagery engagement, which led to three different persuasive outcomes: attitudes toward anti-smoking messages, attitudes toward the website, and participants' behavioral intentions regarding the website. The more participants clicked the slider, the more they felt that they could easily picture the effects of smoking in their mind while browsing the website. This enhanced imagery engagement led to more positive attitudes toward anti-smoking messages such that the messages are believable, informative, insightful, objective, etc. ($B = 0.04$, $SE = 0.02$, 95 % CI from 0.01 to 0.08). It also created more positive attitudes toward the website such that the website was useful, positive, good, favorable, attractive, etc. ($B = 0.04$, $SE = 0.02$, 95 % CI from 0.01 to 0.09), and greater behavioral intention to recommend or forward the website to others ($B = 0.09$, $SE = 0.04$, 95 % CI from 0.03 to 0.20). Figures 5 and 6 summarize the findings of our study.

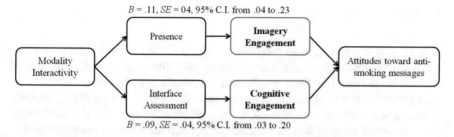

$B = .11, SE = 04, 95\%$ C.I. from .04 to .23

$B = .09, SE = .04, 95\%$ C.I. from .03 to .20

**Fig. 5** The effects of modality interactivity mediated by imagery and cognitive engagement on attitudes

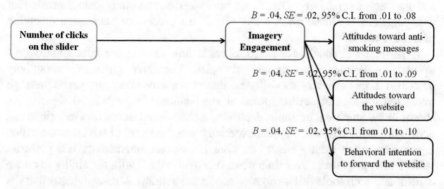

$B = .04, SE = .02, 95\%$ C.I. from .01 to .08

$B = .04, SE = .02, 95\%$ C.I. from .01 to .09

$B = .04, SE = .02, 95\%$ C.I. from .01 to .10

**Fig. 6** The effects of physical interaction mediated by imagery engagement on attitudes and behavioral intention

### 5.4.4 Summary

The three different indicators of user engagement—imagery engagement, cognitive engagement, and physical interaction—all led to persuasive outcomes, using a simple interactive tool, the slider. Participants reported feeling more engaged when the website was equipped with the slider—they reported having more vivid images of the negative outcomes of smoking in their mind and feeling that their imagination and enjoyment were more stimulated by the website. Imagery engagement and cognitive engagement successfully translated into better attitudes toward the persuasive messages delivered by the website, compared with the Control condition, even though the content of persuasive messages in both conditions was exactly the same. Further, the study showed that physical interaction was indeed associated with imagery engagement. Participants reported having more vivid images of negative effects of smoking as they operate the slider, which in turn led to positive attitudes toward the entire website, positive attitudes toward anti-smoking messages, and greater behavioral intention to forward and recommend the website to others.

## 6   Conclusions

This chapter has summarized previous works regarding user engagement in communications, focusing on the importance of user engagement in the context of interactive media. The three most common, significant factors to define user engagement with media are (a) cognitive and emotional focus on media content; (b) attraction, curiosity, and interest in the medium or interface; and (c) voluntary participation of users to distribute media messages. Recent studies about interactive media have proposed and examined three types of interactivity that lead to these cognitive, affective, and behavioral aspects of user engagement—modality, source, and message interactivity. Data from our experimental study demonstrates that user engagement indeed plays a key role in the process of persuasion involving interactive media.

A particular challenge for practitioners is how to integrate conceptual works of user engagement into design principles. The three types of interactivity described in this chapter—modality interactivity, source interactivity, and message interactivity—suggest several practical implications for website designers. As shown in the empirical example, deploying a slide-based interaction technique can add significant value to a website, especially when the goal of the communication is consistent with what a slider can visualize. Source interactivity is a powerful vehicle to engage users over time when it provides them with the ability to create content and with tools that customize media use settings. Message interactivity is able to provide back-and-forth interaction tools to support user-website interaction, such as real-time chat tools or interaction history, and users are particularly engaged when the website delivers the humanness of communication through message interactivity.

Our empirical study shows that imagery engagement, cognitive engagement, and physical interaction all lead to persuasion. The persuasive potential of imagery and cognitive engagement with interactive media has implications in many contexts. A health campaign website that realistically describes symptoms of diseases, a political campaign website that allows users to virtually interact with a realistic avatar of a candidate, and an advertising website that provides 3D product experience could be successful examples of evoking imagery and cognitive engagement through interactive media.

The importance of user engagement with interactive media is not only limited to the area of persuasion. Psychological and behavioral aspects of user engagement with media are important for all areas that involve mediated content through technology. Future studies ought to focus on rigorously examining the effects of specific technological variables on different aspects of user engagement. For example, studies on modality interactivity could investigate how users engage cognitively as well as behaviorally with the newer interaction techniques introduced by emergent technologies such as augmented reality. Investigations into message interactivity can explore the alluring, almost addictive, power of message exchanges through multi-platform messaging applications (e.g., KakaoTalk, WhatsApp), while studies on source interactivity could investigate the greater user agency afforded by increasing customizability of newer media and the relative tension that exists between customization and personalization. In this ever-changing media environment, future studies on user engagement with interactive media will guide us to further understand how to take advantage of new communication technologies.

# References

1. Adamo-Villani, N., Richardson, J., Carpenter, E., Moore, G.: A photorealistic 3d virtual laboratory for undergraduate instruction in Microcontroller Technology. In: 33rd SIGGRAPH 2006 (S. 21). ACM, New York (2006)
2. Agarwal, R., Karahanna, E.: Time flies when you're having fun: cognitive absorption and beliefs about information technology usage. MIS Q **24**, 665–694 (2000). doi:10.2307/3250951
3. Askwith, I.D.: Television 2.0: reconceptualizing TV as an engagement medium. Doctoral dissertation, Massachusetts Institute of Technology, Chicago (2007)
4. Attfield, S., Kazai, G., Lalmas, M., Piwowarski, B.: Towards a science of user engagement (Position Paper). In: WSDM Workshop on User Modeling for Web Applications (2011)
5. Bellur, S., Sundar, S.S.: Interactivity as conversation: Can back and forth interactions affect user cognitions and attitudes? Paper presented at the 63rd Annual Conference of the International Communication Association, London (2013)
6. Bhargava, H.K., Feng, J.: America Online's Internet access service: how to deter unwanted customers. Electron. Commer. Res. Appl. **4**(1), 35–48 (2005)
7. Biocca, F.: Virtual reality technology: a tutorial. J. Commun. **42**(4), 23–72 (1992). doi:10.1111/j.1460-2466.1992.tb00811.x
8. Bucy, E.P.: Interactivity in society: locating an elusive concept. Inf. Soc. **20**, 373–383 (2004). doi:10.1080/01972240490508063
9. Bucy, E., Tao, C.-C.: The mediated moderation model of interactivity. Media Psychol. **9**(3), 647–672 (2007). doi:10.1080/15213260701283269
10. Busselle, R., Bilandzic, H.: Fictionality and perceived realism in experiencing stories: a model of narrative comprehension and engagement. Commun. Theory **18**(2), 255–280 (2008)
11. Busselle, R., Bilandzic, H.: Measuring narrative engagement. Media Psychol. **12**(4), 321–347 (2009)
12. Calder, B.J., Malthouse, E.C., Schaedel, U.: An experimental study of the relationship between online engagement and advertising effectiveness. J. Interact. Mark. **23**(4), 321–331 (2009)
13. Carr, N.G.: The Shallows: What the Internet is Doing to Our Brains. W.W. Norton, New York (2010)
14. Cha, M., Haddadi, H., Benevenuto, F., Gummadi, K.P.: Measuring userinfluence in twitter: the million follower fallacy. In: 4th International Conference on Weblogs and Social Media (ICWSM), vol. 14(1), pp. 8–17 (2010)
15. Chapman, P., Selvarajah, S., Webster, J.: Engagement in multimedia training systems. In: Proceedings of the 32nd Annual Hawaii International Conference on Systems Sciences (1999). doi:10.1109/HICSS.1999.772808
16. Chu, S.C., Kim, Y.: Determinants of consumer engagement in electronic word-of-mouth (eWOM) in social networking sites. Int. J. Advert. **30**(1), 47–75 (2011)
17. Coyle, J.R., Thorson, E.: The effects of progressive levels of interactivity and vividness in Web marketing sites. J. Advert. **30**, 65–77 (2001)
18. Cunningham, T., Hall, A.S., Young, C.: The advertising magnifier effect: an MTV study. J. Advert. Res. **46**(4), 369 (2006)
19. Dobele, A., Toleman, D., Beverland, M.: Controlled infection! Spreading the brand message through viral marketing. Bus. Horiz. **48**(2), 143–149 (2005)

20. Dobrian, F., Sekar, V., Awan, A., Stoica, I., Joseph, D., Ganjam, A., Zhang, H.: Understanding the impact of video quality on user engagement. ACM SIGCOMM Comput. Commun. Rev. **41**(4), 362–373 (2011)

21. Dow, S., Mehta, M., Harmon, E., MacIntyre, B., Mateas, M.: Presence and engagement in an interactive drama. In: Proceedings of the SIGCHI Conference on Human Factors in Computing Systems, pp. 1475–1484. ACM, New York (2007)

22. Evans, D.: Soc Media Marketing: The Next Generation of Business Engagement. Wiley, Hoboken (2010)

23. Eveland, W.P., Marton, K., Seo, M.: Moving beyond "just the facts": the influence of online news on the content and structure of public affairs knowledge. Commun. Res. **31**(1), 82–108 (2004)

24. Falls, J.: What's the value of social media "engagement?" The Financial Brand. http://thefinancialbrand.com/35062/social-media-engagement-in-banking/ (2013). Cited 15 Feb 2015

25. Fazio, R.H., Zanna, M.P., Cooper, J.: Direct experience and attitude-behavior consistency: an information processing analysis. Personal. Soc. Psychol. Bull. **4**(1), 48–51 (1978). doi:10.1177/014616727800400109

26. Green, M.C., Brock, T.C.: The role of transportation in the persuasiveness of public narratives. J. Personal. Soc. Psychol. **79**(5), 701 (2000)

27. Harden, L., Heyman, B.: Digital Engagement: Internet Marketing that Captures Customers and Builds Intense Brand Loyalty. AMACOM, New York (2009)

28. Hayes, A.F.: Introduction to Mediation, Moderation, and Conditional Process Analysis: A Regression-Based Approach. Guilford, New York (2013)

29. Heath, R.: How do we predict advertising attention and engagement? University of Bath School of Management Working Paper Series. http://opus.bath.ac.uk/286/1/2007-09.pdf (2007). Cited 15 Feb 2015

30. Hennig-Thurau, T., Gwinner, K.P., Walsh, G. Gremler, D.D.: Electronic word-of-mouth via consumer-opinion platforms: what motivates consumers to articulate themselves on the internet? J. Interact. Mark. **18**(1), 38–52 (2004)

31. Hu, Y., Sundar, S.S. Effects of online health sources on credibility and behavioral intentions. Commun. Res. **37**(1), 105–132 (2010). doi:10.1177/0093650209351512

32. IJsselsteijn, W.A., de Ridder, H., Freeman, J., Avons, S.: Presence: concept, determinants and measurement. Proc. SPIE, Hum. Vis. Electron. Imaging V **3959**, 520–529 (2000). doi:10.1177/0093650209351512

33. Indvik, L.: Cost Per Like: A Subjective Valuation of Your Facebook Fans. http://mashable.com/2013/04/26/facebook-cost-per-like/ (2013). Cited 15 Feb 2015

34. Jacques, R., Preece, J., Carey T.: Engagement as a design concept for multimedia. Can. J. Educ. Commun. **24**(1), 49–59 (1995)

35. Kalyanaraman, S., Sundar, S.: The psychological appeal of personalized content in web portals: does customization affect attitudes and behavior? J. Commun. **56**(1), 110–132 (2006)

36. Klein, L.R.: Creating virtual product experiences: the role of telepresence. J. Interact. Mark. **17**, 41–55 (2003). doi:10.1002/dir.10046

37. Lee, S.-S. Lee, W.: Exploring effectiveness of physical metaphor in interaction design. In: CHI 2009 Proceedings. ACM, Boston (2009)

38. Li, H., Daugherty, T., Biocca, F.: Impact of 3-D advertising on product knowledge, brand attitude, and purchase intention: the mediating role of presence. J. Advert. **31**(3), 43–57 (2002)

39. Lindgaard, G., Dudek, C., Sen, D., Sumegi, L., Noonan, P.: An exploration of relations between visual appeal, trustworthiness and perceived usability of homepages. ACM Trans. Comput.-Hum. Interact. **18**(1), 1–28 (2011)

40. Liu, Y., Shrum, L.J.: What is interactivity and is it always such a good thing? Implications of definition, person, and situation for the influence of interactivity on advertising effectiveness. J. Advert. **31**(4), 53–64 (2002)

41. Liu, Y., Shrum, L.J.: A dual-process model of interactivity effects. J. Advert. **38**(2), 53–68 (2009)

42. McMillan, S.J.: A four-part model of cyber-interactivity: some cyber-places are more interactive than others. New Media Soc. **4**(2), 271–291 (2002)
43. Mollen, A., Wilson, H.: Engagement, telepresence and interactivity in online consumer experience: reconciling scholastic and managerial perspectives. J. Bus. Res. **63**(9), 919–925 (2010)
44. O'Brien, H., Toms, E.G.: What is user engagement? A conceptual framework for defining user engagement with technology. J. Am. Soc. Inf. Sci. Technol. **59**(6), 938–955 (2008)
45. O'Brien, H., Toms, E.G.: The development and evaluation of a survey to measure user engagement. J. Am. Soc. Inf. Sci. Technol. **61**(1), 50–69 (2010)
46. Oh, J., Bellur, S., Sundar, S.S.: Clicking, assessing, immersing and sharing: an empirical model of user engagement with interactive media. Commun. Res. (2015). doi:10.1177/0093650215600493 [Published online before print September 21, 2015] (in press)
47. Oh, J., Sundar, S. S.: How does interactivity persuade? Effects of interactivity on cognitive absorption, elaboration, and attitudes. J. Commun. **65**, 213–236 (2015)
48. Parsons, T.: Generating 'Engagement' on Facebook Is Just The Beginning. The Financial Brand. http://thefinancialbrand.com/37709/facebook-engagement-roi-metrics-in-banking/ (2014). Cited 15 Feb 2015
49. Plummer, J., Cook, B., Diforio, D., Schachter, B., Sokolyanskaya, I. Korde, T.: Measures of Engagement. Advertising Research Foundation, New York (2007)
50. Rafaeli, S.: From new media to communication. Sage Annual Rev. Commun. Res. **16**, 110–134 (1988)
51. Reeves, B., Nass, C.: The Media Equation: How People Treat Computers, Television, and New Media. Cambridge University Press, Cambridge (1997)
52. Reeves, B., Nass, C.: Perceptual user interfaces: perceptual bandwidth. Commun. ACM **43**(3), 65–70 (2000)
53. Rogers, A.M.: The Virtuous Cycle: Online News, Industry Change and User Choice. Res Pap 104. http://opensiuc.lib.siu.edu/gs_rp/104 (2011). Cited 15 Feb 2015
54. Schlosser, A.E.: Experiencing products in the virtual world: the rule of goal and imagery in influencing attitudes versus purchase intentions. J. Consum. Res. **30**, 184–198 (2003)
55. Shepard, R.N.: The mental image. Am. Psychol. **33**(2), 125–137 (1978). doi:10.1037/0003-066X.33.2.125
56. Slater, M.D. Rouner, D.: Entertainment, education and elaboration likelihood: understanding the processing of narrative persuasion. Commun. Theory **12**(2), 173–191 (2002)
57. Smith, R.E., Swinyard, W.R.: Cognitive response to advertising and trial: belief strength, belief confidence and product curiosity. J. Advert. **17**(3), 3–14 (1988)
58. Steuer, J.: Defining virtual reality: dimensions determining telepresence. J. Commun. **42**(4), 73–93 (1992)
59. Strange, J.J., Leung, C.C.: How anecdotal accounts in news and in fiction can influence judgments of a social problem's urgency, causes, and cures. Personal. Soc. Psychol. Bull. **25**(4), 436–449 (1999)
60. Stromer-Galley, J.: Interactivity-as-product and interactivity-as-process. Inf. Soc. **20**(5), 391–394 (2004)
61. Sundar, S.S.: Multimedia effects on processing and perception of online news: a study of picture, audio, and video downloads. J. Mass Commun. Q. **77**, 480–499 (2000). doi:10.1177/107769900007700302
62. Sundar, S.S.: Social psychology of interactivity in human-website interaction. In: Joinson, A.N., McKenna, K.Y.A., Postmes, T., Reips, U.-D. (eds.) The Oxford Handbook of Internet Psychology, pp. 89–104. Oxford University Press, Oxford (2007)
63. Sundar, S.S.: The MAIN model: a heuristic approach to understanding technology effects on credibility. In: Metzger, M.J., Flanagin, A.J. (eds.) Digital Media, Youth, and Credibility, pp. 72–100. MIT, Cambridge (2008)
64. Sundar, S.S., Marathe, S.S.: Personalization versus customization: the importance of agency, privacy, and power usage. Hum. Commun. Res. **36**(3), 298–322 (2010)

65. Sundar, S.S., Knobloch-Westerwick, S., Hastall, M.R.: News cues: information scent and cognitive heuristics. J. Am. Soc. Inf. Sci. Technol. **58**(3), 366–378 (2007)
66. Sundar, S.S., Xu, Q., Bellur, S., Jia, H., Oh, J., Khoo, G.-S.: Click, drag, flip, and mouse-over: effects of modality interactivity on user engagement with web content. Paper presented at the 60th Annual Conference of the International Communication Association, Singapore (2010)
67. Sundar, S.S., Oh, J., Bellur, S., Jia, H., Kim, H.S.: Interactivity as self-expression: a field experiment with customization and blogging. In: Proceedings of the SIGCHI Conference on Human Factors in Computing Systems, pp. 395–404. ACM, New York (2012)
68. Sundar, S.S., Bellur, S., Oh, J., Xu, Q., Jia, H.: User experience of on-screen interaction techniques: an experimental investigation of clicking, sliding, zooming, hovering, dragging and flipping. Hum. Comput. Interact. **29**(2), 109–152 (2014)
69. Sundar, S.S., Bellur, S., Oh, J., Jia, H., Kim, H.S.: Theoretical importance of contingency in human-computer interaction: effects of message interactivity on user engagement. Commun. Res. (2014). doi:10.1177/0093650214534962. http://crx.sagepub.com/content/early/2014/05/21/0093650214534962 [Published online before print on May 22, 2014] (in press)
70. Sutcliffe, A.: Designing for user engagement: aesthetic and attractive user interfaces. Synth. Lect. Hum.-Cent. Inform. **2**(1), 1–55 (2009)
71. Tavanti, M., Lind, M.: 2D vs 3D, Implications on spatial memory. In: Proceedings of IEEE Symposium on Information Visualization (INFOVIS'01), San Diego, 22–23 October, pp. 139–148 (2001)
72. Venkatesh, V., Davis, F.D.: A theoretical extension of the technology acceptance model: four longitudinal field studies. Manag. Sci. **46**(2), 186–204 (2000)
73. Vorderer, P.: Entertainment theory. In: Bryant, J., Roskos-Ewoldsen, D., Cantor, J. (eds.) Communication and Emotion: Essays in Honor of Dolf Zimmerman, pp. 131–153. Erlbaum, Mahwah (2003)
74. Wang, A.: Advertising engagement: a driver of message involvement on message effects. J. Advert. Res. **46**(4), 355–368 (2006)
75. Webster, J., Ho, H.: Audience engagement in multimedia presentations. ACM SIGMIS Database **28**(2), 63–77 (1997)
76. Wise, K., Bolls, P.D., Schaefer, S.R.: Choosing and reading online news: how available choice affects cognitive processing. J. Broadcast Electron. Media **52**(1), 69–85 (2008)
77. Witmer, B.G., Singer, M.J.: Measuring presence in virtual environments: a presence questionnaire. Presence **7**(3), 225–240 (1998). doi:10.1162/105474698565686
78. Wu, G., Wu, G.: Conceptualizing and measuring the perceived interactivity of websites. J. Curr. Issues Res. Advert. **28**(1), 87–104 (2006)
79. Xu, Q., Sundar, S.S.: Lights, camera, music, interaction! Interactive persuasion in e-commerce. Commun. Res. **41**(2), 282–308 (2014). doi:10.1177/0093650212439062

# A Model of Social Media Engagement: User Profiles, Gratifications, and Experiences

Lori McCay-Peet and Anabel Quan-Haase

## 1 Introduction

Social media encompass a wide array of platforms ranging from popular sites such as Facebook [19] and Sina Weibo [42] to sites geared to niche communities such as Academia, Pinterest, and Ello. While social media share common features that afford engagement through 'two-way' audience interaction, the diversity in design encountered across sites makes it difficult to identify a set of core functionalities [25]. Generally, social media are defined as 'web sites and applications which enable users to create and share content or to participate in social networking' [57]. The uptake of social media by a wide demographic is undeniable despite recent reports stressing the negative implications of social media adoption and use, including privacy threats [66], large-scale experimentation with users [41], and cyberbullying [60]. Americans spend more time on social media than any other Internet activity [1], with 73 % of online adults using at least one social networking site (SNS) and 42 % using more than one [19]. Social media use has become ubiquitous, and a social media presence is an important aspect of self-presentation, social networking, learning, work, and everyday life for academics [28], healthcare professionals [14], university students [20], and consumers [64].

Cracking the secret of the optimal user interface design to spur social media engagement is a major goal of social media research. A key challenge is that user experience is not based on the interface design and unique features of a social media site alone, but is also driven by characteristics of the social network that is responsible for the provision of content. That is, users join social media platforms where they can interact with their peers and obtain access to content that is amusing, surprising, and relevant to their everyday lives. Sites are expected to continually

L. McCay-Peet (✉) • A. Quan-Haase
University of Western Ontario, 1151 Richmond St, London, ON, Canada
e-mail: mccay@dal.ca; aquan@uwo.ca

© Springer International Publishing Switzerland 2016
H. O'Brien, P. Cairns (eds.), *Why Engagement Matters*,
DOI 10.1007/978-3-319-27446-1_9

innovate around what engagement means to their user base, by what methods to increase engagement, and how to provide richer and more rewarding experiences.

Adapting O'Brien's [45] definition of user engagement—'a quality of user experience with technology'—we define social media engagement as a quality of user experience with web-based technologies that enable users to interact with, create, and share content with individuals and organizations in their social networks. In this chapter, we focus on user engagement in the context of social media at the level of the *individual* and *network experience*—i.e. the experiences that motivate users to engage with content created, shared, or endorsed by people in their social networks and encourage them to linger and return. Understanding social media engagement is valuable on many levels. Educators need to understand how student engagement with social media may extend learning beyond the classroom walls; social media research in the context of education will inform teaching practices and have the potential to affect outcomes. Changes in the interface can interfere with users' ability to voice their opinion, or changes can spur awareness and activism around pressing social or political concerns. Social media companies need to recognize how changes to algorithms and interface design will affect engagement; such knowledge will help keep their users satisfied and guarantee frequent returns.

We identify elements of a model of social media engagement from prior research. By examining both tangible indicators of engagement, such as usage and activity counts, and more abstract indicators relating to positive user experiences, we can begin to understand *why* people engage at the level they do, with *what* kinds of social media platforms, and to *what* effect.

## 2 Conceptualizing Social Media Engagement

Much research has attempted to conceptualize social media engagement. There is, however, a lack of overarching models that bring together various elements of the individual and network experience. Our model of social media engagement in context fills this gap by identifying and integrating six overlapping elements.

1. *Presentation of self:* The crafting of a personal profile or virtual self over time signifies identity. The combination of various elements and their respective updates yields a virtual self: a user's name, lists of interests, profile picture, content the user chooses to share, and the manner in which users engage with others through social media.
2. *Action and participation:* Social media sites allow users to perform a variety of tasks such as viewing shared content, posting content, commenting, discussing, and collaborating.
3. *Uses and gratifications:* Users are motivated to adopt and continue using social media for a variety of reasons, ranging from the information to be exchanged to the social benefits to be derived.

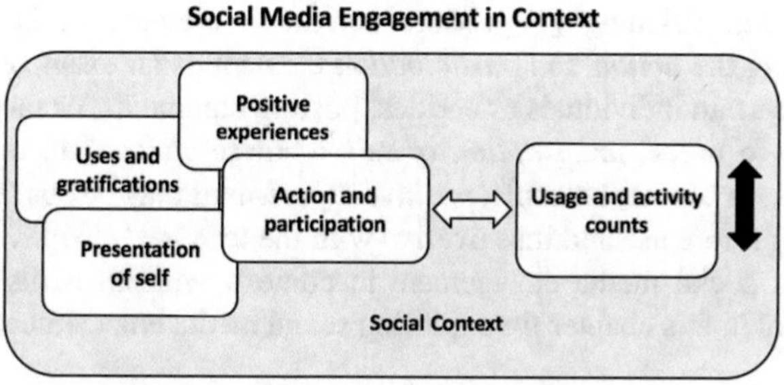

**Fig. 1** Model of social media engagement in context

4. *Positive experiences:* These include the flow, positive emotions, and serendipity, which users may experience during their use of social media.
5. *Usage and activity counts:* Numerical data relating to users' *actions and participation* in a site, which can be presented in real time in raw or aggregate form through numeric values or visualizations (e.g. graphs).
6. *Social context:* Users' social networks within social media sites, including the size and nature of these networks. Social context may be cultural, work, or personal in nature—e.g. a small, close-knit peer group or a large, diffuse network of international social activists.

Figure 1 illustrates our model of social media engagement in context. While each of the six elements is independently useful as a way to both understand and potentially measure engagement, none alone is sufficient. The model proposes that social media engagement may be explained as an iterative and dynamic process that unfolds over time. We use the experience of 'Anna' to exemplify one way in which the model may be used to explain social media engagement.

Anna first engages with various social media by crafting and maintaining a personal profile (*presentation of self*). These social media sites, through features and functions, support and encourage Anna to engage with others in her networks, by enabling her to create content, comment, or simply view other people's profiles and posts (*action and participation*). Anna's social media interactions are motivated by a number of *uses and gratifications* (e.g. social and informational) and the *positive experiences* that underlie her social media usage encourage further engagement, which is reflected in Anna's *usage and activity counts*. Anna is a frequent social media user who often posts her own content and favourites and interacts with others' *action and participation*, helping her to both benefit from and make an impact within her *social context*.

Anna's example scratches the surface of the ways in which aspects of social media engagement may be described. The model's elements may be labelled as motivations, behaviours, outcomes, or indicators or measures for evaluation, and some elements may have multiple descriptors. Aspects of *positive experience*, for example, may include outcomes (e.g. well-being) or motivations (e.g. desire to repeat experience), while aspects of *action and participation* may serve as indicators of engagement (e.g. number of site visits) or describe behaviours associated with social media (e.g. 'listening' [17]). Moreover, the six elements of the model are not discrete. Taking the *action and participation* element as an example, actions such as following certain individuals or entities, posting comments, or favouriting items all contribute to users' *presentation of self* as these actions are often visible to their network. As another example, *positive experiences* may be conceptualized as a motivation for future use and thus overlap with the *uses and gratifications* element. Our model of social media engagement in context, with all of its complexities, serves as a tool in this chapter for exploring social media engagement.

## 2.1 Presentation of Self

A central part of engagement in social media is the crafting of a profile where aspects of the public self—such as pictures, date of birth, and location—are presented. Sundén [58] has termed the process of providing personal information as 'writing oneself into being', stressing both the creative side of this practice and the fact that it is an active and deliberate process that constitutes an extension of one's offline identity [4, 21]. According to research by Young and Quan-Haase [66], users are actively engaged in decisions about what information to share and with whom, rather than being simply passive consumers of content. Users make decisions about what images to include in their profile, what information to share, and whom to connect with via requests and follows, a process that has been described as data curation of the self [25]. The *presentation of self* entails a degree of emotional engagement as users confide information about themselves to their imagined audiences [36], an aspect of their *social context*. The amount of effort that has gone into the *presentation of self* can be seen as a proxy of the relevance that the person gives to their online identity. A good measure of a user's engagement on a social media site then consists of how elaborate their profile is, in terms of the kind and amount of information they have provided as well as the frequency of profile updates (*action and participation*). Maintaining an online self requires investment both in time spent updating the profile and creativity with regard to what to include [20].

## 2.2 Action and Participation

Continued engagement on social media can be attributable to the *action and participation* that social media features afford. For example, Twitter users can create and update their profile (e.g. bio); subscribe to other users' accounts (follow); post text, images, video, and links (tweet); share other peoples' tweets (retweet); reply to tweets (@reply); include other users in their tweets (@mention); or simply read a stream of real-time tweets of those in their network (timeline). Each of these features allows for different degrees of engagement. That is, a retweet requires less time and effort than a reply to a tweet. This differentiation of degrees of engagement has led to some criticisms of measures of engagement with content, as retweets alone cannot show if a user read the content or simply retweeted it without much consideration.

Users of social media sites may vary in terms of the degree to which they participate on these sites. Much research on participation in virtual communities has shown that active contributions come from a small percentage of the community. That is, the large majority only listen in on the conversations without contributing much content. This group has been referred to as 'lurkers' because they are most likely to read posts and messages, but not to post themselves. It is important, however, not to dismiss the relevance of this group to our understanding of engagement. As Crawford [17] argues, 'listeners' 'are actively logging in and tracking the contributions of others; they contribute a mode of receptiveness that encourages others to make public contributions' (p. 527).

When users have a 'voice' [17] by contributing content, they may spark further interest and engagement in other users. Through more participatory activities, such as @mentioning and @replying, users are not simply putting content out there for others to see, but are also encouraging others in their network to respond, disagree, and share with others. In 2008, when Dave Carroll's guitar was broken on a United Airlines flight, he took to social media, recording and posting a music video on YouTube that went viral with a staggering number of views and tweets, retweets, and @replies on Twitter [23]. The Carroll example not only illustrates the power consumers—celebrities and noncelebrities alike—now wield through social media, but how engagement, through a feedback loop of *action and participation*, makes it possible for content to go viral, a network-wide indicator of engagement that can create significant spikes in *usage and activity counts*.

## 2.3   Uses and Gratifications

What motivates social media engagement? *Uses and gratifications* (U&G) theory is the most common approach to the study of motivations behind social media use and behaviour [6] and one of the most useful [49, 50]. U&G is a media and communications theory that explains media selection and continued use through peoples' needs and satisfactions. Smock et al.'s [56] web-based survey of 267 undergraduate students found that three dimensions of use predicted time spent on Facebook: (1) relaxing entertainment, (2) expressive information sharing, and (3) social interaction. Thus, U&G is useful for explaining motivations behind social media engagement. For the purposes of this chapter, examples of prior U&G research associated with social media have been selected for discussion (see Table 1). For more background on U&G, Reinhard and Dervin [52] provide an introduction to its history, theory, and applications, and Quan-Haase and Young discuss its applicability to social media [50]. While there are several motivations for social media adoption, two of the most salient themes throughout the literature are social and informational factors [32, 68].

**Table 1** Findings from a selection of U&G studies of social media

| Research | Social media | Motivations for use |
|---|---|---|
| Brandtzaeg & Heim (2009) [6] | Various Norwegian SNSs (e.g. Underskog and Biip) | Get in contact with new people; keep in touch with friends; general socializing |
| Coursaris et al. (2013) [16] | Twitter | Information, relaxation, social interaction |
| Joinson (2008) [33] | Facebook | Social connections, shared identities, content, social investigation, social network surfing, status updating |
| Papacharissi & Mendelson (2011) [47] | Facebook | Habitual pastime, relaxing entertainment, expressive information sharing, escapism, cool and new trend, companionship, professional advancement, social interaction, and meeting new people |
| Quan-Haase & Young (2010) [49] | Facebook and instant messaging | Pastime, affection, fashion, share problems, sociability, and social information |
| Whiting & Williams (2013) [64] | Social media | Social interaction, information seeking, pastime, entertainment, relaxation, communicatory utility, convenience utility, expression of opinion, information sharing, and surveillance/knowledge about others |
| Zhang & Pentina (2012) [68] | Weibo | Professional development, emotional release, information seeking, citizenship behaviour, social connection, visibility, self-expression, and interaction with Weibo |

### 2.3.1 Social

Table 1 reflects several perspectives on socially grounded personal, professional, and community or network motivations for social media use. People go to social media to keep in touch with friends [6], for companionship [47], to share problems [49], and for social interaction [16, 47, 64] in general. Sharing everyday life experiences on social media enables feelings of belonging [12] and creates a sense of online community [33, 68]. An important aspect of social factors that encourage engagement is the *social context* of social media users; this includes networks of individuals in a common field of work such as those found on sites like LinkedIn, which are sustained by people motivated to interact with others for the purposes of professional development [68] and advancement [47]. Social media also helps users pass time in a fun and entertaining way through social interaction [47, 64, 68], which has the potential to contribute to *positive experiences*. And finally, some people have broader motivations for social media usage, such as those associated with citizenship behaviour [68], which may be spurred by the *action and participation* of others in the user's networks.

Perhaps one of the most noteworthy findings has been the association between social media usage and social capital return. Social capital is defined as the resources—actual and potential—that a person can obtain from their social networks [5, 15]. Key gratifications obtained by users of social media are bonding and bridging social capital [48]. Bonding social capital refers to connections with strong ties: those individuals with whom one shares an intimate bond. By contrast, bridging social capital refers to linkages with weak ties: people one associates with, but with whom one is not close. The results of a series of studies revealed that individuals who engage with their Facebook networks show greater levels of both bonding and bridging social capital [20]. What is less clear is whether higher levels of engagement yield higher levels of social capital and thus increase motivations for social media use. A study by Young and Quan-Haase [66] showed an association between the amounts of information a person disclosed on Facebook (*presentation of self*) and their network size (*social context*). In this study [66], higher disclosure, as measured by the range of information types disclosed, was associated with larger networks. This indicates that perhaps investments in one's profile (*presentation of self*) and frequency and range of posts (*action and participation*) can lead to higher levels of social capital in terms of network size (*social context*) and increased social motivation for social media use (*uses and gratifications*).

### 2.3.2 Informational

While the social aspects of social media have garnered a great deal of attention in the literature, social factors are insufficient to fully explain what influences social media engagement [29]. One of the strongest gratification themes in the literature is information seeking and sharing. Prior research has tended to be general in its exploration of the informational motivations of social media use, e.g. sharing 'information' [16] or 'content' [33]. However, other research has been more explicit, specifying qualities or types of information such as 'expressive information sharing' [47] and 'social information' [49] or motivations in the form of behaviour such as 'information seeking' [63]. What is clear is that social media provide an alternative means to traditional media of gathering and relaying a variety of types of information. And while search engines like Google and Yahoo! provide a sophisticated means for seeking specific kinds of information, social media provide a complementary means for sharing and discovering information in a *social context* ranging from social to political to health topics [40, 51]. Often a user's social network has a good understanding of what kinds of news and sources of information may be relevant to a person's current life situation; this kind of targeted information sharing is not available in traditional media.

Social media engagement is in part stimulated by others' *presentation of self* and *action and participation*: the provision of interesting tidbits of information, stories, and reports and the inclusion of popular culture that a user may otherwise have missed. Social media is about staying 'in the know' about what is trending, what people in one's social network are reading and commenting on, and what is considered 'newsworthy'. Nonetheless, not all social media are considered equally information oriented. Some sites are described as serving more of a social function [44], while others are thought to be more information oriented [26, 32, 35]. Kwak et al. [35] found that 78 % of user pairs on Twitter are one-way rather than reciprocal; that is, a Twitter user may follow a celebrity or a news station, but the user is not likewise followed by the celebrity or news station. Perhaps even more telling, '67.6 % of users are not followed by any of their followings in Twitter. We conjecture that for these users Twitter is rather a source of information than a SNS [35]. Below, we briefly examine peoples' use of social media for news gathering and the exchange of everyday life and work information.

## News

Though the credibility of news available through social media is a source of concern [2], it serves to keep people informed of what is happening in their local community and to provide and receive first-hand accounts of events unfolding around the world [8, 31]. While most Americans prefer to get their news directly from a news organization, they are doing so via multiple sources including social media [2]. More than half of respondents to Pew's social media survey reported they obtained their news from social media sites such as Reddit and Twitter [26]. Thirty percent of Americans reported that they incidentally consume news on Facebook; that is, people visit Facebook for reasons other than to obtain news but encounter news while interacting on the site [44]. Rather than replacing traditional sources such as print, radio, and television, social media provides an additional means for people to consume and engage with news by:

1. Spreading the news and thereby determining what is newsworthy in their social networks
2. Providing their opinion of news items by adding user-generated content
3. Creating their own news, by starting a blog or post on a specific topic of their interest [2]

These three types of engagement have an immediate effect on social media *usage and activity counts*. It is no wonder then that Twitter encourages users to live-tweet unfolding events, arguing that it increases follower growth and retweets, and it also 'drives engagement on Twitter and builds buzz' [61].

## Everyday Life and Work Information

Social media 'fill a surprisingly useful role in everyday life information seeking' [55] and the larger people's social media networks are, the more information sources people have at their disposal [32]. While social media has been criticized as a platform where people can keep their network informed of mundane activities, such as what they ate for breakfast [27], at the other end of the spectrum, people find and share consumer, business, and special event information and learn new things [64]. Social media also enable people to encounter and maintain awareness of professional or work-related information [67]. Through social media, university students share information about social functions, friends, and academic information [3, 18, 49], making these sites valuable resources. Moreover, people can engage others through social media by asking questions and then getting a timely response [9].

Even though social media sites vary in their reciprocal nature [35], the majority of sites share features that enable a higher level of engagement than seeking, encountering, and maintaining awareness of information in traditional media allows for. Social media sites enable user-specific information dissemination and facilitate discussion of relevant topics that further feed the information available to its user base and create the kind of *social context*—dynamic and information rich—that has the potential to attract and maintain user interest and a high degree of engagement.

## 2.4  Positive Experiences

Pew reports that 63 % of Facebook users log on to the site at least once a day, with as many as 40 % logging onto the site numerous times throughout the day [19]. Fifty-seven percent of Instagram users visit the site at least once a day (with 35 % doing so multiple times per day), and of those who use Twitter, 46 % are daily visitors (with 29 % visiting multiple times per day) [19]. What makes users of social media sites come back for more—what is driving these *usage and activity counts*? Important aspects of social media engagement are the *positive experiences* that compel an individual to return to the site and the attempt to recreate those experiences or seek out new ones. We examine three such *positive experiences*: flow, emotion, and serendipity.

### 2.4.1  Flow

A key concept of user engagement is Csikszentmihalyi's notion of flow, an experiential psychological state of total or deep involvement 'that is so desirable that they wish to repeat it as often as possible' [29]. It is, therefore, no wonder that social media use is often likened to addiction in the popular press [54] and usage and activity counts are popular as a quick and dirty measure of user engagement in the context of social media. Survey research on undergraduate students who identified themselves as heavy Facebook users found that the site was used to communicate and maintain friendships; the playfulness, subject involvement, and focused attention students perceived they experienced through Facebook use helped to explain students' deep involvement in the SNS [11].

### 2.4.2 Emotion

People react to external stimuli through positive emotions such as comfort and pleasure or negative emotions such as social rejection and disgust, which may prompt approach or avoidance behaviours [30]. Social media engagement has been shown to be linked to the emotionality of the content presented on these sites, including (1) the emotions associated with the *presentation of self*, and (2) the emotions that result from various levels of *action and participation* [34]. In terms of the crafting of the self, social media engagement can be an emotional experience: the content presented is a reflection of our identity. What we present and how others engage with this content via likes, retweets, and favourites influence our sense of *involvement*, 'a cognitive and emotional response to media' [46]. Second, the emotions expressed through social media content, such as posts or comments, are central to engagement. Findings from case studies on social media-based public forums indicate that angry discussions were more influential (e.g. garner more replies) than those characterized by anxiety [13]. In the second case study at the end of this chapter, we examine research that shows how both negative and positive emotions in response to social media content influence users' level of social media engagement [34].

### 2.4.3 Serendipity

Serendipity is 'an unexpected experience prompted by an individual's valuable interaction with ideas, information, objects, or phenomena' [39]. Serendipity is a *positive experience* relating to the use of social media, resulting from a dynamic, messy information space that is unpredictable and full of surprises. McCay-Peet et al. [38] found that social media environments may be better at leading to the unexpected, a facet of serendipity, than websites, databases, and search engines. Serendipitous experiences are often social in nature, involving a transfer of knowledge or information between people [37], a function for which social media platforms are aptly designed (see *uses and gratifications*). While the 'noise' within social media and its potential to distract can be a source of negative experiences, social media also afford positive user experiences: discovering unexpected and useful resources, meeting new people, finding consumer products, becoming informed of news, and helping people make connections between ideas.

Distrust of mainstream media due to its perceived potential to distort and provide imbalanced coverage has led some people to turn to social media. Through research on news-reading behaviour, for example, Yadamsuren and Heinström [65] found that some people use social media such as Boing Boing, a collaborative blogging site, to get their news incidentally or serendipitously from sources they perceive are more transparent. Research also indicates that postgraduate students come across information related to their academic work serendipitously on social media, which encourages further engagement with social media. The students recognize that time spent engaging on social media (*action and participation*) is an investment in serendipity both from the perspective of the person sharing content and those exposed to it. And while each parcel of time allotted to social media may not pay off in the form of serendipitous discoveries, for those times it does, it is worth the effort [18] (*uses and gratifications*).

## 2.5 Usage and Activity Counts

From a broad, economic perspective, the level of activity or the number of monthly active users (MAUs) on social media is the industry's primary measure of user engagement and an indicator of a social media site's financial health [10]. Researchers have also equated repeat visits to social media with user engagement. Pew, for instance, reported, 'Facebook and Instagram exhibit especially high levels of user engagement: a majority of users on these sites check in to them on a daily basis' [19]. However, we refer to *usage and activity counts* here also as those numbers that are presented to individual users in raw and aggregate form that serve to create a feedback loop of engagement.

There is an abundance of numbers on social media, exemplified through the social network Academia, a platform for academics to share their research. The site allows scholars to easily monitor the number of people who, for example, (1) follow their work, (2) view or download their papers, and (3) view their profiles. Various data relating to users' interactions with Academia content are collected, summarized, and visualized for each profile. A map of the world, for example, indicates the country of origin of those who viewed an Academia profile in the past 30 days. These numbers, raw, aggregate, and visualized, may not only serve to give users a sense of self-worth as Michael Harris [43] suggests, but may also influence, for example, whether academics continue to upload papers and follow other academics' work. As previously mentioned (Sect. 2.2), the summaries of users' *action and participation* have the potential to influence further *action and participation*. Moreover, usage and activity counts also provide a type of summary of the social media user for others to view—e.g. how many people downloaded or liked the content they shared—which may or may not mirror the identity the user is attempting to reflect (*presentation of self*).

## 2.6 Social Context

User engagement is shaped by the *social context* in which interactions take place in social media. Different contexts necessitate the use of diverse indicators, measures, and indices of engagement because norms, values, and customs will vary. Also the role played by the content shared varies greatly across contexts, reflecting the many *uses and gratifications* of social media. Though there are few barriers within social media to share content, some social media are more associated with one type of information than another (e.g. leisure versus work) due to their technological affordances (e.g. image and text oriented) and because some social media attempt to attract a specific demographic (e.g. professionals, academics). Moreover, within social media sites, who people imagine their audience to be affects what information they share [36] (*presentation of self*). While some people choose to mix the personal with the professional through a single social media site, others choose to create separate profiles to reflect the context of their social media contributions, for example, scientists who keep a separate personal and professional Facebook account [62]. Distinctions made by users between their various social media accounts, and accounts bound within disparate *social contexts*, may suggest differences in the type, quality, and level of engagement in each. We examine the social context of digital humanities scholars' user engagement in the first case study to follow.

## 3   Conclusions

In this chapter, we propose a model of social media engagement which comprises six related elements: (1) *presentation of self*; (2) *action and participation*; (3) *uses and gratifications*; (4) *positive experiences*; (5) *usage and activity counts*; and (6) *social context*. Together, the elements paint a picture of the degree and quality of social media engagement that helps explain why people choose to adopt social media and continue to engage with it. We mainly focus on the positive side of user engagement by discussing how social media can promote feelings of belonging to a community and enable people to keep up with the news. However, there is also a growing body of literature on the negative aspects of social media engagement which raise a number of important questions.

1. *Manipulation of content.* For those planning a trip, wishing to buy a product online, or pondering the legitimacy of a company, there is often a wealth of user reviews or indicators (e.g. 'likes'), which help consumers make informed decisions; but buyer beware. Some companies exist to create false reviews and inflate reputations [24]. How can false user engagement be vetted?
2. *Unpaid workforce.* Social media users are creating content and the 'buzz' which helps drive social media engagement [61], increasing the bottom line of social media companies [7]. Is this fair? Can and should engagement be monetarily compensated?
3. *Engagement extremes.* Is it possible to be too engaged with social media, so much so that people are crashing their cars while using social media [22]? Is engagement something that should always be increased, encouraged?
4. *Numbers obsession.* Many of the social interactions we have online have been reduced to sheer numbers [43], e.g. votes on Reddit submissions, follower counts on Twitter, and blog post views. How is the numbers focus impacting users' self-worth? Should it be mediated?

While engagement is framed by the social media industry as a numbers game with higher being 'better', the questions above suggest a need to look beyond *usage and activity counts* to understand how to build sustainable social media engagement.

Exploring abstract experiences such as flow, emotionality, and serendipity from both positive and negative perspectives may be particularly fruitful for unlocking *why* people engage at the level they do with different types of social media and to *what effect*. Future research on user engagement with social media may examine, for example, whether some people avoid social media due to the same experiences that draw others to it (e.g. flow, serendipity). Moreover, what interface features support social media engagement and what features may also help curb engagement when disengagement is preferable? Understanding these more complex elements of engagement will help inform the design of social media to the benefit of users.

## Case Studies of Social Media Engagement

We discuss two case studies to illustrate the usefulness of the model of social media engagement to the study of user engagement in different kinds of social contexts. Case Study 1 explores how digital humanities scholars engage with their community (*social context*) on Twitter through modes of *action and participation*, scholars' motivations for engagement (*uses and gratifications*), and the *positive experiences* derived from engagement. Case Study 2 examines how the networked transmission of emotion (an aspect of *positive experience*) on Facebook through the *presentation of self* (e.g. pictures, updates) influences *action and participation* (e.g. posting comments, likes).

## *Case Study 1: Digital Humanities Scholars' Use of Twitter*

This case study examines user engagement in the social context of scholarly digital communication among digital humanities scholars. Specifically, it draws from data collected as part of a multi-year project, 'Digging DH', which examines the role of electronic resources and social media in the scholarly practices of digital humanists (see DiggingDH.com). The focus on digital humanities scholars is pertinent, as these scholars have been described as early adopters of social media and have also reflected on what their engagement on these sites means for their scholarly practice [59]. What motivates these scholars to participate and engage with content on Twitter? As part of the larger Digging DH project, 15 semi-structured interviews were collected in 2013 at the Digital Humanities Conference with graduate students, faculty, scholars, and practitioners [51]. We identified engagement in the context of scholarly communication among digital humanities scholars that map onto three of the elements of social media engagement outlined in this chapter.

## Uses and Gratifications (Informational and Social)

The content of a tweet yielded the greatest level of engagement; often timely discussions, controversial topics, or personal disputes led to the involvement of large segments of the community. For digital humanities scholars, social media engagement was primarily motivated by finding and sharing information and disseminating research as well as the building of new connections with fellow digital humanities scholars who shared their interests.

## Action and Participation

The amount of time spent on Twitter varied considerably among scholars. Some were heavy users of Twitter and owned multiple accounts, while others were only sporadic users, visiting Twitter primarily during conferences as a form of backchanneling (see also [53]). For example, some described viewing their Twitter feeds when there was a conference they were unable to attend, providing a means to follow conference discussions from afar. There were also variations in how people engaged with content on Twitter. Not all users were equally active participants; some indicated they felt most comfortable as 'listeners' [17] or 'lurkers.'

## Positive Experiences

Twitter represented a creative filler of downtime; one reported, 'I tend to use Twitter in interstitial moments in my day. So if I am catching public transport or if I am sitting in front of a TV and not entirely engrossed in my program'. This finding fits well with the U&G literature, which reports that one of users' primary gratifications is pastime (e.g. [47, 49, 64]). Scholars also noted the importance of Twitter as a means to discover unexpected information sources (serendipity), which is in accord with the U&G finding of informational motivations (e.g. [16, 33]). Scholars stumble upon content on Twitter, keeping them informed of research in their field without searching for it. When Melissa Terras, a digital humanities scholar, tweeted and blogged about her research papers (*presentation of self; action and participation*), she observed a drastic increase in the number of monthly downloads of these papers [59], suggesting others in her field were able to encounter her research via social media. Terras' experience also underlines the importance of listeners to social media engagement; the visible increase in downloads encouraged Terras to continue blogging about her research and encourage other researchers to do the same, even though not all listeners necessarily retweeted her posts or commented on them (*action and participation*).

However, just as positive experiences have the potential to increase social engagement, negative experiences have the potential to decrease it. Engagement on Twitter had a negative connotation for some scholars because it distracted them from their work. Scholars also described feeling overwhelmed by the amount of content and the difficulty of engaging deeply with short snippets of information.

In summary, in the context of scholarly communication among digital humanities scholars, social media engagement on Twitter demonstrates large variability in terms of *uses and gratifications, action and participation*, and *positive experiences*. Findings from the Digging DH project provide insights into how social media engagement may impact scholarly process and output.

## Case Study 2: The Facebook Experiment

Our second case study is based on a research paper, which examines emotional contagion—the transfer of emotional states—on Facebook [34]. Findings inform our understanding of the relationship between *positive experiences*, emotion in particular, and other elements of the model of social media engagement including *presentation of self* and *action and participation*.

Experiments were conducted by computational social scientists on the popular social media site Facebook to debunk the widely believed assumption that when you are immersed in an environment in which people share positive posts, updates, and images depicting others having fun, this leads to feelings of social inadequacy and even depression. In other words, the expression of positive emotion on social media can trigger negative emotion in others.

Two experiments ran for 1 week in 2012 and manipulated the amount of positive and negative content that randomly selected users ($N = 689,003$) would see in their news feeds. Each experiment had a control and experimental condition with a sample size of approximately 155,000 per condition. For the two experimental conditions, the researchers made changes to Facebook's ranking algorithm, filtering content to reduce the amount of negative or positive content visible in users' news feeds, though all content was still accessible by viewing friends' content directly (e.g. via friends' walls).

Though the study has been criticized for ethical problems relating to privacy and informed consent [41, 63], the results provide some insights for our understanding of social media engagement. Specifically, it illustrates that engagement can occur at a deep level without much awareness on the part of users and demonstrates the relationship between *positive experiences* and different elements of the model of social media engagement, namely, *presentation of self* and *action and participation*.

### Presentation of Self

In contrast to popular belief, the Facebook experiment found that exposure to emotions led users to express the same emotions (i.e. emotional contagion) through their posts and comments (*presentation of self*). For example, those users in the reduced negative emotion condition wrote posts in the days that followed with a lower percentage of negative words and a higher percentage of positive words.

## Action and Participation

The research also found that the omission of emotional content, whether negative or positive in nature, led to what the researchers referred to as a withdrawal effect:

> People who were exposed to fewer emotional posts (of either valence) in their news feeds were less expressive overall on the following days, addressing the question about how emotional expression affects social engagement online [34].

In other words, emotion appears to share a relationship with level of *action and participation*: lower levels of emotion lead to lower levels of *action and participation*.

Findings from the Facebook experiment have implications for designers of social media and their users. The experiments show that the emotional valence of content—positive or negative—has the potential to influence *action and participation* and thus *usage and activity counts*. The findings underline the potential of sentiment analysis to understand spikes in uses and activity counts. The success of the experiment also raises ethical concerns. The research suggests that changes to algorithms that effectively manipulate emotion are possible: increasing the amount of emotional content seen in users' news feeds can raise *usage and activity counts*. Should this power to manipulate go unchecked? As we asked in the chapter conclusion above, is social media engagement something that should always be increased, encouraged?

**Acknowledgements** This paper was funded by SSHRC Insight Grant No. R3603A13 given to A. Quan-Haase, a Western ADF internal grant, and by GRAND NCE, subproject NEWS2 & DIGHUM.

# References

1. Adler, E.: Facebook is crushing all other social networks in the time each user actually spends on the site. Business Insider. http://www.businessinsider.com/ (2014). Cited 14 Jan 2015
2. American Press Institute: The media insight project: the personal news cycle. http://www.americanpressinstitute.org/ (2014). Cited 14 Jan 2015
3. Bonds-Raacke, J., Raacke, J.: MySpace and Facebook: identifying dimensions of uses and gratifications for friend networking sites. Individ. Differ. Res. **8**(1), 27–33 (2010)
4. Bortree, D.S.: Presentation of self on the Web: an ethnographic study of teenage girls' weblogs. Educ. Commun. Inf. **5**(1), 25–39 (2005)
5. Bourdieu, P., Wacquant, L.: An Invitation to Reflexive Sociology. University of Chicago Press, Chicago (1992)
6. Brandtzg, P.B., Heim, J.: Why people use social networking sites. In: Ozok, A.A., Zaphiris, P. (eds.) Lecture Notes in Computer Science, vol. 5621, pp. 143–152. Springer, New York (2009)

7. Brown, B.A., Quan-haase, A.: "A workers' inquiry 2.0": an ethnographic method for the study of produsage in social media contexts. tripleC **10**(2), 488–508 (2012)

8. Cao, Q., Lu, Y., Dong, D., Tang, Z., Yongqiang, L.: The roles of bridging and bonding in social media communities. J. Am. Soc. Inf. Sci. Technol. **64**(8), 1671–1681 (2013)

9. Carmichael, G. (gailcarmichael): Anyone at Carleton_U know the name of the main department in charge of student records? I forget!. Twitter. https://twitter.com/gailcarmichael/status/502116574850187264 (2014). Cited 15 Jan 2015

10. Chan, E.: Twitter assuages growth concerns for now as shares soar 35 pct. Yahoo! Finance. http://finance.yahoo.com/ (2014). Cited 14 Jan 2015

11. Chan, W.W.L., Ma, W.W.K.: The influence of playfulness and subject involvement on focused attention when using social media. J. Commun. Educ. **1**(1), 16–27 (2014)

12. Chen, G.M.: Tweet this: a uses and gratifications perspective on how active Twitter use gratifies a need to connect with others. Comput. Hum. Behav. **27**(2), 755–762 (2011)

13. Choi, S.: Flow, diversity, form, and influence of political talk in social-media-based public forums. Hum. Commun. Res. **40**, 209–237 (2014). doi:10.1111/hcre.12023

14. Chretien, K.C., Kind, T.: Social media and clinical care: ethical, professional, and social implications. Circulation **127**(13), 1413–1421 (2013)

15. Coleman, J.S.: Social capital in the creation of human capital. Am. J. Sociol. **94**(Suppl.), S95–S120 (1988)

16. Coursaris, C.K., Sung, J., Van Osch, W., Yun, Y.: Disentangling Twitter's adoption and use (dis)continuance: a theoretical and empirical amalgamation of uses and gratifications and diffusion of innovations. Trans. Hum.-Comput. Interact. **5**(1), 57–83 (2013)

17. Crawford, K.: Following you: disciplines of listening in social media. Continuum **23**(4), 525–535 (2009). doi:10.1080/10304310903003270

18. Dantonio, L., Makri, S., Blandford, A.: Coming across academic social media content serendipitously. Proc. Am. Soc. Inf. Sci. Technol. **49**(1), 1–10 (2012)

19. Duggan, M., Smith, A.: Social media update 2013: 42 % of online adults use multiple social networking sites, but Facebook remains the platform of choice. Pew Research Internet Project. http://www.pewinternet.org/ (2014). Cited 14 Jan 2015

20. Ellison, N.B., Steinfield, C., Lampe, C. The benefits of Facebook "friends:" Social capital and college students' use of online social network sites. J. Comput.-Mediat. Commun. **12**, 1143–1168 (2007)

21. Gibbs, J.L., Ellison, N.B., Heino, R.D.: Self-presentation in online personals the role of anticipated future interaction, self-disclosure, and perceived success in Internet dating. Commun. Res. **33**(2), 152–177 (2006)

22. Gorman, R.: Woman, 32, dies in head on crash seconds after Facebook post from behind wheel about how she loved Pharrell hit Happy. Daily Mail. http://www.dailymail.co.uk/ (2014). Cited 14 Jan 2015

23. Greenfield, D.: Response to Dave Carroll YouTube video: 9 tweets. Social Media Today. http://www.socialmediatoday.com/ (2014). Cited 14 Jan 2015

24. Griffith-Greene, M.: Fake online reviews: 4 ways companies can deceive you. CBC News. http://www.cbc.ca/ (2014). Cited 14 Jan 2015

25. Hogan, B., Quan-Haase, A.: Persistence and change in social media. Bull. Sci. Technol. Soc. **30**(5), 309–315 (2010)

26. Holcomb, J., Gottfried, J., Mitchell, A.: News use across social media platforms. PewResearch. http://www.journalism.org (2013). Cited 8 Sep 2014

27. Hough, M.G.: Keeping it to ourselves: technology, privacy, and the loss of reserve. Technol. Soc. **31**, 406–413 (2009)

28. Housewright, R., Schonfeld, R.C., Wulson, K. Ithaka S + R | Jisc | RLUK UK Survey of Academics 2012, pp. 1–92 (2013)

29. Huang, L.-Y., Hsieh, Y.-J., Wu, Y.-C.J.: Gratifications and social network service usage: the mediating role of online experience. Inf. Manag. **51**(6), 774–782 (2014)

30. Jarymowicz, M.: Understanding human emotions. J. Russ. East Eur. Psychol. **50**(3), 9–25 (2012). doi:10.2753/RPO1061-0405500301

31. Java, A., Song, X., Finin, T., Tseng, B.: Why we twitter: understanding microblogging. In: Proceedings of the 9th WebKDD and 1st SNA-KDD 2007 Workshop on Web Mining and Social Network Analysis, pp. 56–65. ACM, New York (2007)

32. Johnson, P.R., Yang, S.-U.: Uses and gratifications of Twitter: an examination of user motivation and satisfaction. In: Proceedings of Annual Association for Education in Journalism and Mass Communication Conference. http://citation.allacademic.com//meta/p_mla_apa_research_citation/3/7/6/3/6/pages376367/p376367-1.php (2009). Cited 14 Jan 2015

33. Joinson, A.N.: 'Looking at', 'looking up' or 'keeping up with' people? Motives and uses of Facebook. In: Proceedings of the Twenty-Sixth Annual SIGCHI Conference on Human Factors in Computing Systems, pp. 1027–1036. Association for Computing Machinery Press, New York (2008)

34. Kramer, A.D.I., Guillory, J.E., Hancock, J.T.: Experimental evidence of massive scale emotional contagion through social networks. Proc. Natl. Acad. Sci. USA **111**(24), 8788–8790 (2014)

35. Kwak, H., Lee, C., Park, H., Moon, S.: What is Twitter, a social network or a news media? In: Proceedings of the 19th International Conference on World Wide Web – WWW '10. p. 591. ACM, New York (2010)

36. Marwick, A.E., Boyd, D.: I tweet honestly, I tweet passionately: twitter users, context collapse, and the imagined audience. New Media Soc. **13**(1), 114–133 (2010)

37. McBirnie, A., Urquhart, C.: Motifs: dominant interaction patterns in event structures of serendipity. Inf. Res. **16**(3), Paper 494 (2011)

38. McCay-Peet, L., Toms, E.G., Kelloway, E.K.: Examination of relationships among serendipity, the environment, and individual differences. Inf. Process. Manag. **51**, 391–412 (2015)

39. McCay-Peet, L., Toms, E.G.: Investigating serendipity: how it unfolds and what may influence it. J. Assoc. Inf. Sci. Technol. **66**(7), 1463–1476 (2015)

40. McDonnell, M., Shiri, A.: Social search: a taxonomy of, and a user-centred approach to, social web search. Program-Electron Lib. **45**(1), 6–28 (2011)

41. McNeal, G.: Facebook manipulated user news feeds to create emotional responses. Forbes Magazine. http://www.forbes.com/ (2014). Cited 14 Jan 2015

42. Millward, S.: Check out the numbers on China's top 10 social media sites. TechInAsia. http://www.techinasia.com (2013). Cited 14 Jan 2015

43. Mirani, L.: What it feels like to be the last generation to remember life before the internet. Quartz. http://qz.com/ (2014). Cited 14 Jan 2015

44. Mitchell, A., Kiley, J., Gottfried, J., Guskin, E.: The role of news on Facebook: common yet incidental. http://www.journalism.org/2013/10/24/the-role-of-news-on-facebook/ (2013). Cited 14 Jan 2015

45. O'Brien, H.: Exploring user engagement in online news interactions. Proc. Am. Soc. Inf. Sci. Technol. **48**(1), 1–10 (2011). doi:10.1002/meet.2011.14504801088

46. Oeldorf-Hirsch, A., Sundar, S.S.: Posting, commenting, and tagging: effects of sharing news stories on Facebook. Comput. Hum. Behav. **44**, 240–249 (2015). doi:10.1016/j.chb.2014.11.024

47. Papacharissi, Z., Mendelson, A.: Toward a new(er) sociability: uses, gratifications and social capital on Facebook. In: Papathanassopoulos, S. (ed.) Media Perspectives for the 21st Century, pp. 212–230. Routledge, New York (2011)

48. Putnam, R.D.: Bowling Alone. Simon & Schuster, New York (2000)

49. Quan-Haase, A., Young, A.L.: Uses and gratifications of social media: a comparison of Facebook and instant messaging. Bull. Sci. Technol. Soc. **30**(5), 350–361 (2010)

50. Quan-Haase, A., Young, A.L.: The uses and gratifications (U&G) approach as a lens for studying social media practice. In: Fortner, R.S., Fackler, P.M. (eds.) The Handbook of Media and Mass Communication Theory, pp. 269–286. Wiley, Hoboken (2014)

51. Quan-Haase, A., Martin, K., McCay-Peet, L.: Online conversation and information management on Twitter: preliminary findings of interviews with digital humanities scholars. Paper presented at the Social Media & Society International Conference, Toronto (2014)

52. Reinhard, C., Dervin, B.: Media uses and gratifications. In: Eadie, W. (ed.) 21st Century Communication: A Reference Handbook, pp. 506–516. Sage, Thousand Oaks (2009). doi:http://dx. doi.org/10.4135/9781412964005.n56
53. Ross, C., Terras, M., Warwick, C., Welsh, A.: Enabled backchannel: conference Twitter use by digital humanists. J. Doc. **67**(2), 214–237 (2011)
54. Sethi, L.: Social media addiction: 39,757 years of our time is collectively spend on Facebook in a day! Dazeinfo. http://dazeinfo.com/ (2015). Cited 14 Jan 2015
55. Sin, S.-C.J., Kim, K.-S.: International students' everyday life information seeking: the informational value of social networking sites. Libr. Inf. Sci. Res. **35**(2), 107–116 (2013)
56. Smock, A.D., Ellison, N.B., Lampe, C., Wohn, D.Y.: Facebook as a toolkit: a uses and gratification approach to unbundling feature use. Comput. Hum. Behav. **27**(6), 2322–2329 (2011)
57. Social media. (n.d.). Merriam-Webster online. http://www.merriam-webster.com/dictionary/ socialmedia. Cited 14 Jan 2015
58. Sundén, J.: Material Virtualities: Approaching Online Textual Embodiment. Peter Lang, New York (2003)
59. Terras, M.: Adventures in Digital humanities and digital culture heritage. Plus some musings on academia. Melissa Terras' Blog. http://melissaterras.blogspot.ca/2012/04/is-blogging-and-tweeting-about-research.html (2012). Cited 14 Jan 2015
60. Throop, B.B.: Cyberbullying has 'hugely disproportionate impact on women and girls'. CBC News. http://www.cbc.ca/ (2014). Cited 14 Jan 2015
61. Twitter: Best Practice: Tweet in the moment. http://media.twitter.com/best-practice/tweet-in-the-moment (2014). Cited 14 Jan 2015
62. Van Eperen, L., Marincola, F.M.: How scientists use social media to communicate their research. J. Transl. Med. **9**(1), 199 (2011)
63. Verma, I.M.: Editorial expression of concern and correction. Proc. Natl. Acad. Sci. USA **111**(29), 10779 (2014). doi:10.1073/pnas.1412469111
64. Whiting, A., Williams, D.: Why people use social media: a uses and gratifications approach. Qual Mark Res. **16**(4), 362–369 (2013)
65. Yadamsuren, B., Heinstrm, J.: Emotional reactions to incidental exposure to online news. Inf. Res. **16**(3), paper 486 (2011)
66. Young, A.L., Quan-Haase, A.: Privacy Protection Strategies on Facebook. Inf. Commun. Soc. **16**(4), 479–500 (2013)
67. Yuan, Y.C., Zhao, X., Liao, Q., Chi, C.: The use of different information and communication technologies to support knowledge sharing in organizations: from e-mail to micro-blogging. J. Am. Soc. Inf. Sci. Tecnol. **64**(8), 1659–1670 (2013)
68. Zhang, L., Pentina, I.: Motivations and usage patterns of Weibo. Cyberpsychol. Behav. Soc. Netw. **15**(6), 312–7 (2012)

# Conclusions

Heather O'Brien and Paul Cairns

Throughout this book, we have seen the importance placed on user engagement by researchers representing a variety of disciplinary perspectives and working in diverse technological domains. A major conclusion we can draw from the contributed chapters is that engagement is an important mediator of the user experience. This is stated explicitly by Wiebe and Sharek who place engagement squarely between students' goals and learning outcomes in eLearning environments. Although it may not be as explicitly (or simply) stated in other chapters, this centrality is a common theme. Engagement is positioned as a mediating variable between user characteristics, motivations, and preferences and individual's ability to locate information, be entertained, learn, or connect with content or others. It is intertwined with the tasks people perform and the complexity of these tasks, as well as the content conveyed and how it is delivered. Ultimately, the hope is that user engagement will affect some kind of change in users for the better—be it affective, cognitive, or behavioural.

In addition to the importance placed on user engagement in each chapter, there is also a shared emphasis on the use of theoretical frameworks and technology design.

With respect to theoretical frameworks, Flow Theory in particular was utilized by authors (e.g. McCay-Peet and Quan-Haase; O'Brien; Wiebe and Sharek) to acknowledge the tensions between "work and play" in the engagement equation. Wiebe and Sharek and Cairns both draw upon self-determination theory (SDT) to emphasize the need for motivation, both "at a particular point in time" (Cairns) and when "people to perform effortful tasks" (Wiebe and Sharek), as a key aspect of

H. O'Brien (✉)
iSchool, The University of British Columbia, Vancouver, BC, Canada
e-mail: h.obrien@ubc.ca

P. Cairns
University of York, York, UK
e-mail: paul.cairns@york.ac.uk

© Springer International Publishing Switzerland 2016
H. O'Brien, P. Cairns (eds.), *Why Engagement Matters*,
DOI 10.1007/978-3-319-27446-1_10

engagement. Lastly, uses and gratifications is used by Cairns and McCay-Peet and Quan-Haase to discuss why people play games or interact through social media. Collectively, all of the authors draw upon theories to try to explain human behaviour, motivation, and decision-making.

The chapters also critique existing models and present emerging ones. These models are major contributions of their respective chapters, well suited to their respective contexts, and informed by empirical research and testing. What is also interesting to note is that each of these emerging models includes different elements and yet has three central factors: affect, behaviour, and cognitive. So it would seem that there is an appreciation that user engagement needs to be thought of from the perspective of the whole person, rather than only what they do with technology; in fact, what people do as a result of interacting with technology is equally attended to by the contributors. Both existing and emerging models are tempered by the idea that social interaction is essential. Wiebe and Sharek call it "a very powerful force in shaping the motivation to engage" and it is embedded in media and social media experiences, the competitive nature of digital games, and the development of eHealth virtual communities of practice.

With respect to design, it is the sole focus of Sutcliffe's chapter, but it is also touched on in other chapters. Kostkova, for instance, richly illustrates eHealth engagement using concrete examples of developed technologies, including one that incorporates digital storytelling; others discuss the role of multimedia (Cairns), communication affordances (McCay-Peet and Quan-Haase), and interactivity and imagery (Oh and Sundar). Wiebe and Sharek propose that an engaging eLearning environment should "both engender and support motivation to learn, limit barriers to engagement, provide feedback as to a student's progress towards their learning goals, and provide a robust environment that adapts and supports learning based on a student's current affective and cognitive state". However, translating these characteristics into design practice is not an easy task (Sutcliffe; Oh and Sundar).

One unexpected insight related to design comes from Edwards and Kelly and concerns the "representational stability" of the interface. While we might expect that familiar interfaces are crucial for maintaining search engagement, they state, "altering the traditional interface to include elements that allow users to reflect on their own behaviours, and compare them to others, can potentially improve user engagement". Thus the idea that stable interfaces are best is questioned here, and this leads to considerations of how much instability users can tolerate and how to design interfaces that balance the need for stability and instability depending on the user, the task, and the given point in time.

This brief synopsis of the theoretical and design elements of the book's chapters demonstrate that we have some degree of crossover: we draw upon the same theories in some cases, place importance on the design of digital technologies, and support modelling the cognitive, affective, and behavioural aspects of engaged users. However, these chapters are highly diverse with respect to how the context of the interaction impacts user engagement: within a given domain, the characteristics of technology users and the outcomes of value determine the kind of engagement we are designing for and its duration (short term vs. long term). Thus we must stop and ask ourselves, "Are we all on the same page? Is *my* engagement also *your* engagement?" and, related to this, "Should it be?"

It is highly unlikely that engaging with healthcare information feels the same to users as engaging in a boss battle in a digital game! That being said, there are common elements between these experiences because they are performed using an interactive technology, where users are mentally and physically active and where applications and devices are, in some sense, inanimate until our interaction makes them behave and take on an animus, i.e. games are not anything until someone starts to play them. Yet this could also be said of books, which may or may not be read digitally.

The question becomes how digital engagement differs from nondigital engagement, and this is complicated by the fact that the digital and nondigital aspects of our lives coexist. For example, a group of friends eating dinner together might use their smart phones to verify the name of an actor using Internet Movie Database (IMDb), and the conversation might then shift from the previous topic to other movies in which he has played a role. Are the friends engaged in IMDb or the conversation now that the two have become intertwined?

As we conclude this book, we think that a number of broader issues bear mentioning. Firstly, there is a fine line between healthy and problematic relationships with technology, and thus engaging users may pose ethical implications. This issue is touched upon briefly by Cairns in his discussion of digital games, and McCay-Peet and Quan-Haase make reference to social media "engagement extremes". For the most part, however, we did not address the potentially negative consequences of user engagement in this book. Our stance is that user engagement can contribute to positive outcomes for individuals and society by enhancing the tasks we already perform, such as learning, searching for information, playing, and communicating, especially when the motivation to do so is not intrinsic to the user. We expect that people will and should disengage from technology and that this is a "necessary part of the process" (Wiebe and Sharek). Our goal is that the disengagement occurs because users need time to reflect, rest, live their lives, etc., and will re-engage when they have the need to do so.

Yet this position is a statement about what we, as a society, value. For example, eHealth and eLearning technologies may aim to change behaviour, but not every user is open to changing his/her behaviour! It also speaks to the pervasiveness of technology in our work and personal lives such that we cannot help but engage. Thus the agency of technology users, ubiquitous computing, and societal norms combine to create an ethical conundrum that has been broached through studies on Internet and video game addition, but not specifically with regard to engagement. To what extent does engagement contribute to unhealthy outcomes for users? What level of engagement is "too much"? Is engagement with a learning system "good" and an online gambling portal "bad" engagement? Should systems disengage users? If so, how and when should this be done?

Secondly, McCay-Peet and Quan-Haase raise the issue of "numbers obsession" and question whether the way in which social interactions have been reduced to "sheer numbers" is negatively impacting social media users' self-worth. They remind us that this quantification of human computer experiences is monitored not only by the corporations that operate social media sites, search engines, etc., but by users themselves.

But what about the nature of data that is produced through our technological interactions as an indication of our engagement? Is it exploitative or necessary to ensuring the viability of these corporations? The data we generate is used to understand our patterns of engagement to increase the likelihood that we will continue to use online services and applications, but the "Facebook Experiment" case study by McCay-Peet and Quan-Haase demonstrates that content and design can be manipulated without users' knowledge or consent. How does this affect the public's trust and willingness to engage with such technologies in future? When does changing the interface for the purposes of enhancing engagement cross an ethical line?

These ethical questions are not restricted only to the study of user engagement. But we must ponder them as we seek to look beyond the micro level of the human-computer interaction to understand the macro level implications of engagement on individuals and society.

In conclusion, in the chapter "Theoretical Perspectives on User Engagement", we speculated that a universal definition of user engagement would be difficult if not impossible to achieve. We might also question, given the new models proposed in various chapters, whether a general model of user engagement is also possible or even desired. Perhaps it is not so much about sharing a unified vision as it is clearly articulating the scope, anticipated outcomes, and unique characteristics of our users and domains that shape the meaning of engagement for us. This may lead to a clearer picture of what engagement looks like within and across technological domains, which would contribute to theory and application, e.g. design strategies crafted for specific types of engagement.

Despite the fact that engagement manifests differently for different kinds of user experiences, we are still proponents of developing a flexible, middle range theory of user engagement that works in tandem with practice. Testable propositions of what engagement is and is not in the context of digital interactions will build a solid basis for evolving this area of research and connect cross-disciplinary perspectives of user engagement.

Printed in the United States
By Bookmasters